BAD MORMON

BAD MORMON

A MEMOIR

HEATHER GAY

G

GALLERY BOOKS

New York   London   Toronto   Sydney   New Delhi

Gallery Books
An Imprint of Simon & Schuster, LLC
1230 Avenue of the Americas
New York, NY 10020

First Gallery Books trade paperback edition September 2024

GALLERY BOOKS and colophon are registered trademarks of Simon & Schuster, LLC

Simon & Schuster: Celebrating 100 Years of Publishing in 2024

For information about special discounts for bulk purchases, please contact Simon & Schuster Special Sales at 1-866-506-1949 or business@simonandschuster.com.

The Simon & Schuster Speakers Bureau can bring authors to your live event. For more information or to book an event, contact the Simon & Schuster Speakers Bureau at 1-866-248-3049 or visit our website at www.simonspeakers.com.

Interior design by Jaime Putorti

Manufactured in the United States of America

10 9 8 7 6 5 4 3 2 1

Library of Congress Control Number: 2022044358

ISBN 978-1-9821-9953-1
ISBN 978-1-9821-9954-8 (pbk)
ISBN 978-1-9821-9955-5 (ebook)

To Ashley, Georgia, and Annabelle

When I think of the three degrees of glory now,
I think of my heaven, my eternity, my legacy . . .
My three daughters.

> you are my sun,
> my moon,
> and all of my stars
> e. e. cummings

CONTENTS

Author's Note   ix
Prologue   xi

PART ONE

BAD DAUGHTER

1   Feels Like Home   3
2   Domo Arigato, Mr. Roboto   15
3   Tell Me Lies, Tell Me Sweet Little Lies   27
4   I'm a Puzzle, I Must Figure Out Where All My Pieces Fit   35
5   Nightswimming   45
6   Rise and Shout, the Cougars Are Out   61
7   Your Life, Little Girl, Is an Empty Page   73

PART TWO

BAD MISSIONARY

8   Love Is A Temple   85
9   Called to Serve Him, Heavenly King of Glory   111
10 Le Chaleur Humaine   117
11 I Got So High That I Saw Jesus   125
12 My Heart Will Go On   137

CONTENTS

PART THREE

BAD WIFE

13 Lost on You   145

14 Secure Yourself to Heaven   151

15 God Gave Me You   155

16 Which Part Is Mine?   161

17 I'm Harboring a Fugitive, Defector of a Kind   165

18 Somewhere That's Green   169

19 Put Your Shoulder to the Wheel, Push Along   175

20 If You Loved Me, Why'd You Leave Me?   179

PART FOUR

BAD MORMON

21 I Can Breathe for the First Time   189

22 There Must Be Fifty Ways to Leave Your Lover   195

23 The Hill I'm Walking Up Is Getting Good and Steep   201

24 Looking for Heaven, Found the Devil in Me   207

25 In My Life, I Love You More   217

PART FIVE

BAD ASS

26 All of These Lines Across My Face   225

27 Only Girl (In the World)   239

28 A Diva Is a Female Version of a Hustla   253

29 Started from the Bottom, Now We're Here   265

30 I Think Life Chose Me After All   271

Epilogue   279

Acknowledgments   283

About the Author   299

AUTHOR'S NOTE

The official name of the Mormon church is the Church of Jesus Christ of Latter-day Saints. The full name was given by revelation from God to the prophet Joseph Smith in 1838. For almost two hundred years, we called ourselves Mormons; it was the name of our book, our lessons, our songs, our marketing campaigns, our website, and a church-produced movie titled *Meet the Mormons*.

In 1990, one of the church's apostles, Russell M. Nelson, spoke out against using the term "Mormon" and instead encouraged members to use the official name, "the Church of Jesus Christ of Latter-day Saints." He was publicly reprimanded by the prophet Gordon B. Hinckley, who encouraged that the nickname "Mormon" be embraced. In 2018, when Nelson advanced to the office of prophet himself, getting rid of the nickname became one of his first orders of business. He proclaimed that the Lord had impressed upon his mind that using the proper name of the church was not negotiable and commanded that members stop referring to themselves as Mormons and instead only as members of the Church of Jesus Christ of Latter-day Saints.

He then asked the rest of the world to respect this new commandment and refrain from using "Mormon" and "Mormonism" when referring to church members, doctrine, culture, and lifestyles unique to the Church of Jesus Christ of Latter-day Saints.

Originally, I tried to follow the prophet and the church's style guide and use the full and proper name. But when I realized that I had used the word "Mormon" nearly two hundred times, it became clear that the Church of Jesus Christ of Latter-day Saints was perhaps a bit belabored.

I have chosen to use "Mormon" and "Mormonism" as they are words with which I have found resonance since birth. Both monikers are used throughout the story in order to speak to my lived experience and my identity. This is not meant to offend or dismiss the identities of those who feel otherwise.

You'll soon find that this choice is only one of the many ways that I am a Bad Mormon.

PROLOGUE

I was thirty thousand feet above Death Valley contemplating my life.

It was sinking in. *We were making a TV show!* I pressed down hard on my lower lip to keep from smiling. I needed to stay serious and acknowledge the gravity of the situation; this was a life-altering moment! If I went on television and exposed everything I'd been hiding from my friends, family, and church, there would be devastating consequences. But inside, the girl who grew up on MTV's *Real World* and Lauren Conrad's *The Hills* was euphoric. Maybe this was my golden ticket.

As I flew back to Salt Lake City from Los Angeles, I caught a glimpse of my reflection in the cloudy airplane window. With my polyester cap-sleeved blouse and quickly deflating three-barrel curls, I looked like a tried-and-true frugal Mormon, not a starlet of the stage or screen. I asked myself, *Is this really happening? Does reality television seriously want* me?

This didn't happen for sensible, church-bred, landlocked single moms like me. In my small, insular world, there were few things I knew like the back of my hand, the Book of Mormon being one and the book of reality television being the other.

Years of reality television consumption had taught me that *nothing* hides from the cameras. You can't expect to go on television pretending to be something you aren't. The viewers will see right through you.

From the time I was born, I'd been indoctrinated to think in terms of binaries. Black or white, right or wrong, everything could be traced back to good or evil, God or Satan. There was no gray area, no in between. You could choose Hollywood, but you'd have to give up heaven. You can't have both. With cameras in my face, my hand would be forced in one direction or the other.

Which route would I take? Would I pretend to be naive about the absurdities of my faith and hide behind my Mormon upbringing? Or would I use this opportunity as a chance to escape and finally come out of the closet I'd been hiding in? Would I risk my eternity, my church, my community, my family, for a *sizzle reel*?

I thought about my life, what I had imagined it would be and what it had become. I thought about my daughters and the life I desperately wanted to give them. How the fairy tale had all imploded. How the impact had revealed all the cracks in my faith. There was no putting Humpty Dumpty back together again. There was no moral dilemma to wrestle with. No real decision to be made. This was my way out.

It's all happening.

When an opportunity like this comes along, you grab it with both hands, kid. You grab it with both hands.

the whole truth is like the story of a wave unfurled

—DAR WILLIAMS

BAD MORMON

PART ONE

BAD
DAUGHTER

CHAPTER 1

FEELS LIKE HOME

Nestled in a suburban Colorado cul-de-sac in an unassuming cottage rambler on quiet Ivy Way, I sat peering out my bedroom window. I imagined myself as queen of the castle observing my kingdom below. My room was on the second floor and high enough to observe both the static familiarity of my own backyard and the unexplored wilderness just beyond my neighborhood. Leafy aspen trees shaded our playhouse and trampoline, the spindly branches growing low enough to display my mom's hand-painted wooden birdhouses. There were potted geraniums on the patio and a weathered soccer ball long forgotten in the basement window well. Adjacent to the swing set was a custom-built wooden sandbox filled with half-buried plastic shovels, pails, and tiny trucks, their wheel axles forever frozen by grains of sand.

This corner of heaven was my domain, and its perimeter was clearly defined by a six-foot-tall teakwood fence my dad had built and stained with help from family and friends. It created an impressive and imposing boundary complete with a private gate. The gate not only allowed us direct access to the undeveloped land preserve bordering our property but also kept our home private from the passing traffic and the vast landscape. We were safe and set apart, with access to the outside world when and if we needed it.

I had been told on more than one occasion not to go through the gate without my parents, but their warnings never stopped me from dreaming. *What good is a queen if she's not striving to expand her kingdom?* The longer I gazed at the mounds of dirt and prairie grass bordering our neighborhood, the more I felt them calling to me.

My mom and I had been reading aloud the book *Incident at Hawk's Hill* and I had become fixated on the story of young Ben, a six-year-old boy on the frontier who wandered away from his home and is nurtured, cared for, and fed from the teat of a wounded badger separated from her cubs. This story spoke to me and my maternal instincts. I was convinced a lost child could be living in the field outside my suburban Denver neighborhood, but I'd never know if I didn't leave the safety of my bedroom. If I was going to find a badger den and an actual feral child to rescue and raise as my very own, I would have to venture through the forbidden gate, not just dream about it. And so it was, after weeks of gazing out my window imagining my destiny, I finally dared to try.

The lock had been positioned just high enough to allow a taller, more responsible person to go through the gate, close it, and then return to the backyard by reaching over the top of the fence to unlatch the lock from the other side. The secret to the gate was twofold: you had to be tall enough, and you had to know exactly where on the fence the lock was located. Once shut, the gate was virtually undetectable from the surrounding fence and out of reach to any adventurous six-year-old.

Opening the gate had been easy. I was small but resourceful enough to boost myself up and unhinge the simple latch, but once I stepped through to uncharted territory, the gate slammed shut, and the lock clicked back into place. I panicked. I couldn't tell where the normal fence ended and the gate to my backyard began. The distant, intermittent cars that I had once watched passively from my bedroom window immediately became unbearably loud and fast. I doubted my ability to *ever* cross the street alive, and certainly not while holding anything feral. My ambition had exceeded my ability, and I understood why my parents had built the fence and been explicit about the rules.

Because they loved me.

Because they wanted to protect me.

Because they knew it was dangerous; they knew there was no way back.

On the other side of the gate, it was all so clear. I was locked out of my life, locked away from my family, abandoned in the lone and dreary world. The adventures I had planned forsaken, the good intentions I had nurtured long forgotten. Outside the gate was bad. Inside the gate was good. And I needed to get back home.

Screaming for help was an option, but it would (1) reveal my disobedience, and (2) most likely go unnoticed. I couldn't control my heaving sobs, but I kept my head down, my long mane of wavy hair hanging around my face just enough to conceal my shame. I wanted to disappear. I kept my eyes glued to the sidewalk and tried to walk with purpose to avoid being kidnapped or, worse, being asked by a Good Samaritan if I needed any help.

Once I reached my street and saw our house crest around the corner, I broke into a run. I didn't bother to gather myself or wipe my tears or even come up with a cover story. I ran right through the front door, headed straight up the stairs to my room, and dove face-first into the pillows on my bed. I vowed never to tell a soul and never to leave the sanctity of my kingdom again.

I told myself that from then on, I would only look for badgers and feral children within the confines of the backyard. I didn't need or want to go beyond the blasted gate. The lesson I learned left an imprint. The rules were there to keep me safe, not to stifle my ambitions. If no badgers or orphans appeared in my backyard, it was probably for the best.

The small voice inside my heart continued to whisper, *You can make all your dreams come true*, and I really believed it. The world was mine for the taking, and there was nothing I couldn't do if I set my mind to it. What could possibly go wrong? Who could possibly be against me?

I don't know the exact time I realized that the world was created for more than just me, but I like to think I had a good nine or ten years of absolute, egocentric, ignorant bliss.

Everything in my life confirmed my identity, my faith, and my future. Until it didn't.

I was planned for, prayed for, and prepared for long before I even knew it was my turn on earth. Perfectly spaced and perpetually pampered, I was the third child and the second daughter born into what I believed was one of God's chosen families. But to anyone else, we appeared to be typical suburban Americans.

I was one of six children, three girls and three boys. The births of my older and younger siblings were stacked within eighteen months of each other, but I was born with years of cushion in the blessed middle.

My sister Jenny and brother Tyler had birthdays a mere fifteen months apart and were five and four, respectively, when I arrived. I was the only child at home when they went to school, so I had my mom all to myself. My little sister, Nancy, was born four years later, and this sacred gap between siblings gave me just enough undivided attention to confirm my birthright.

I was what they called a BIC in my church, which meant I was "born in the covenant." A daughter of the Most High God sealed for time and all eternity to devout, temple-married parents. BIC is only on your church membership record if your parents are married in the temple before you are born. "Children of the covenant" are natural heirs to the blessings of the priesthood and, according to the prophet Russell M. Nelson, part of a strain of sin-resistant souls with special promises and responsibilities. If you are born to parents married outside of the temple, you aren't a BIC. You can still be admitted into the highest level of heaven, but it requires a work-around. You are grafted onto the family tree as a branch, but you will never be of the covenant line.

Born in the covenant: Mormon flex.

I may have had "BIC" on my church membership record, but growing up, I didn't know what "covenant" meant. I didn't even know that we were religious. I just thought that we were better than everyone else. I had no idea the sacrifices or oaths my parents had taken in order to assure that their children were part of "the prosperity of promise." I just thought they were following the recipe for a typical family, with the secret ingredient of the gospel making us deliriously happy. We were Mormons, and Mormons had it figured out. We were doing something right. We were thriving. We had the world on a string.

Mormonism was our way of life, the only way of life, because we loved it. And we believed it.

Our faith came with perspective, balance, and humor. It was all-American. We were service oriented. We had fun. We had refreshments at every get together. We loved pinewood derbys, road shows, and girls' camp. Our youth leaders indulged us with water balloon fights and ice cream socials. We would meet for activities at the vacant church buildings in the middle of the week and hang out afterwards to run through the darkened hallways feeling safe and silly and sneaky all at the same time.

We didn't hang crucifixes or focus heavily on sin, we knew the rules and we assumed no one would ever break them. We didn't forgo birthday parties and Halloween. We didn't cover our hair with veils or wear prairie dresses with tennis shoes. We seemed normal. We seemed practical. Our priests weren't cloistered away in monasteries, they were married volunteers who wore sport coats and Christmas ties.

I had never heard anyone at church say anything garish like "Praise Jesus!" or raise their arms uncontrollably and speak in tongues. Of course, we believed in the speaking in tongues and in the praising of Jesus, but we would never actually do it out loud. I had been taught that people who loved God like *that* were fanatics. We were the one and only true church on the face of the earth; we had the restored gospel, the priesthood, the Book of Mormon, and a living prophet that spoke to God. We had everything. We didn't need to shout it from the rooftops, all we needed to do was show up and share.

When other people spoke of their religions, I would think, *Forget religion, what we have is so much better. We have a way of life. A plan of happiness, a proven system. It works if you work it.* I wanted to share the gospel! I wanted to help the world! I was blessed to be born into the covenant, born into the faith, and I knew I had a duty to share it with those who were less fortunate.

We had the answers to all the tests. And "man's search for meaning" would undoubtedly lead everyone right to our front porch, where we would be waiting like *Dateline NBC*'s Chris Hansen on *To Catch a Predator* with a pitcher of sweet tea and a smile.

"Hello! Come on in! Pull up a chair. Let's get started."

Where did we come from? What is our purpose here on earth? Where will we go when we die? I could answer these questions with confidence from the time I could speak. Everyone else was floating through life without a purpose, without a plan, and without the perfect love that we had as a family. I believed in my family and our religion like I believed in America, and from my window at the center of the universe, I couldn't tell the difference between the two.

My parents both grew up in Utah surrounded by members of the church and Mormon culture, but they eventually moved away. I was born in Carmel, California, where my dad was studying Russian at the Language Defense Institute on the Monterey Peninsula. My parents were Mormon, but they weren't weird. I wasn't one of those run-of-the-mill Utah girls, I was a Carmel-by-the-Sea California girl, and I planned on living a life worthy of the distinction.

My father started his career in the FBI investigating bank robberies and eventually found his way into Russian counterintelligence, which forced him to relocate frequently. My mom, his wingman and wife, happily followed, creating homes without complaint in multiple states around the nation. By the time I was five, she finally said, "Eight is enough." After seven states, she wanted to take root. My dad left the FBI and accepted an assignment with the Bureau of Land Management, hunting thieves of historical indigenous sites in Denver, and my mom settled in to make the Mile High State her home sweet home for good.

My mom's early years of marriage always seemed like a grand adventure to me. I imagined how she learned to adapt and represent from sea to shining sea, living in a new state almost every two years, stopping only long enough to make a few friends and have another baby: Utah (Jenny), Minnesota (Tyler), Washington State, California (me), Virginia, Texas (Nancy), Colorado (Logan and Casey). Eventually, each state she made a home in would be immortalized in a series of framed batiks along our staircase and mantle in Denver. I would study each landmark etched out in ink and wax and imagine my parents all across America, making friends, making memories, making homes.

Mom was a BIC, born in the covenant, like me and like the generations before her. Her ancestors were oxcart pioneers that had traveled across the plains and settled in Ogden, Utah. When I imagine my mom in her prime, she resembles a young Katherine Heigl: perpetually youthful, deep brown eyes, and a big, brilliant smile. The oldest of six children, her youngest brother was barely born when she began having babies herself. In high school, she was a member of the 4-H Club and a white-gloved song leader, cheering in her green and white Hillcrest Huskies uniform. She was self-reliant and resourceful, working after school every day and saving up to buy her own braces and contact lenses. She wasn't afraid to spend a pretty penny to look pretty.

When she first met my dad, she was a Chi Omega at Utah State. He was a smooth-talking Sigma Chi who wore white jeans and penny loafers with no socks. She said she fell for him because he was a sharp dresser and drove a convertible VW Bug.

"What can I say?" she'd muse. "He looked like he came from money." *Eye roll.*

My dad had not come from money; he had been raised by a cruel father and a well-meaning Mormon mother of meager means. The Scouting program and church youth groups had been his saving grace, and he worked hard for everything he had. He was influenced by bishops who later became apostles to the prophet. But his home life didn't compare to the love and stability my mom had grown up with. And that did not go unnoticed. "We are who we come from" was a recurring theme in our church culture. My mom's attempts to explain the rationale in marrying my dad served both as a cautionary tale for first impressions and as an explanation for how a prize like her fell for someone with a less-than-perfect pedigree.

"I was tricked," she would joke. "He charmed me!"

Her destiny from that fateful moment on was to be on a fast track from sorority girl to stay-at-home mom. She was engaged, married, and pregnant within the year. The families decorated the wedding breakfast tables with black-eyed Susans in her honor. At the reception, her bridesmaids wore custom-sewn dotted-swiss gowns in a rainbow of pastel colors with puffed sleeves and empire waists.

My mom was an enigma, a sarcastic tour de force who was supremely competent in all the creative arts. If you wanted to turn in a winning essay or art-fair project, you wanted my mom as your consultant. She knew how to sprinkle salt on my watercolor painting of an ocean wave to make it foamy, how to add a topless mermaid on a rock outcropping to a drawing of an island to create intrigue, how to use words like "ermine" and "gilded" to describe something regal.

She always smelled of Paco Rabanne and could wear red lipstick without it smearing or getting on her teeth. The kind of mom who added a dollop of Cool Whip and a bendy straw to your glass of milk just because she knew it would thrill you. I'd follow her around the house like a groupie and watch her sit on the end of her bed with a compact mirror, applying her makeup slowly and methodically, the mascara wand hovering in midair if she was distracted by the soap operas on the television in her bedroom.

"Oh, Heather, don't watch this. It's not for kids," she would say, her eyes glued to the screen.

Those words filled me with illicit joy. She would say the same thing to me when I got to stay up late to have her comb my hair and set it in pink rollers or twist it into braids. I learned to hand her the comb or curler as slowly as possible to extend the task and prolong our time together. All my other siblings were in bed, and I considered these moments alone sacred. I'd sit quietly while her hands worked their way through my hair.

When she was finished, I'd creep onto my stomach and push my body back until it was level with the couch and out of her line of vision. The stakes were high. Any sudden movement or sound would remind her of my presence and get me unceremoniously sent to bed before the first note of the *Hill Street Blues* theme song played on the twenty-four-inch screen in the dimly lit living room.

I could tell which shows were for kids and which shows were not for kids based on the main characters. If they seemed like they could be Mormon—a father with a briefcase and a mother with an apron—then the show was safe to watch. If they did not seem Mormon—a mother with a briefcase and a father nowhere to be found—it was best to turn the channel. Because of my community, I had been surrounded by a specific type of faith, a specific type of success, that was easy for me to recognize. I would see a mom and a dad with kids on television or in a movie and it was obvious to me that if they seemed happy and well-adjusted, then they were most assuredly Mormon.

The Partridge Family? Mormon.

Tom Hanks? So Mormon I could taste it. Even as a bachelor disguising himself as a woman on *Bosom Buddies*, he still seemed Mormon. Peter Scolari, too. To me, they were just well-meaning Mormon guys working the system until they found wives.

Dick Van Patten? A good-time guy driving a minivan with eight highly independent children? Now, that is a *Mormon* man. And not just a Mormon man but a *bishop*. He'd never make it to the Big 12 apostle status—he was too easygoing for that—but he would definitely be a bishop. And not just any bishop, a *fun* bishop. The kind who would keep your secrets and not make you break up with your boyfriend. The kind who would encourage his son to marry a soap star and a Real Housewife of Beverly Hills. With a Dick Van Patten by my side, anything was possible.

CHAPTER 2

DOMO ARIGATO, MR. ROBOTO

I was not a golden child. I was not a problem child. I was, like my birth number, somewhere right in the middle. My parents described me as a deep thinker and a deep sleeper, wetting the bed regularly and haunting the house with my occasional sleepwalking. But I was also intuitive and pragmatic—most likely a result of the pioneer, make-do, can-do gravitas embedded in my DNA.

Sometimes that type of confidence leads directly to tragedy.

I was inspired by a recent *Jetsons* episode where Rosey, the robot housekeeper, used her extendable arms to accomplish all her household chores. I decided to try opening the curtains using my own extendable claws—a pair of my mom's sewing scissors. I was a smart kid, I had learned the ways of the world, I had been outside the backyard gate, but I never imagined that my robot pincers would cut the curtains.

All I wanted to do was open the curtains without ever touching the fabric. The plan was to extend my robot forceps, pinch the curtain, pull it aside, retract my robot arm, and look out the window. I approached the task robotically, scissors open. When I went to pinch the fabric between the blades, I applied a whisper of pressure and was shocked to see them clasp tight instantly, slicing a tiny crescent moon right in the middle of the diaphanous fabric. *I was in the shit*. It was an unwelcome and unexpected complication.

When my mom arrived home to the brighter-than-usual living room, she saw the pillar of light descending directly onto the carpet and gasped in horror. I feigned ignorance but was immediately sent to my room as the only suspect. I sat upstairs, paralyzed on the end of my bed for what seemed like twelve days but was probably less than an hour. In my solitude, I retraced the steps of my failed engineering experiment.

I would never just cut a hole in the curtains. That would be a terrible thing to do. And I didn't want to do terrible things. At least, I didn't *think* I wanted to do terrible things. But maybe I did, because here I was. There was a hole in the curtain, and I had caused it.

When my dad walked into my room, he had the swagger of a seasoned detective with an open-and-shut case. I'm sure he thought, *This kid will be easy to crack. She's the only suspect, she left the weapon at the scene of the crime, she has no alibi, and she's seven years old.*

He was wrong.

The more I stood steadfast in my denial, the more my parents upped the ante. They took it upon themselves to try to break me, to pry a confession. They marched me down the stairs to the living room. I saw the robot forceps on the side table and felt betrayed by their sudden transformation back into scissors. My dad stood me in front of the curtains and had me lift my hand with my arm out straight in front of me. My fingers measured the exact height of the hole. I didn't even flinch.

My mom tried appealing to my emotions.

"These were my brand-new curtains, Heather. And they're ruined. They're ruined!"

Silence.

I knew the evidence was stacked against me, I knew the stakes were high, but I had not cut a hole in the curtains. My robot forceps had experienced a malfunction.

I'm sure my parents feared they had a bad seed. Not only had I been caught eating dry cake mix, I also could not stop biting my nails or humming loudly whenever I was around food. They had plenty of other things to be worried about without adding a demonic robot alter ego. There was no place in their Plan of Happiness for a child who broke the rules, followed her own path, and caused them to explain the meaning of holes in the curtains.

I wonder if there was any part of them that was impressed at the strength of my resolve, my commitment to my innocence. My stoicism under pressure. Hadn't they taught us to always remain steadfast and firm in our beliefs? Wasn't our faith built on being able to withstand the slings and arrows of man while remaining valiant? These were the lessons from Family Home Evening and Sunday school that I had taken to heart. I couldn't see how I was getting it so wrong now.

Claiming that I hadn't cut a hole in the curtains didn't feel like a lie. And if it was a lie, it wasn't a delectably sweet lie. It didn't feel good on my tongue. It didn't feel creamy. I was trying to make sense of my mistake, rationalizing and justifying in order to excuse a seven-year-old's imagination. If I believed I wasn't wrong, I wasn't wrong. If I believed it was true, it was true. If I was good, how could I also be bad? These were the concepts I'd already internalized, even though I was only in the second grade, and now they had somehow failed me. I didn't yet know that I was already steeped in the lifeblood of devout religion: denial, denial, denial.

My father tried to laugh off the fact that he couldn't break me. No face, no case. He wasn't upset, just deeply, *deeply* concerned about my refusal to cop to the crime. Pushed to his absolute limit, he was left no other choice than to revert to the most basic punishment: a simple spanking. I wasn't struck in anger; it was one short, dispassionate, flat-palmed whack, but I cried my little broken, innocent heart out.

I was beginning to learn the gendered roles of behavior. My parents didn't want a steely-eyed warrior for a daughter, they wanted someone obedient and kind. She didn't have to be a quivering sack of hysteria, but she should at least crack under pressure at FBI interrogator levels. I would have to do better. I would try to be softer.

I didn't know the difference between a Willa Cather pioneer or a Brigham Young pioneer, and no one ever bothered to tell me. I devoured every book in Laura Ingalls Wilder's *Little House on the Prairie* series and assumed they were Mormon like me. The only differences I could determine between her family and mine appeared to be Pa's penchant for his pipe and the occasional celebratory swig of whiskey, both offenses that I chalked up to old-fashioned frontier failings. I figured with my faith and pioneer ancestry, I was just a modern-day Laura Ingalls Wilder, a frontier girl with all the comforts of modern life and the fullness of the restored gospel. I knew I'd never know the simple joy of corncob dolls gifted on Christmas morning, but I was pretty sure that if pressed, I could make a balloon from a pig's bladder.

When it came time to attend school at Homestead Elementary, the transition from *Little House on the Prairie* to little house on the Homestead was seamless. My local public elementary school was brand new and smelled like fresh paint and chemically treated carpet. Everything about Homestead Elementary was based on the theme of westward expansion. Every grade had a pioneer trail and therefore to me was evidence of the Mormons' contribution to the American frontier. Kindergarten and first grade began on the Pony Express, then every year students advanced: Oregon Trail, Chisholm Trail, Genesee Trail, and the lofty sixth-grade Santa Fe Trail. The walls had murals of covered wagons and yoked oxen—the same type of oxen I had seen in pictures upholding the sacred baptismal fonts in the temple. The type of oxen that represented marriage, equally and eternally yoked for time and all eternity. Each covered wagon spoke of my ancestors and their journey from persecution to religious freedom.

Everything at the school resonated with me and my family's faith. We were the descendants of noble pioneers, and therefore I had a deep personal connection to every single trail in every single grade. I was sure of it. I was an actual trailblazer, so in my heart Homestead Elementary belonged to me and my family more than it did to any other student.

On Sundays, all school friends and activities were forbidden. If anyone outside of the church invited us to socialize, we would politely decline and explain, "Sunday is a family day." Saturdays were for playing sports, Sundays were for going to church. We arrived on time, starched and stiff in our Sunday best, and sat attentive for all three hours. We'd come home hungry and happy and gather for a family meal of fork tender

Crock-Pot roast, Rhodes rolls, and frozen green peas, eating and talking and laughing until our stomachs and hearts were overflowing with family togetherness. We'd stagger to stand with our bellies full and lazily retreat together to watch the Broncos game. On any given Sunday, the cadence of a football game on a television in the background can elicit the same spiritual stirrings in my heart as a choir of heavenly angels, and I just know in my bones that the church is true.

My mom aspired to run our home like a tight ship. She wrote out chore charts and delegated tasks and made sure all hands were on deck at dinnertime.

As soon as I was old enough to be assigned chores like the big kids, I felt I had finally made it as a human being. On well-organized days, I'd return home from school to a three-by-five notecard on the counter. Each child had a designated card, and each card had our designated chores. The older kids' cards were written in cursive, but mine was still in babyish print to make it easy for me to read. My tasks and chores gave me a sense of pride, a sense of belonging.

Around the age of eight, when my chore cards advanced from feeding the baby a bottle to feeding the family a casserole, I knew that I'd finally arrived. My mother entrusted me with a green bean casserole, and I immediately committed the recipe to memory. Two cans of green beans, one can of cream of mushroom soup, a splash of Worcestershire, a pinch of salt, a dash of pepper, a frozen bag of Ore-Ida Tater Tots. Mix wet ingredients in a bowl (bowl and spoon already on the counter) and pour into a nine-by-twelve casserole dish (also already on the counter). Cover with Tater Tots (still in the freezer). Preheat the oven to 350 degrees, bake until the Tots are golden brown, then remove using the oven mitts and trivet (again, already on the counter).

I was steeped in the noble art of cooking, cleaning, and homemaking, a sacred, dutiful ritual that instilled in me a self-esteem and self-worth derived from the things I could control.

I know it took twice as much time to write down the step-by-step instructions and lay out all the tools as it did to do the actual chore itself, but it didn't matter. My mom loved me and was willing to make the sacrifice. She was smart enough and *mom* enough to teach me, to stack the deck in my favor. To build the skill set I would need to survive. She was giving me a fighting chance.

Church friends were like family; we were all bound together by our common identities and membership. Growing up in Denver, if you had a church friend who was cool and lived in your neighborhood, you were one of the lucky ones. I learned that pretty early when I watched my parents befriend other "cool" Mormon families in the Willow Creek First Ward.

The Gillespies were a family of all boys. They also were a family who raised Scottish Terriers. I remember my parents loading all of us into the family Econoline to go to their house to witness the birth of a litter of puppies. They had created a blanketed space in their laundry room, with a child's gate protecting the mama dog and her pups. The Gillespies let us gather around and watch her birth each baby puppy in the sac, then tear the sac open with her teeth and nuzzle it to life. It was miraculous. *God loves a terrier.*

I felt like Fern in *Charlotte's Web*, soaking in all the farm life around me. I wasn't grossed out. I was inspired. I had witnessed the miracle of birth and was therefore fully prepared for any midwife emergency should one occur. Thanks to Brother and Sister Gillespie opening their home birth and hearts to our family, I felt confident that I knew enough to nuzzle any newborn creature to life.

At church, we referred to everyone as "Brother" and "Sister." "Mr." and "Mrs." were never used when referring to other church members. I would never say Mrs. Gillespie's Scottish Terrier had puppies. She was always *Sister* Gillespie. It didn't matter if I saw her at the store or in Sunday school, to greet her as anything other than Sister never occurred to me.

On one fateful day, I saw her in the King Soopers checkout line and excitedly called her name to get her attention. "Sister Gillespie!"

My mom gently grabbed my arm and whispered, "Call her *Mrs.* Gillespie when we are in public. Or Becky." *Becky? Was she kidding?*

"People don't understand when you say 'Sister,' and it sounds weird. They will think she's a nun or something."

A nun? Like Fraulein Maria in *The Sound of Music*? Was she Mormon, too? I didn't get it. I didn't understand why saying "Brother" and "Sister" was weird in public but not in private. No one explained that calling members of the church Brother and Sister established a very specific and deliberate social perimeter around our community. A quick code to identify an ally. A toe-tap under the bathroom stall. I couldn't explain it, but I had already internalized it. I had shaped my instincts around it. I could trust *Brother and Sister* Gillespie with anything. But I would give a big side-eye to *Mr. and Mrs.* Gillespie, and I would die before I trusted *Becky* with a goddamn thing.

I loved Mormonism so much that I wanted everyone in my orbit to be exposed to that kind of joy, that endorphin rush of righteousness. We would invite someone to an activity like a barbecue or a picnic, but we wouldn't mention that it was religious; instead, that element would have to be a wonderful surprise.

When I opened the fridge and saw two bottles of Martinelli's sparkling apple juice, my interest was piqued. When I asked, my mom explained that my dad had a business associate, Craig. He and his wife, Melissa, were struggling to conceive and my parents had invited them over for dinner. Craig and Melissa weren't Mormon. And, as such, their otherness was apparent. "Are they members?" was always the first question we asked. All the people in my parents' immediate circle were Mormons. This would be a first. I knew something was up.

"They are doing everything they can to have a baby," my mom explained. "Sometimes the church can help with these things."

I didn't know how or why specifically the church could help, but it made sense to me that they were the ones to ask. If you were in trouble, the church was there on the double—better than the Bloodhound Gang. We had systems to feed, clothe, house, and employ every church member. If this couple desperately wanted a child, if this couple desperately wanted *anything*, the church could provide it, but they would have to get baptized first.

After dinner, we gathered in the living room. It was time for the wonderful surprise. My dad gave a tiny speech about faith. We sang "As I Have Loved You," a hymn that began as a children's primary song but was so popular it was canonized in the adult hymnal; I knew every word, and I sang with all my heart. The spirit filled the room, and I felt tears form and my throat tickle with emotion. The gospel is true!

My dad asked if we could kneel in prayer, and for only a second it broke the reverie. We all slid off our couches and chairs and knelt in unison. The couple was, understandably, a beat behind, not being accustomed to such an immediate physical transition. We waited patiently with our arms folded. As soon as they safely assumed the same position, I bowed my head and closed my eyes. My dad's prayer was simple and heartfelt.

"Dear Heavenly Father, we are so grateful to be gathered here today as family and friends and to be able to feel of thy love for each and every one of us. We are grateful for the many ways that thou hast blessed our lives. We are grateful for the gospel, and we know it is true. We are grateful for the Book of Mormon and for the joy it brings into our home. We are grateful for the prophet Joseph Smith and for the sacrifices that he made to restore to the earth the fullness of the gospel of thy Son, our Savior, Jesus Christ. We pray that thou might bless our friends, Craig and Melissa, that they will be able to feel of thy love, to feel of thy Spirit that is here tonight, and to be rewarded in their righteous endeavors to create a family here on this earth."

I opened my eyes. I wanted to see if they were feeling what I was feeling or if my dad had dipped too deep into the divine. Their eyes were closed, their arms folded, their faces strangely passive. I had expected tears or emotions, but I understood that might be embarrassing for them in front of us, so I let it slide and closed my eyes again.

"Bless them with patience and with faith and with the strength they need as they experience these trials. Bless them with the understanding that if they endure it well, they will be strengthened as a couple and as future parents. We thank thee for all that thou hast given us, and we pray for all these things this night, in the name of Jesus Christ, Amen."

During my dad's prayer, I felt my heart expanding, confirming my love for my family, my testimony of the gospel, and imbuing me with a sense of strength and security. Craig and Melissa had to feel it, too. And if they didn't, they probably weren't ready to be parents anyways.

CHAPTER 3

TELL ME LIES,
TELL ME SWEET LITTLE LIES

Whenever we traveled outside our hometown borders, my mom transformed into a detective trained in profiling members of the LDS church. If there were other members of the church out there, she was going to find them. She was Angela Lansbury looking for clues in her own unscripted series, *Mormon, She Wrote*. If we happened to cross paths with another member, she would make the connection, and we would instantly go from being absolute strangers to being sisters in Zion.

I would watch my mom in action, alert as a prairie dog, eavesdropping on conversations or keenly observing other families. Her back would be tense and upright as she pretended to grope around in her purse for a nonexistent pen or a half-eaten roll of spearmint Certs.

"I think they are members," she would say quietly through gritted teeth. If I started to pester her with questions, she would shush me and shake her head, as if to say, *Not now! We don't want them to know we are observing them.* Once we were out of earshot, she would divulge her investigative theories.

"I think they are members. I can just *tell*. And I'm pretty sure I saw a garment line."

I can't see a bare shoulder or kneecap without thinking about the garment line. I can't see a garment line without thinking about how I wore garments for twenty years, took them off, and never wore them again.

The first time I realized that other people didn't wear sacred garments was a rude awakening. My dad was one of my soccer coaches, and it was his team T-shirt that revealed his not so secret underwear.

The soccer team's name was the Cracker Jills. It had beaten out the 7Ups by popular vote and immediately made me doubt my team's discernment. I didn't get it. I had voted for the 7Ups. What did Cracker Jills even mean? Firecrackers? Cracker Barrel? It made me feel uneasy and unathletic.

Our head coach, a seasoned marathon runner in short corduroy OPs, had a trimmed blond beard and mustache and was not Mormon. Occasionally, he lost his temper during practice and spiked a soccer ball in anger or whispered "Godammit" under his breath, and when he did, I cringed with anguish. I felt what can only be described as pure pity for families who had to live like that . . . with occasional *swearing*. These people needed Jesus in their lives. At our first practice, he explained the origin of the team name, oblivious of his poor lost soul: "It's like the candy Cracker Jack, except we aren't boys, so we are calling ourselves the Cracker Jills."

Eventually, both the name and the team grew on me. I loved being a part of the Cracker Jills. I was the only member of the church on the team, and I loved playing soccer with these exotic peripheral friends. The thrill of the competition, the metallic taste in the back of my throat from running too fast, the smell of the grass, the stats of the teams, the oranges at halftime, I looked forward to all of it.

My dad signed on as assistant coach for a few of the years, and my mom made the coaching staff custom T-shirts with tiny red fuzzy iron-on letters. The shirts were white and thin, slightly more transparent than a heavy Hanes T-shirt, and trimmed at the neckline and sleeves with red binding. Emblazoned in a tiny arc across the chest, evenly spaced and ironed on with love: C R A C K E R J I L L S.

I'll never know or be brave enough to ask anyone what started the fight on the sidelines that day. My dad was probably challenging a bad ref call or calling out a heel raise on the throw-in. Whatever was considered normal banter and parental sideline coaching in the 1980s would get you thrown off the field and kicked off the team in today's safe-sideline spectator rulebook.

Voices were raised, and the background chatter grew silent. Suddenly, as I was running down the field in my perforated double-ply polyester, I became aware that the kerfuffle on the sidelines involved my dad and that everyone was watching. I saw him roll his eyes, shake his head from side to side, and mumble as he began to storm off.

As soon as his back was turned, the other parent yelled out, "That's right! Take your daughter and your funny underwear and go home!"

The blood rushed to my ears, and time stood still. Funny underwear?

My dad flipped around and charged at the man, grabbing his T-shirt with both hands. He was raging. The other guy braced himself, and they stood there heaving and holding each other at arm's length like two elks with their horns interlocked. A few bystanders shouted at them to knock it off, as concerned parents on the sidelines quickly separated them.

My dad's comb-over had been shaken in the altercation, and while his friends pulled him away from the fracas, he smoothed his hair back into place and muttered angrily, never looking away from the man he was forced to retreat from. What had this guy said? Why was he teasing my dad about something as stupid as underwear?

My dad didn't wear funny underwear. My dad wore garments. He was prone to sporting a one-piece romper with a back flap. Perhaps not really a flap so much as overlapping fabric that created a closed effect until you bent over or pulled the two overlaps apart in order to use the bathroom. It was exactly like my mom's garments, except hers were made of a silky material and had lace trim. That's the only underwear I had ever seen them wear, but I had never really thought it was something to make fun of. And more important, why did this guy care about my dad's underwear?

I had been folding my parents' garments in the laundry for nearly a decade. It was just underwear to me. I didn't know there was anything unusual about it. None of us did. When my little brother came across an advertisement in the Sears catalog for children's long johns, he was overjoyed. "Mom! Dad! LOOK!" he squealed, running into their bedroom with the pictures displayed. "Garments for KIDS!"

I had no idea that there were sacred symbols sewn onto the garments in distinct places to remind them of covenant promises and associated penalties. I assumed that the stitched symbols were my mother's quick needlework, darning the snags in my dad's shirt so his nips didn't poke out. I figured he was using a sharp pen or wearing jackets with exposed zippers or corners that could snag and tear his undershirts . . . in the exact same place every single time. But the second this guy called out my dad's underwear, I began to reevaluate everything. My thoughts were swirling, and in horror I realized that my parents did indeed wear funny underwear.

I don't remember anyone talking about it on the ride home. I don't even remember who was in the car. My ears were still ringing as the blood began to retreat from my face. Once we reached the house, I immediately looked for my mom in order to ask her about the man's accusations, but she was nowhere to be found. I felt paralyzed. I couldn't even change out of my soccer uniform. The lumps in my throat and my chest were so tight that I felt physical pain.

Where was my mom?

She had probably attended every one of my soccer games dutifully, but I have no memories of her being there or cheering on the sidelines at any of the games. I'm not sure why, but it confirms the fact that when my dad was around, his presence eclipsed the sun. My mom fell in line and became his helpmeet; everyone else disappeared. I look at pictures from my soccer games now and see that my uniform was clean and ironed, my socks and shin guards were matching and bright. My hair was always parted down the middle into two golden Dutch braids with matching ribbon. A solid hour of unpaid labor that I counted on so that I could enjoy time with the real hero in all of our rewrites: Dad.

I waited impatiently for my mother to return home, standing stoically in front of the living room window, watching for her and secretly peeking through the now-replaced unmarred curtain. Every car that came around the corner caused my stomach to jump. It felt like hours of waiting and waiting and waiting. Finally, my mom pulled around the corner and into the driveway.

As she unloaded the car, I rushed out and tried to talk to her, but my voice was thick with tears and tension.

"Mom, Mom!" I croaked.

She looked over. "What's wrong?" she asked.

"Mom. " Big inhale. "Dad got in a fight, and this guy yelled at him, and he made fun of Dad."

I couldn't bring myself to tell her about the underwear. It was too shameful, for reasons I didn't exactly know.

My mom froze, a bag of groceries cradled in each arm.

"What do you mean, Dad got in a fight? A fight? He was in a fight?"

Her questions came at me rapid-fire. She seemed highly fixated on the fight, so much so that I realized it wasn't the fight that had bothered me nearly as much as the slanderous remark about the underwear.

Why wasn't she asking how he'd made fun of Dad?

"Where's your dad?" she asked.

"I don't know! " I cried. And the tears sprang anew from my eyes, hot and furious. The knot in my throat tightened, and I couldn't express to my mom what was truly wrong.

All I had to say was, "Mom, is there something about Dad's underwear that I should know? That man on the soccer field acted like he had seen Dad's underwear, and there's no way to make that make sense."

It could have been a simple conversation. But I couldn't ask it. I didn't want to acknowledge it. All I knew was that I didn't want to have a dad who wore underwear that other people knew about, and this guy knew about my dad's underwear. In fact, he was so confident that he hurled the insult as if he'd been waiting his whole life to say it. Something in my heart shifted in that moment. I realized that people knew we were different, *special*, even, but they might not admire us for it.

Later that night, my parents casually addressed the skirmish on the sidelines.

"I think he said 'funny underwear' because you could see the outline of my garment top through my shirt, " my dad explained.

My mom seemed irritated. "John, low-cut garment tops make everything so obvious. Just wear the ones with the T-shirt neckline. There is no need to sport an 'eternal smile.'"

My dad made a few jokes and reluctantly agreed that my mom was right. Everyone carried on eating their corn on the cob and their rice and Russian apricot chicken like it was no big deal. Lesson learned. Change up your garment tops to better align with your fashion choices and avoid being mocked. The thin cotton of the Cracker Jills custom tee had betrayed my dad, it had betrayed the covenants of the garment, and it had betrayed me.

I soothed myself by pretending to believe the tale my parents were spinning. Garments weren't something to make fun of, garments were cool. That guy was not making fun of anything more than the obvious fashion faux pas in front of him: the wry eternal smile of my dad's funny underwear.

CHAPTER 4

I'M A PUZZLE, I MUST FIGURE
OUT WHERE ALL MY PIECES FIT

Matt Geary was a barrel-bodied strawberry blond with white lashes and freckles. Matt had been in my classes since kindergarten and was the foil by which I gauged all my scholarly pursuits. We tested in the same percentile, we checked out the same books at the library, we raced each other to finish our math worksheets, and pretended it wasn't a big deal if we didn't win a poster award at the book fair.

When it came to playing Around the World for multiplication tables, Matt and I were often the last two remaining in a heated stand-off until the teacher finally declared a tie and we happily shared the victory. Matt was my friend and my equal. I didn't feel better than him, I felt exactly like him. When our teacher turned our classroom into a pretend news station for a week, she assigned different students to be field reporters, cameramen, and writers. She asked Matt and me to be the anchormen. I was Victoria Corningstone and he was my Ron Burgundy, minus the misogyny. We sat at the news desk and carried the entire show. *You stay classy, Homestead Elementary.*

The summer before sixth grade was in many ways the end of my innocence—my last great summer. My last summer racing Matt in made-up relays and scraping pennies off the bottom of the pool. I went from believing I could do anything to actually doing *anything* for the boys to pay attention to me. When I showed up outside Santa Fe Trail for my first day of school, I hardly recognized Matt and my other male classmates, who, between our last field day and back-to-school night, had somehow become men. Puberty had slapped them right out of their straight denim jeans from Sears and landed them in cargo pants, rugby shirts, and a vat of Drakkar-scented pheromones.

I was too tongue-tied now to challenge them in Around the World, and I no longer wanted to shame them in multiplication-table defeat. They were too cute to embarrass publicly. I wanted what they had: sex appeal and self-divinity.

If I was looking for a balance to my tween hormonal urges, I turned to the church. Being big and brazen was fine until it came time to finding a man, a task that required a strict dedication to being small, quiet, and dutiful.

In the church, everyone graduates from primary at the age of twelve. Boys are separated into a quorum of men and are given the Aaronic or preparatory priesthood by the laying on of hands. Mormon men can trace their priesthood back to Jesus Christ himself. They believe Christ's priesthood was lost and then miraculously restored by the prophet Joseph Smith.

If they can keep their hands and minds clean, they are endowed with the power to bless and pass the sacramental bread and water to the congregation; collect tithes and fast offerings; administer blessings to the sick and needy; and baptize men, women, and children by immersion with full authority.

Girls, however, are separated and given a different set of responsibilities. The purpose of the Young Women Organization is to guide and nurture daughters of God as they become covenant women and to help each one prepare for her divine role as a daughter, wife, and mother.

Every Sunday, we'd meet in a classroom to learn about our divine role in God's kingdom. No power was bestowed upon our heads, no trajectory presented to preside and provide for the world. Instead, we were simply given a list of qualities that God wanted us to emulate. We'd stand up from our folded chairs as a group and recite in unison the Young Women motto with reverence, precision, and hope.

> *We are daughters of our Heavenly Father, who loves us. And we love him. We will stand as witnesses of God at all times, and in all things, and in all places as we strive to live the Young Women Values which are: Faith, Divine Nature, Individual Worth, Knowledge, Choice and Accountability, Good Works, Integrity, and Virtue.*
>
> *We believe as we come to accept and act upon these values we will be prepared to strengthen home and family, make and keep sacred covenants, receive the ordinances of the temple, and enjoy the blessings of exaltation.*

We'd pray that someday, someone (preferably our future beaux) would see these qualities in us and ask us to be their helpmeets, supporters, and wives for time and all eternity. I was only twelve, but I knew that if this was the menu the men were ordering from, then by God, I was going to make sure I exemplified every one of these qualities, even if none of them spoke to my natural talents.

Shouldn't a sense of humor be somewhere on the list? Where was the value for a generous laugh? What about an affinity for memorizing lines from books and movies? Wasn't unsinkable ambition something to strive for? It felt meager to pin all my hopes and dreams on the ability to make and keep sacred covenants or strengthen home and family. "Strengthen" felt so diminished for a girl who could build a shelter out of a toothpick and some duct tape. *Please, oh, please let me make and keep sacred covenants, strengthen your home, and give you a family. Please take me to the temple so I can enjoy the blessings of exaltation.*

Everything I was learning to become was in preparation for finding a man, because my salvation was contingent on it. And like other things in Mormonism, they'd already given me the answers to the test. I would lead with the Young Women Values, with the tip of the iceberg, and find a prince to take me to the temple. The rest of the qualities that lay dormant under the surface would be a wonderful surprise.

Every Wednesday night, we had a youth activity where we worked on embodying these Young Women Values. Occasionally, we'd join up with the boys, and coed mayhem sent our hearts aflutter. But for the most part, it was just the girls, and as the saying goes, girls just wanna have fun. Activities ranged from crafts and roller-skating to tying fleece blankets for the care centers and hospitals. Our leaders found ways to teach us the principles of the gospel and womanhood while still making it fun. Treats were always included, and if your Young Women leaders were "cool," those Wednesday nights as a tween unsupervised by siblings or parents were the devil's playground.

It was easy to stand out among the Mormon girls. I was confident. I had cool clothes and cool parents. I felt the flair of natural leadership and leaned into being a ringleader of all things subversive.

It wasn't hard to do. In a world where a bare shoulder or a Starbucks cup can get you ousted, titillating a few twelve-to fourteen-year-olds with some Laffy Taffy jokes makes you an instant hit. Unfortunately, Need for Endless Attention was not one of the Young Women Values nor a goal I could write down in my Personal Progress Workbook.

One particularly adventurous Wednesday evening, we loaded into our youth leader's van to go out for ice cream. Emboldened by our little field trip, I started engaging passersby by leaning out the window and being obnoxious. Obnoxious was a shadow value that fell somewhere between Choice and Accountability and Good Works. It came very naturally to me.

"Hey, how does your hot dog taste?"

It was not my finest work, but it certainly wasn't a career ender. I yelled it at an unsuspecting middle-aged man in the car next to us, who barely looked up from what he was eating to acknowledge me or my question. I may have gotten a few giggles from my friends for my boldness, but by then, I was already moving on to new material, new cars at new stop lights, and new victims for my coded food innuendos.

"Heather, roll the window up."

My youth leader was not amused, and from her white knuckles on the steering wheel and her steely gaze straight ahead, I knew I had gotten the hook. The car banter comedy show had been unceremoniously canceled with no future dates pending. I sheepishly rolled the window up and offered to surrender the front seat to some other aspiring comedian. Tough crowd. Let them have a crack at it. Once a heckler gets to you, it's best to call it a night.

The day following my ill-fated stand-up routine, as I was practicing the piano, I saw my mom go into my dad's office and sit down in one of the blue leather upholstered chairs. His office had two large white-trimmed French doors, and from my seat on the piano bench, I could read their body language with my peripheral vision. Someone was in trouble, and I prayed it wasn't me. Quick-tempered trouble for walking through the pile when she was sweeping or asking if friends could sleep over in front of other adults would be easily tolerated. A minor flare-up followed with an oppressive and exaggerated, "I'm sorry, geez," and the offense was forgotten as quickly as it had occurred. But this conference behind the French doors seemed serious. They weren't just parenting, they were plotting.

My mom got up from her chair and opened the door, beckoning me to join them. Part of me was thrilled to be invited to join their congress of the minds, but I had to remind myself that this was most likely going to end badly.

My dad laid it all on the line and didn't leave a moment for defense.

"We heard about the things you shouted from the car. You're going to call Sister Chesser and apologize. You're going to be grounded from hanging out with any of your school friends. You can be with your church friends, attend your church activities, and stay home with your siblings. And finally, we want to talk to you about why you are really acting like this."

"Acting like what?" I asked incredulously.

"Sometimes, when we aren't feeling good about ourselves, we act out. Your mom and I think that you may be feeling insecure about your appearance and your weight, and so you're acting obnoxious to get attention. We want you to start exercising daily. You and I can go on a walk every morning before breakfast, and it won't interfere with any of your other activities. I'll wake you up at five-thirty a.m., and we can walk the parkway and get back in time to read scriptures with the family. If you lose a little weight, you'll feel better about yourself, and you'll start to get noticed in positive ways."

I pretended to protest, but my throat was flooded with tears. I was humiliated, I was angry, and I was sad. Everything my dad had said was more or less true, as hard as it was to hear. He was willing to say the things that needed to be said even if they were unpopular. I was in that awkward tween phase. I knew it was true, and I knew how the world saw me, but I wanted my dad to see me differently. I wanted him to pull me aside and say, "I'd rather you be funny and brave and occasionally look obnoxious than for you to think you have to be small and quiet and nice in order to be good."

But in their counsel, my parents saw their twelve-year-old leaning into being loud over ladylike, crude over cultured, chubby over chaste, and they feared the worst. They knew things about the world that I didn't. They knew things about our faith and our culture that I didn't, and they wanted to keep me safe within the parameters that would bring me the most happiness in this life and for eternity. They wanted me to keep sweet, pray, and obey, because it would make my life easier.

Because they loved me.

Because they wanted to protect me.

Because they believed it was dangerous; they believed there was no way back.

Every day for the next few months, until the weather changed and it was too cold to tolerate, my dad shuffled into my darkened bedroom at five-thirty a.m., gently shook me awake, and waited silently for me at the foot of our stairs. I grumbled, I stalled, I faked sick on more than one occasion. But my dad never wavered. We'd set out walking along Homestead Parkway, past the fields of prairie dogs and badgers, past the country cottages with calico curtains and window seats, past the occasional car where a man might randomly be sitting and eating at the wheel. No matter how strong the urge, I refrained from making any food-related observations about the man, the myth, or the hot dog.

Because of my dad's background in the FBI, not only was he disciplined enough to take his daughter on daily walks, but when the Denver Temple Committee came recruiting for security detail, my dad was at the top of the list. The Temple Committee was a special task force composed of successful, righteous, and skilled Colorado Mormons. To be asked to serve on the Temple Committee was prestigious, the type of role my dad was made for.

"Dad is going to drive the prophet!" my mom proudly announced.

For several weeks before the temple was dedicated, it was open to the public for tours. Most attendees were surprised to learn that inside the large cathedral-like buildings, there were no worship halls, no crosses, no giant stages on which to hold services. Instead, the temple consisted of auditoriums with rows and rows of white and beige upholstered chairs. Additionally, there were many little rooms designed for specific rituals: washings and anointings, deep baptismal fonts, administrative offices, laundry services, locker rooms, waiting rooms, and secret chamber rooms.

When the temple was dedicated, a special church service was performed inside the highest of holy rooms, the celestial room, where the people seated can sit face-to-face with the living prophet and his counselors. Participants hear him speak, hear him pray, and participate in the Hosanna Shout in the presence of God, His angels, and us, His witnesses here on earth.

I had never been inside a temple, I had no idea what to expect, but because of my dad's position on the Temple Committee, our family had special access to the dedication ceremony. I had an actual golden ticket. And not just a ticket to the waiting room, but a ticket to the Front Row Joe celestial room.

I planned my outfit meticulously: a two-piece set made of sweat-shirt material, a straight skirt and boxy long-sleeved top in light pink with silver abstract flowers. The prophet and his apostles would all be dressed in white from head to toe: suit, tie, jacket, pants, socks, patent-leather shoes. I wanted to be respectful of the palette and avoid wearing anything that detracted from the reverence and pageantry of the sacred event. My sister wore royal blue satin, and I thought it was in such poor taste.

Before we piled into the car, my mom handed me a delicately embroidered handkerchief folded into a perfect square.

"Here," she said. "You're going to need this later when we dedicate the temple."

"What's it for?" I asked.

"You'll see."

At the dedication, after we sang a few hymns and heard a sermon, it was time for the handkerchief's spotlight moment. The prophet, Ezra Taft Benson, approached the white podium and invited everyone to rise and participate in the Hosanna Shout. Dramatically, he pulled a white handkerchief from the inside pocket of his white jacket and raised it above his head.

I looked to my mom, she nodded, and I immediately understood. I snapped my perfect white square into a shape similar to the one the prophet had above his head. No sooner had I assumed the white flag of surrender than the prophet shouted, "Hosanna!"

The entire celestial room followed in sync: "Hosanna! Hosanna! To God and the Lamb!"

The syncopation was surprisingly sophisticated, and the intensity with which everyone was rhythmically slicing the air with their handkerchiefs seemed absurd. When had they all gotten together and rehearsed this? I burst out laughing. I couldn't help it. I was thirteen, I had a pink phone in my bedroom shaped like the letter H, I listened to Yaz and Madonna and doubled up my Swatch watches. I was not prepared to stand straight across from the living prophet and follow his drill-team routine like an erratic windshield wiper that had gone absolutely haywire.

I glanced over at my mom, and she was staring straight ahead.

Death stare.

Poker face.

If she thought this was weird, she was not showing it.

The collective "Hosannas" from the group muffled my spontaneous laughter and disguised my shock. I swallowed my smile and snapped to attentive reverence as swiftly as the handkerchiefs flew through the air. I finished out the Hosanna Shout with my Aqua Net bangs, my Revlon Zinc Pink lips, and a little flourish of the wrist. I had not only ushered in the spirit of the Lord to the Denver temple, but it also felt like I had participated in my first flash mob with the prophet in the celestial room: Mormon flex.

CHAPTER 5

NIGHTSWIMMING

I don't know if it was puberty or personal growth, but over time, I slowly began to peek from behind the iron curtain. Junior high introduced me to an entirely new group of non-member friends. And instead of shining, I was turning the white missionary field of Denver to a dingy gray with my poor example. I experienced my first sips of alcohol (a Fuzzy Navel at Jessica Miller's bat mitzvah); my first tingles below the Mason-Dixon Line, (a slow dance with a scruffy Jewish hunk to Cutting Crew's "I Just Died In Your Arms Tonight"); and several clumsy attempts at heavy petting (sneaking out to meet up with the neighborhood Casanova on the greenbelt outside the tennis courts). I wanted to be good, but it was so easy to be bad. I was beginning to wander off onto the wrong path, and if my hot-dog jokes weren't warning enough, my blue eyeliner should have been.

I had recently discovered the *TV Guide*, and what began as a simple quest to learn more about *Fraggle Rock* turned into a pastime of cruising the *Guide* for "not meant for kids" content. If a show had adult situations, profanity, nudity, or violence written in the fine print, it earned a one-way ticket onto my watch list.

Most of the good stuff didn't air until well after my bedtime. Occasionally, the stars would align, and I'd find myself alone and unsupervised for just long enough to catch the beginning of *Cannonball Run* or the opening shootout in *Big Bad Mama*. I'd sneak into my parents' bedroom and silently advance the channel on the cable box to number fifty-five (HBO); then I'd blindly press the volume button down several times for good measure before I'd even risk turning the television on.

Once the illicit program flickered to life, I'd watch it standing up, the volume barely above a whisper, my hand poised above the power button the entire time. As soon as I heard my mom's Volvo round the corner to our house, I'd turn the TV off, change the cable box back to its original channel, silently float down the stairs, and resume practicing the piano before her Weejuns hit the welcome mat. I was hoping to learn the tricks of the trade in seduction and give myself an edge over the competition. I knew it was a hot-dog-eat-hot-dog world out there in the battle of the sexes, and I planned on succeeding with the boys using a few of the unspoken Young Women Values.

I didn't want to be a bad seed, but here I was. I began to pray fervently for help to know what to do. There weren't a lot of church members to cling to in Denver, and none of my other friends had to follow the strict guidelines I did. I was not keeping up with the cool kids, and I started compromising my values to fit in. I prayed for strength and guidance. I wanted to repent and be purified of my base instincts. I prayed every morning and every night and wrote in my journal about my hopes and fears. I wanted to be better, but I didn't know how. And then Heavenly Father answered my prayer.

My dad had advanced in his career from the Bureau of Land Management to president of an oil and gas company, but the market was crashing, and the franchises he had owned as a side gig, Arby's and Major Video, suddenly became his main focus. His business partners wanted to expand the Major Video franchise into Utah. My parents presented the move to us as a family, around the dinner table.

"Dad is going to be opening three stores in four years in Salt Lake City. It's a very exciting opportunity for our family," my mom announced.

My older siblings immediately protested, Jenny was graduating from high school, and Tyler was going into his senior year at Cherry Creek High. I was getting ready to start ninth grade and was looking forward to heavy petting with high school boys. The younger siblings seemed unfazed, if anything excited about living closer to their cousins.

I wanted to lean into my teenage angst and brood over all the ways moving to Utah was going to ruin my life, but there was a nagging deep in my gut that told me this move was just what I needed. A fresh start, a clean slate. Heavenly Father wanted to get me out of Colorado. I was not strong enough to withstand what I was going to face in high school. The temptations were too, well, tempting. *The force is strong with this one.* I wanted the boys with the cargo pants and hair gel, and I was willing to put my Barbies and badgers away to get their attention. It was a recipe for disaster.

Moving to Utah was the change in environment I *thought* I needed. Once we arrived and settled in, I assumed it'd be like a trip to Grover's Corners, where the girls were wholesome and earnest, the boys a little backward and shy, and hot-dog jokes nowhere on the menu. I wouldn't be drowning anymore, trying to balance my commitment to the church and the normal teen behavior of a secular friend group.

One of my first nights hanging out, I met up with two girls from my new friend group at Geppetto's, a pizzeria just up the street from our junior high. Christie had brought her older brother, and he had brought a friend. They both had been drinking and arrived a little lit up. I felt surprised about the situation, but these were the good kids. Who was I to be the buzzkill?

As the night progressed, my friend kept encouraging me to make out with her brother's friend, Mark: "Just do it. He's so cute, and he's totally into you. I think you guys would make the best couple."

He was cute, but he was awkward. I felt like they might be setting me up to kiss a toad instead of a prince.

"Is he cool? Am I going to regret this?"

I didn't want my first make-out in Utah to set the bar too low. And something about it didn't feel right. They reassured me that he was cool enough, and we should definitely make out. Tonight. No need to wait.

He wasn't hard to seduce, and after a few horrible, sloppy mouth chews, I came up for air and removed myself from his tentacle embrace. It was so stupid, and I regretted it immediately. I called my older brother for a ride, and as soon as he pulled up, I jumped up and got out of there.

On Monday morning at school, the air felt different in the hallways. There were a lot of sideways glances and a different mood around the lockers. I shrugged it off and tried not to take it personally. A few class periods later, as I approached the lunchroom, it became clear that the chill in the air was directed at me. My friend Gretchen walked up to me with a strange, glazed smile on her face.

"Did you make out with Mark Frazier?" she asked, while grinning from ear to ear.

"Um, kind of. Why?"

Her smile stayed frozen, and her gaze never left mine, but her lips moved, and she yelled out, "You guys, it's true! She said it's true!"

A few girls ran to her side and stared me down. Gretchen's eyes lit up as she informed me of my faux pas: Mark Frazier was Regina's boyfriend.

The corners in the hallway darkened, and I heard a buzzing in my ears. What she was saying didn't make sense. Christie and Mandy were both good friends with Regina. And they knew I was friends with Regina, too. If she had a boyfriend, they would know about it, and they would tell me. I didn't know the lay of the land yet. I had just moved in. I was still figuring out how to find the bathrooms on the second floor of the school. And these so-called friends had encouraged me to make out with Mark, had practically insisted, knowing that I would be betraying Regina. It was a setup. It had to be. Why would they do that? It was Housewife Tradecraft 101, an omen of my future. And now I was going to have to figure out what to say to Regina.

Our paths didn't cross until seventh period honors English class with Mr. Gill. My soon-to-be former crowd of friends tightened the circle and let me know that they were Team Don't Steal My Man and that I had committed the ultimate offense. I was worried. I had only been going to this school for a few weeks, and my reputation would not survive a scandal. Especially one of this magnitude. And now I had to face Regina, and she had to be furious.

I walked into the classroom and immediately locked eyes with her. She got up from her desk in the front row and walked towards me. I sat in the chair, and she crouched down by my desk. Before she could speak, I blurted out my apology. "Regina, I'm so sorry about Mark. I didn't know. I was with Christie and Mandy, and they didn't tell me, and I asked them if it was OK. I never would have done that if I had known you were dating him."

"We weren't really dating. I can't date until I'm sixteen, but I definitely liked him. . . . And it's OK. I'm not upset with you. I know you didn't realize. What I'm most upset about is the fact that he was drinking. I feel really betrayed and let down that he would do something like that."

I agreed with her. Drinking alcohol was a character flaw and an indication of his unrighteousness and deficient morals. Regina was no slouch, and she wasn't about to cast her pearls before any swine. Mark was kicked to the curb, and our friendship took off to the races. I knew I could count on her to keep me in line. She was an anchor in a storm that was growing by the day.

The lines between good kids and bad kids, right and wrong, wayward and obedient were getting blurred again, and I found myself adrift in a sea of changing values and relative morality. I was born with a proclivity for all things sinful so it was easy to backslide into temptation. My clean slate was getting cloudy. Wherever you go . . . there you are.

When we first moved into the neighborhood, my dad called an old friend from our ward in Colorado who lived in the area and asked him directly who I should be friends with. He wanted to make sure I was hanging with the right kids, the good kids. He didn't care if it made him seem backward to ask such questions. He wasn't afraid to say what he knew was unpopular.

This plan would have worked if we had been back in Denver, where the groups were clearly divided between partiers and Mormons, for example. But in Holladay, Utah, everyone was Mormon, and a lot of the Mormons partied. I had thought moving to Utah was a trip back in time, but the longer I lived there the more I realized I had been duped.

A lot of my friends were just living double lives and keeping their sins secret. The camouflage was nice for a while, allowing me to partake of the small wonders of the wayward world while still charting my course for celestial glory. But it felt like the goalposts kept getting moved, and it became harder for me to tell the difference between right and wrong, dabbling and indulging in the wages of sin.

One summer night, I snuck out and upped the ante on my usual night games. My friend's parents were out of town, and a group of us from the neighborhood were going to hot-tub past curfew at his house. I snuck back home around two a.m., and as I came sidling in the sliding glass door, I heard my dad stir. Thinking fast, I kicked my flip-flops off, half closed my eyes, and shuffled to the refrigerator, pretending I was disoriented and possibly thirsty. My dad came into the kitchen, immediately suspicious: "What are you doing up?"

"I'm just getting a drink of milk."

He continued to press me. "Were you just outside?"

I dismissed him. "Outside? What are you talking about? I'm half-asleep."

I faked a yawn and sauntered casually out of the kitchen and straight upstairs into my room. I tried to consciously slow my breathing down and quell my hummingbird heartbeat as I curled up under the covers. Within minutes, I felt a presence at my side. I slightly opened one eye and saw the silhouette of my dad's face and the outline of a key piece of evidence. One single wet, grassy flip-flop.

Busted.

Much to my mortification, my dad drove me down to where all my friends were still hot-tubbing. He made his presence known, storming onto the scene.

Surprised by the fairly innocent happenings, my dad said, "I don't appreciate my daughter being down here in the middle of the night."

My prayer came out suddenly, instinctively, and surprisingly in the voice of Rhonda from *Grease 2*.

Oh, God! Please don't say anything you guys. Oh, God! This isn't happening. I'm so embarrassed. I don't want to die a virgin.

Then my friend Clayton, one of the many unrequited loves of my life, said to my dad, "I think she's old enough to make her own decisions." That kind of courage was equal parts thrilling and terrifying: stand up to my dad, but also be just like him.

Never raising his voice or breaking a sweat, my father said, "I'm the one who decides what decisions she makes."

I always felt that my dad was deeply invested in my chastity and in my reputation. So much so that he would load me into the car at two a.m. and drive me through the neighborhood to make sure I wasn't being taken advantage of. We were new in town, but he was always a dad first. He put his principles ahead of being liked or being cool in the community. My dad loved me so much that I knew he would break somebody's arm if they so much as touched me.

I had a deep love and testimony of the gospel and my faith. I was attending church, attending seminary, keeping enough of the rules, and keeping enough of the faith. Regina and Gretchen were the Lion and Tin Man to my Dorothy. They had grown to become my best friends, and as long as we never strayed from the path, the Yellow Brick Road would lead us directly to the Wizard.

Part of my growing dedication to the gospel required me to have quarterly interviews with my local bishop. A bishop's primary objective is to be the shepherd and father of the ward, and part of doing that means connecting directly with the youth. It was a treat to have the bishop sit in on one of our Young Women's classes on Sundays or come visit us at girls' camp for a testimony meeting. With the young men, he was even more involved. Scout camp, snow caves, the youth spaghetti dinner, and the annual Lake Powell extravaganzas.

Bishops, for the most part, were the well-adjusted, wealthy, shining examples of the patriarch's role in the Plan of Happiness. In addition to being a mentor, leader, and friend, the bishop was also the shepherd of our sexual purity. The teenage years can be tough on those who follow a moral code of no sex with yourself or others.

The boys would complain about their bishop interviews because they often required what many bishops called the check-in method. At the end of every day, a young boy struggling with masturbation would call the bishop to let him know how he had fared when it came to fantasizing about the fairer sex. "Good day today, Bishop" meant he had weathered the storm without any cloudbursts. "Bad day today, Bishop" meant he had fallen victim to the five-fingered devil himself.

The church holds these purity principles to be sacred. Breaking the Law of Chastity is tantamount to murder, and that's the doctrine, not the culture.

I was grateful I didn't have to deal with the same scrutiny as my male counterparts and secretly wondered which boys might be flooding their bishops with bad-day calls because of me. Most of my bishop's interviews were short and sweet; I made sure to pause after each question to look thoughtful and not rehearsed.

"Are you staying morally clean? How are your thoughts? Are you having dirty thoughts?"

The pattern of questions was usually rapid-fire and perfunctory, like he was brushing his teeth, and I knew how to get through unscathed.

"Keep up the good work," he'd say, with a tender hand on my shoulder as he escorted me out of the office.

This interview, however, had a different energy to it. Right after the small talk and right before the morality closer questions, my Dick Van Patten, cool-dad bishop took a sharp left turn, paused, and asked me stoically, "Do you ever touch yourself?"

Touch myself? Why was he asking me this? *I touch myself all the time, Bishop. I mean, I wash my face, I scratch my legs, I fold my arms, I clasp my hands. How am I supposed to answer this question?*

He must have sensed my hesitation, because he started tapping his pen on the table. He put both arms behind his head and leaned back in his recliner chair and said, "I don't know why the Spirit is telling me this. But I feel that this is an issue in your life, and the Lord wants me to talk to you about it. If there's something you need to tell me, now's the time. Go ahead and get it off your chest. I can't help you fix it if I don't know exactly what we are dealing with."

I don't know what we are dealing with either, Bishop. You've got me confused with a different type of girl. I was boy crazy, not sex crazy. I wanted a man. I wanted Dick Van Patten. I wanted Tom Hanks. Someone safe and soft with thinning hair and a dad bod. I wanted a man who was just grateful to have sex. I never thought about what I'd get out of it. I kissed a lot of boys because I was searching for a prince, not pleasure. I imagined sex would be a communion of souls and minds.

His questioning continued, and I was filled with shame as I remembered the times I had watched *Big Bad Mama* muted and breathless, listening for the sound of a car in the driveway. I remembered the boys I'd flirted with, the seductions of a fifteen-year-old with braces and an uneven chest. I couldn't drive a car, but I was learning how to drive a teenage boy crazy. The push and pull of pretending you wanted to go farther but then finding your conscience right before he unclasped your bra. Was I supposed to tell my bishop about *Mandarin Orange Sunday*, the sultry paperback I quietly snuck out of a local garage sale that told the tale of Solange, a sexually adventurous woman who enjoyed post-coital omelets with her brawny lover, Sven? (I had read a particularly titillating scene aloud to Regina, prompting her to snatch the paper-back from my toe-curled grip and fling it over a chain link fence into an abandoned lot.)

Every impulse, every dirty joke, every rushed dark grope from a boy that never developed past a house party. Was this what he wanted to talk about? And why? I wasn't having sex. I wasn't masturbating. I was coming to church; I was doing my best. And talking about it was the last thing I wanted to do with anyone, let alone a fifty-year-old father of four.

But I also didn't want to make him mad. I didn't want to expose his false inspiration; I didn't want to call his bluff. I didn't want to accuse him of lying for the Lord. He said the questions were weighing on Jesus's mind as well. A fact I found even harder to believe. I was stuck, and I didn't know what to do.

He had the power to pick up the phone and call my parents and express concern that he'd just had an interview with me and felt I was being evasive. A phone call like that would end my life as I knew it. Evasive didn't mean I was fifteen and uncomfortable, evasive meant I was having sex and covering it up.

"Is there anything you regret that you need to resolve?" he persisted.

Hell, yes! There are about eighteen things I regret just in the last ten minutes. I need to resolve the six ways plus Sunday that I've imagined what might be interpreted as masturbating every time you've tapped your pen on the counter.

Sitting across from Bishop Crawley, I truly believed that he had seen my soul and that God had told him I was a hot-blooded woman.

There I sat, alone in a room, not in front of a priest behind a grate but face-to-face, with a man I would be bobbing for apples with at the fall carnival next week. A man with a daughter in my algebra class. A man who took me and my siblings to Baskin-Robbins after a church activity if we pleaded. There I sat at fifteen, fully believing and committed to the gospel, and yet my bishop—my spiritual leader, my family friend—looked me dead in the eyes, rocked back and forth in his chair, and waited. Waited for me to tell him about all my dirty thoughts and deeds.

And then, because it's your neighbor, because it's your father's family friend, because you feel bad for the guy, because you want the interrogation to end, because you want to try the repentance process, because you must be guilty or he wouldn't be asking, you feel compelled to tell him what he wants to hear. You imagine describing deeds not done but dreamed of and dark moments you hoped would never see the light of day.

You feel pressure to confess because it's John Crawley—it's Dick Van Patten. And he already thinks he knows. You know exactly how it will play out if you sing like a canary, so you tell yourself it's not dirty, it's just his duty, and confess just a little, not a lot.

"I guess I have some things I should clear up. But I'm not sure what I need to talk about with you and what I can clear up on my own."

I wanted to give us both an easy out. Maybe this was just a part of the job he hated. But if he hated it, I couldn't tell.

He lowered his voice. "Was there penetrative sex?"

"No."

Now would be the time for him to say, *Welp, sounds like my part is done. Go with God, little girl. Keep up the great work.*

But he continued. If I unlatched this gate and walked through to the other side, I would be on a slippery slope. The questions could go anywhere.

"I guess I've participated in, ummmmm, petting?" I cringed saying the word and immediately tried to bury the quickly surfacing image of my cat. I needed to stick to the assigned vocabulary list and a hopefully minor offense.

"Heavy petting?" he asked. "Who initiated the contact? Who touched whom first? Did you touch him, or did he touch you?"

"Uhhhhhhh . . . it was kind of a hot jumbled mess of a make-out, so we were never not touching each other. But I guess he 'touched' me first." *Abort! Abort mission!*

"Just your chest, or did he touch you in other places?" *Just my chest, but I'm intrigued.*

"Over the clothes or under the clothes?" *Yes, and yes, please.*

"Any skin-on-skin contact?" *Just the thin white cotton of his briefs, Bishop.*

"Did he orgasm?" *I hope so. To make all of this uncomfortable questioning worth it.*

"Did you orgasm?" *I hope not, because I didn't notice.*

"Did it happen more than once?" *Unfortunately, no. But if it happens again, will this false confession cover future misdeeds?*

I didn't answer truthfully, but I didn't pretend to be perfect. I didn't tell him too much or too little, it was just enough. I said nothing of Fuzzy Navels or stolen wine coolers, I stuck to chastity because that was the only path the bishop pursued that day. He gave me some stern warnings about playing with body parts, mine and others, and then wrapped the interview up and told me I was free to go. He did not walk me to the door, he did not place a hand on my shoulder. He just sat there, rocking back and forth in his office chair, and watched me walk away.

I could tell he was disappointed. He didn't look at me the same way he had before the interview. Righteousness through obedience was the true goal, not righteousness through experience and I always regretted crumbling under the pressure that day. I should've kept my mouth shut. I should've lied.

When my friend's older sister got married, we all headed over to the reception to see her dress and her basketball-star groom. I knew nothing of the clothing or endowment ceremony yet. Or how it related in any way to marriage. The temple to me was just a beautiful castle and the only place where marriage actually counted.

The reception center was full of families dancing, eating, and celebrating the new nineteen-year-old bride and her twenty-two-year-old groom. The air was rife with excitement and anticipation. There was no denying that everyone in the room was thrilled, and that her family was breathing a collective sigh of relief. Her life was beginning! She did it!

I wandered off to a side room and noticed that they had her wedding video playing on loop. The soft primary music I had heard since birth floated in the background, and I was mesmerized by the slow dissolving images of the bride in her dress and veil outside the temple, surrounded by family, by love, by God.

I felt my heart actually ache. *This is what I want. This is who I want to be.* I wanted the white wedding outside the giant temple. I wanted a virgin groom with a mission and ambition on his résumé. I wanted my family to celebrate and embrace me as I started my life as a wife and mother. I didn't want to do anything to sabotage this chance. I didn't want to randomly make out with some loser and disappoint my future husband one day. I wanted to be perfect. I wanted to be pure. I wanted the fairy tale.

I doubled down on my personal prayer, my commitment to fasting once a month, and my daily scripture study. I read from my Book of Mormon every night, even if it was just a verse. I felt spiritually strong and my testimony of the truthfulness of the gospel was growing. I wanted to be good. I wanted to be righteous. I wanted to be worthy of the companionship of the Holy Ghost.

After graduating high school my dad took me and my friends, Regina and Gretchen, on a camping trip to the San Juan River to celebrate. We scouted a campsite high up on a red rock ridge overlooking the goosenecks of the river and the backdrop of the high, steep, marbled rock. It was a cathedral carved out of the canyon, and it made me feel deeply connected to God.

After a dinner of seven-layer enchiladas from the Dutch oven and a dessert of Pepperidge Farm coconut cake, we made our way around the campfire on a flat rock ledge. It was the perfect stage for a concert. Regina stood up and began to sing, "Down the Via Dolorosa, in Jerusalem that day . . ."

She sang of Christ the King, on the way to Calvary. The acoustics made her sound like she was backed by a full orchestra. I felt the spirit of God surrounding us, and every star in the sky testified to me that the church was true and that Jesus was a Mormon. I was graduating high school, and I wanted to keep that feeling with me forever. We were three BICs well on our way to see the Wizard, and our friendships were deepened by our shared beliefs and spiritual bond.

CHAPTER 6

RISE AND SHOUT,
THE COUGARS ARE OUT

After high school, I got a full-ride scholarship to the University of Utah for piano performance. Thanks to the dutiful lessons of my homemaking mother and my Mormon desire to fill my house with music, I had been a child prodigy in Colorado, winning state competitions and performing around the nation.

My mom interviewed all the best teachers, arranged auditions with the best piano performance professors at University of Utah, Brigham Young University, and Utah State. She had spent half my childhood sitting on the piano bench next to me, painstakingly teaching me note by note and practicing the curriculum my teachers, Bernard and Carolyn Shaak, assigned.

My mom deserved to win the piano competitions as much as I did, and when my wanton teenage ways became more burden than blessing, she resigned herself to letting me retire from the classical piano circuit and start playing the pop music I yearned for. When it came time to audition for a scholarship, I put away "Jessica's Theme" and "What I

Did for Love" and instead wowed the admissions committees with the Chopin étude I had previously learned and performed when I was just eleven years old. It impressed them enough to award me a full-ride scholarship in addition to the feather in my cap.

However, the University of Utah was not the school my parents wanted me to attend. A full ride was nothing compared to the pride and joy of having a daughter at the premier, faith-affirming institution: Brigham Young University.

Brigham Young University is where our family believed the best Mormons went to college—the corn-fed, home-bred descendants of trailblazing pioneers. The consensus in our home was, if you can get into BYU, you go. "Enter to learn. Go forth to serve."

The real allure of BYU was the flood of righteous men fresh off their missions who returned to Provo looking to find a woman to seal in the new and everlasting covenant. Parents wanted their daughters at BYU because that was where the eligible boys were. If you could get married in the faith, it was a fast track to a life of happiness and eternal glory. What parent wouldn't want to ensure those conditions?

So my parents made me a deal. They said, "We'll pay you the equivalent of your scholarship, and we'll pay for your first year at BYU, but then you're on your own."

Challenge accepted. I went to BYU.

At school, I always tried to color inside the lines. I was terrified I'd be expelled if I didn't. It was the job of all of us to police each other, to make sure that we weren't painting the white roses red. My roommates knew who went to church each Sunday, and which boyfriends stayed over too late. They saw if Domino's dropped a pizza on a porch on the Sabbath. They knew who had gotten handsy with the guy passing out the sacrament. We were either exposing each other or covering for each other. Either way, the concept of secrecy, of harboring double lives, bred like bacteria in a Petri dish.

The childish antics and unique sense of humor that had set me apart growing up weren't as charming at BYU. I found myself bobbing in a sea of similar-minded Mormon girls looking to wed with genetic dowries much finer than mine. When you're surrounded by the truly sweet, even a raspberry can seem sour. I was standing out for all the wrong reasons. I was too big, too loud, and too much. I wanted to become marriageable, and that meant I'd need to shelve whatever foolish ideas were filling my brain and replace them with self-care, self-improvement, and an eye single to the glory of a groom.

I had ambition. I had drive. I was entrepreneurial. I started counting my calories and counting my coins. I turned to work, the one thing that had always been there for me even when the boys weren't.

My first job that didn't involve a cash register was a writing gig at a company in Salt Lake City called Wasatch Education Systems. My older sister Jenny had been working full-time at the front-desk reception area for more than a year. She was the main gatekeeper for the president and vice president of the company, and her influence at the top of the corporate food chain exceeded her title. Her job required absolute attention from nine a.m. until five p.m., with a headset, a transfer board, and constant phone calls, visitors, and meetings.

She had one blessed hour off for lunch and every day we raced against time to make the most of it. We would jump in the car, find a place to eat, and return back before the phones started ringing again.

Our days were spent gearing up for lunch, racing through lunch, and then recovering from lunch. It was my dream job.

Jenny, at twenty-three, was almost nine months pregnant. She left school at BYU after she got married and immediately started working to cover her husband's tuition. To everyone around us, she was living the dream. Went to BYU, found a man, bought a house, and had a baby. Her path was one clean, continuous line. Once she had the baby, she'd be kissing Wasatch Education Systems and her life as a receptionist goodbye forever. She was counting down the days, but I was dreading having her leave.

Our lunch hours together were cherished times for me, when we laughed and bonded and experienced each other in an element outside of our house and family. Businesswomen bonding over salads. She was so good at her job, and everyone at the company loved her. The fact that they had hired me was evidence of such. I loved watching her shine, and I was proud to be her sister. I wasn't going to let her down.

I didn't want to brag around the office, but I was a published writer by the age of seven. My poem in second grade, "Purple Mountain Majesties," won a school contest and was published in the *Rocky Mountain News*. I was shocked to learn it had won and terrified to learn it would be published. It was some last minute non-rhyming drivel where I lazily regurgitated lyrics from "America the Beautiful" and a school song, "Colorado! Where a Man Can Walk a Mile High!" There was hardly any thought behind any of it, and I was ashamed. I was surprised they didn't accuse me of plagiarism but instead rewarded me with a byline on the front page of the supplemental arts section of the newspaper.

I imagined a celebratory parade in my honor where I'd be prancing like the emperor in my new clothes, only for a child from the audience to shout, "But she hasn't got anything on! She's just taken bits and pieces from her favorite songs and jumbled them on the page."

In high school, my AP English teacher, Carol Spackman Moss, had to wrangle more than a few *Cosmopolitan* magazines from me in class. But she gave me an A++ on my essay about Toni Morrison's *Beloved*. I entered the schoolwide "My America" speech contest on a whim two years in a row and placed both times. I won four hundred dollars the first year and a respectable two hundred fifty the year after that. I listed all of these things on my résumé .

There were a few gems I also left off. I had been known to pen my own romantic scenes from Harlequin paperbacks from time to time. Mostly to titillate my friends, but also because it came easily to me. My mom stumbled on one of my more impressive tales about a heaving stallion with a furious gallop and his golden-haired maiden, but if she was shocked by the content, she didn't show it.

"Hmmph," she said, while handing me back the pages. "Descriptive."

I couldn't believe she wasn't freaking out. Certainly she had to know I was alluding to sex when I spoke of riding a bareback horse. Maybe I wasn't a good writer after all, or maybe I had gotten sex all wrong. I didn't know, but I didn't ask. She either trusted me enough to know my stories were merely fantasies or she didn't examine it closely enough to read between the lines.

Despite my accolades and detailed stories about Arabian horses, I was convinced that it was my sister Jenny who had sold the company on my abilities, and once she left for maternity leave, I'd be abandoned and exposed.

She promised me that her having a baby wouldn't keep us from hanging out. Instead, we would just advance to lunching without time constraints. Casual, hours-long lunches where we wouldn't be forced to rush our tostadas or forgo pasta e fagioli soup and unlimited breadsticks altogether. Neither of us realized that I would still be limited by working and that motherhood would become all-consuming. Our lunches as two working gals together were over forever. She left to be a full-time mom and never looked back.

After I left Wasatch, I moved to Provo and applied to work at Electric Beach, the social hub and only choice for a tanning salon at BYU. Fairly quickly, I got promoted to manager and started hiring and firing girls at will. I loved the work and scheduled myself for every available shift. If I had time to lean, I had time to *clean*, and I always wanted to be at work.

I realized that having a job was my thing. I was the only one who was always there, ready to put a girl in a RUVA bed for twenty-five minutes or sell the most expensive tanning lotion to Donny Osmond: Helix, fifty dollars. I wanted to be surrounded by my customers and employees more than I wanted to be ice-blocking with other BYU coeds in my Family Home Evening group on the weekend.

When I did hang out with friends, I had a tendency to take a leisurely activity and theorize about a way to monetize it. I made it my business to make everybody's business better.

At a summer barbecue my sophomore year, a friend brought over rock beads, watch faces, and fishing line. She showed us how to craft our own rustic bracelet watches with little nubs of polished turquoise, agate, and tiger's eye. The work was intense, but the results were beautiful.

I beckoned to our business-owner friend. "Charlie, check this out. We need to sell these in your stores."

Charlie Freedman was a legend around campus; he had started not one but three discount retail stores called DownEast Outfitters and was in a position to make or break our imagined careers.

"How much did it cost you to make?" he asked. I consulted with my friends and did a rough calculation of our raw materials.

"About sixty-five dollars," I proudly exclaimed.

Charlie laughed. "In order for those to sell at my store, you need to make them for less than ten dollars, so I can buy them for twenty and sell them for fifty."

"That's impossible!" I replied.

"Then find something else to sell."

Challenge accepted. I immediately factored in the materials on a watch and realized that one watch had enough rock beads to make fifteen pairs of earrings. I pitched the idea without hesitation.

"What if I sell you earrings?"

Charlie walked over to our craft table, looked me in the eyes, and said, "Make some earrings I can sell for around six dollars, and we will see how they do."

The following Monday, I walked into DownEast Outfitters with a basket full of fishhook earrings crafted, carded, and branded with my first company name: Steelhead Designs. I cast my line, and the fish were biting. The earrings practically leaped off the store countertop into the bags of the customers. In a matter of months, I had built display cases, style storyboards, and a wholesale account with the local bead supplier thanks to Charlie's cosign. I used my income from the tanning salon to fund the production of the earrings and watched the purchase orders grow. I had accounts with all three of the local DownEast Outfitters locations, and then I expanded to the gift shops at Sundance, Bridal Veil Falls, and Jackson Hole before I had the courage to try for the really big fish on Steelhead Designs' radar: Nordstrom.

Nordstrom turned my little earring gig into a pretty big deal. A year later, the sales were significant enough for me to be a contender. My professor let me know that I had been nominated for the Entrepreneur Student of the Year award, and I was thrilled, but I assumed I'd never win. But because I'd been innovative in my approach for outsourcing labor, because I'd impressed the committee with my rapid growth and market-share increase, because I'd done it all while working full-time as a tanning engineer, I won BYU's Entrepreneur Student of the Year Honorable Mention my junior year. (I lost to the student who came up with 1-800-CONTACTS.) But no one cared. No one mentioned it. Being a businesswoman was not a mark of success in my family nor my community. If I brought it up, they just asked if I was dating anyone and changed the subject.

My college years were a tempestuous time for BYU, feminism, and stepping outside of the box. In 1993, BYU revoked Cecilia Farr's status as a professor because she had privately advocated a pro-choice position on abortion and someone turned her in. I was pretty sure I was pro-choice, but I was smart enough never to say that out loud around my friends. I went to a "gathering" on campus to show support for Dr. Farr and to challenge BYU's actions. (Protests are prohibited on campus without written permission.)

While I was there, in the front row of the crowd, a *Daily Universe* photographer snapped a picture with me at the center.

The next day, a photo of the protest along with the headline about Cecilia Farr were both on the front page of the school newspaper. My heart froze. I didn't want to look like a protester. I didn't want my professors to think I was anything but dutiful. I was terrified that a photo like this would flag my account and that I would be called into the Honor Code office. I was one phone call away from falling to my knees and losing more than I bargained for just because I supported a fired professor who identified, off-campus, as pro-choice. The Honor Code knows no bounds. It can find you anywhere and arbitrarily revoke your student status at any time.

David Knowlton, another professor at BYU, briefly mentioned the church's missionary system at an independent Mormon forum. He then made some disparaging remarks about LDS architecture and, surprise, got a pink slip. The church is very proud of its mid-century modern meetinghouses. *Don't go there, David. It won't end well.*

Gail T. Houston, one of my English professors, was devastated to hear that she got the boot because she admitted to praying to Heavenly Mother. Any tremor of feminism created a tidal-wave reaction within the administration. The message was clear: toe the line or abandon ship. If you didn't surrender yourself, the Honor Code office was happy to have you walk the plank.

Officially, BYU has stated that Farr, Knowlton, and Houston did not have their contracts renewed because of their lack of scholarship, not because of their opinions. It wasn't an environment to question, to explore identities, to try new experiences. If you went through the forbidden gate, it slammed shut, and you couldn't find your way back.

It was rumored that if it was a slower day at the watchtower, the Honor Code office kept themselves busy by researching Utah county booking records and calling in anyone who had been booked into jail. You already had a criminal record and court fees, but now you would also be kicked out of school and forfeit your tuition.

If your bishop felt you went too far with your boyfriend, he was compelled to inform the Honor Code office. A low-grade, up-the-shirt moral violation could have you suspended. And with that came a whole other litany of woes. Enrolled in classes? Not anymore; you were automatically dropped from all of them. Living in student housing? Not anymore; you would be evicted. And if you were evicted due to an Honor Code suspension or investigation, you were still responsible for the rent through the semester. If you worked on campus or for the school, that was gone, too. You were immediately fired. It was not the type of environment where you were free to be a good-time girl and regret it in the morning. You flashed your tits and someone told? You were going home in a body bag of shame and debt.

I knew distinctly the times when I had heard the Spirit whisper to me and I chose to ignore it or to let logic, laziness, or cynicism dismiss my intuition. I believe I felt a distinct prompting to go visit my grandmother in Salt Lake City while I was in Provo at BYU. It was a forty-five-minute drive, not preventative but not convenient. And as a BYU student with two jobs, a home business, and a full class load, I continually found reasons to cancel my trip.

Feeling guilty, I called her and made a plan to take the drive and visit her the following week. Then I got tired, or busy with work, or distracted by life, and I didn't go. Two days later, my dad called to tell me that she had passed away. The air was sucked out of the room, and I felt dizzy. God had spoken to me, and I had ignored it. And look what happened. I was Kevin McCallister in *Home Alone*, spilling Pepsi on the pizza. *Look what you did, you little jerk.*

A few weeks later, I flew home for Christmas and saw my dad laid bare by this loss of his mother. She had been married to a man we never talked about, unless it was to complain about how mean he was. She was from a long line of devout, Mormon pioneers. But she had married a man outside the faith and suffered because of it. When he died, she refused to do his temple work. She had no desire to reunite with him in the Celestial Kingdom and procreate forever. *Good riddance. Good day, sir.* As a widow, she volunteered and worked in the church genealogical center until the day she died. Never remarrying, never being sealed in the temple to her spouse, fulfilling her destiny as a minstering angel on earth and then in heaven. She had raised my dad and his siblings with next to nothing, no support, and the shame of having a spouse who was never the assistant coach of the soccer team.

Two apostles attended her funeral to speak and give tribute to my grandmother. Joseph B. Wirthlin and M. Russell Ballard had lived in my dad's neighborhood growing up and knew our family well. When Elder Ballard was giving his eulogy, he looked out at all of her grandchildren seated in the church pews and decreed an apostolic blessing from the pulpit. He blessed us as her descendants with additional gifts and protection if we continued to keep the commandments and honor her legacy as valiant latter-day saints. Apostles at a funeral: Mormon flex.

Christmas break that year was thick with grief, and we tiptoed around my normally jubilant father, who, in the wake of the loss, seemed much more fragile.

One afternoon, I found myself attempting to imbue a little Christmas cheer by lazily playing our favorite holiday songs on the piano. My dad casually walked into the piano room and laid down on the couch. I amped up the ornamentation and tried to play "Jingle Bells" as gently as possible.

In almost a child's voice, he meekly asked me to play his favorite hymn, "How Great Thou Art," and I immediately obliged. By the time

I reached the chorus and arpeggio of "Then sings my soul, my Savior God to thee," the dam in his heart broke wide open. He began to cry, his hand shielding his eyes, his body wracked with sobs. I had never seen him upset like that before, and I never saw it again. A son grieving his mother and perhaps grieving what could have been if she had married a different man. If she had given him a different father. I took note. Martyrdom is so conflicted.

"Promptings are important," my dad always said. "You need to learn to listen to them in life. Those are the moments that matter."

Watching my dad cry on that couch reignited my desire to make him proud. I never wanted to see him this hurt again. I vowed to not let my natural self eclipse my spiritual self anymore.

I wanted the love, serenity, and protection that my family and church provided. No longer would I question or long to leave the Americana world of enamel, painted piggy banks and embroidered, monogrammed Christmas stockings. Our white-bread wonderland was a marshmallow world that I would no longer take for granted. It was our birthright to be better, and when you have the Hilton name, why would you ever give it away? Why eat the fruit of the tree when it rids you of Eden?

CHAPTER 7

YOUR LIFE, LITTLE GIRL, IS AN EMPTY PAGE

Despite the cold, dark winter of the Honor Code's domain, when I returned to Provo and my job at Electric Beach, I was happy to provide patrons the sights, sounds, and sun of summer all year round. Rich or poor, Honor Code–abiding or defying, we made the UV rays shine down on all of them. Our beds did not distinguish between saint and sinner. Electric Beach was a safe space for everyone. Even older men with sugar-daddy potential.

When James Barnes sauntered up to our counter, he seemed out of place for the average college student customer. I asked if he had any questions and geared up to pitch him on buying a bottle of lotion. I got seven percent of the store's gross lotion sales, and the only customers who ever splurged on them were the ones not paying tuition. He was an easy mark. I had him fill out the customer card and began to enter his data into the computer.

Name: James Barnes.

Address: Idaho. *Hmmmm. Not local but not far.*

Birthdate: October 5, 1963. *1963?*

He was thirty-three years old. Definitely had discretionary income for our finest bronzing lotion. I started with a quick speech about the damage caused by the sun's rays and the danger of a tan that fades too quickly and glided right into the different pricing tiers of lotions that could prevent all of these woes.

He was amused, and I saw him smiling at me in a way I wasn't used to. I was comfortable around older men asking me questions. After all, I had been interacting alone with my church leaders since I was eight years old. But none of those bishops ever smiled at me in a way that made me feel anything like this. His smile was beckoning. *Thank you, Big Poppa!*

I was good at flirting with boys, but I was not prepared to flirt with a real live *man*, out in the wild.

"Don't stop." He encouraged me. "I want to hear more about the products you're selling."

"Oh, it's not a sales pitch. My job as the manager is to keep you safe and keep you tan. The best way to do both of those things is with a quality lotion."

He burst out laughing. "I'm impressed. Are you a business major?"

I was smiling now too, in a way that I had never smiled at my bishops, either.

"No," I scoffed playfully. "I'm majoring in humanities."

He seemed surprised. "Well, I'll buy whichever lotion you recommend the most, not because you're selling it but because you're keeping me safe."

I selected the second most expensive one.

After I rang him up, I confessed. "Calling my sales pitch 'not a sales pitch' is my actual sales pitch."

When he returned from his tanning bed bronzer and bolder, he lingered at the counter until I could talk.

"Well, here's my sales pitch," he proclaimed. "I think you should have dinner with me. I'm not selling you on the idea, I'm just recommending it out of the kindness of my heart."

Dinner? With a man? I'm not ready!

He picked me up at six o'clock sharp two days later at the salon and walked me to his car. He had a silver Mercedes, and he opened my door for me. When I sat down, I noticed he had a dashboard cover with his name embroidered on it. Weird flex but a nice reassurance that the name on his car and the name on his customer card were one and the same. If he was perpetrating a fraud, he had gone to great lengths to hide it. We started driving up the canyon toward Robert Redford's Sundance resort. *If I forget to tell you later, I had a really good time tonight.*

"Have you ever been to the Tree Room?" he asked.

"No, I haven't." *I've never been anywhere.*

"They built the restaurant around this giant tree because they couldn't bear to cut it down. It still grows right in the middle of the restaurant. You're going to love it."

He was right. I did. He held my hand and led me down the rough-hewn log stairs and pulled my chair out so I could sit facing the giant tree. He commandeered the menu and ordered several different things, describing each of them to me in detail. We ate and laughed and talked, and I fell head over heels in love. I wanted him. I wanted this life. I wanted to eat food men had ordered for me and face trees that were too beautiful to cut down. Everything looked better, smelled better, tasted better because he was there. Or because it was expensive. Or both. Either way, it didn't matter to me. *Sweet dreams are made of this. Who am I to disagree?*

The waiter asked him if he would like a nightcap, and he casually asked if they had any Drambuie.

While the server left to get his drink, he used the opportunity to take my hand in his. He interlaced our fingers and traced my palm with his thumb. When his drink arrived, he raised the snifter up and tilted it to catch the light.

"Do you see the flecks of gold?" *Yes, dear God, yes. I see it all. Take me now.*

"Drambuie is a golden Scotch whisky liqueur." He swirled it in the glass and held it up to my nose. "Smell this. "

I closed my eyes and inhaled deeply. Too deeply, because I heard him chuckle. My eyes snapped open.

"It's incredible, right?"

I nodded lamely.

"Drambuie comes directly from the hills of Scotland and is infused with honey, spices, and one very special ingredient." He took a sip and handed me the glass. "Drink some, and then lick your lips."

I held the glass to my lips and swallowed. It burned, but it wasn't bitter. I licked my lips and could taste the hills of Scotland, I could feel the passion of William Wallace, I could hear the groan of the Loch Ness Monster from the deep.

He leaned in across the table. "Did you taste it?"

"Uh-huh. Um, yeah. I think so." *Take me. I believe. It doesn't matter what you ask me to do. I'm going to do it. Drambuie me all night long.*

He dipped my finger in the glass and put it in his mouth, pulling me closer. I was about to climb across the table or climb the trunk of the giant namesake tree in front of me. He took my finger out of his mouth and held on to my hand.

"The secret ingredient is heather."

He put his other hand under my chin and pulled my lips to his. He kissed me softly and slowly at first, and I could taste the Drambuie and the honey and the hills of Heather on his tongue. "They harvest the natural heather and then infuse it into the whisky. It's subtle, strong, and rare. Just like you." *Check, please.*

We made out in the parking lot of the restaurant until the windows fogged and the last kitchen worker locked the door. *On this night of a thousand stars, let me take you to heaven's door.* I was blissful. On the drive home, we held hands, and I fought the urge to climb over the console and into his lap. When we arrived back at the salon, I kissed him goodbye. He said he would call me in the morning. I floated home and dreamed of Scottish moors and Mercedes dashboard covers.

When my roommates woke up, they cornered me and begged to know every detail. I began describing my night, minus the Drambuie. I didn't want them dismissing this guy without a fight. They didn't seem to be impressed. Not with his charm. Not with his Mercedes. Not with his ability to fog up the windows.

"Who is he? Why is he still single at thirty-three? It's strange."

I wanted to blurt out, "He's not even Mormon" but that would just make the situation worse.

"He's either addicted to porn or he's out to seduce you and leave you scorned, Heather. You should stay away. I don't think you should go out with him again. He's too old to be single and too old to be dating you."

"What will ever come of it? If you're not going to marry him, what's the point?"

They had a point. There was no point. More dates would lead to more Drambuie, and more Drambuie would lead to him tasting all my secret ingredients. It was better not to play with fire. I would snuff out the flame of James Barnes before I got burned.

He called several times the next day, but I was too afraid to answer and also resisted the idea of having to tell him I couldn't see him again. Every cell in my body wanted to see him again. He was sexy and funny and successful and smart and into me. Why couldn't we have a torrid affair? I didn't need to *marry* him. I could just have a *relationship* with him. A one-night stand. And then move on to a nice Mormon boy and get married in the temple. But I knew that wasn't how it worked. Everyone wants to marry a girl who's naive, not all-knowing. I wanted to be a prize for my future husband. All of his calls went unanswered and unreturned. There would be no harvesting of this Heather.

Despite my attempts to be small, to be quiet, to be sweet, to not sparkle too much but just enough, I still found my graduation date approaching without a ring on my finger.

The writing was on the wall. My sister Jenny had gotten married at nineteen. And yet there I was at twenty-one. I had a humanities degree from BYU, a managerial position at a local tanning salon, and a burgeoning business, but I felt like a complete loser because I wasn't married. I had run out of options. My anchor had left me adrift.

I didn't know what to do. I had already overshot the mark. The Young Women Values had led me up to the gate, but it wasn't up to me to unlatch it. I was treading an unmarked path on my Plan of Happiness. I had done all I was supposed to do, and I was scared that if I left the stock pond of BYU, I'd flounder in the open sea.

I had never had anyone in my life encourage me to do anything past this point. No mention of an advanced degree. No mention of an actual career. No mention of travel, or adventure, or a gap year. The map only led to marriage, so I didn't know where to go next.

I was wallowing in my pain and coping the best way I knew how— eating Pop-Tarts and reading *Prince of Tides* on our living-room couch— when Regina, my tried and true, came down the stairs and stood at my feet.

"Hey, I just talked to my mom, and she felt impressed to tell you that if you have ever considered serving a mission, she will help pay for it."

I sat up abruptly and brushed the Pop-Tart crumbs off my chest.

"Are you serious? She said that?"

"Yes," Regina replied, almost as surprised as I was.

Serving a mission had been a charged subject for her. She was a go-getter, a super-achiever, the type of Mormon girl who would serve a mission and be admired for it. However, she had prayed and pondered and decided that the Lord wanted her to pursue her education more than he wanted her to pursue new converts to the church.

She was in the same position as me: graduating without a prospect for marriage but she didn't seem consumed with it like I was. She seemed to have a plan for her future that didn't immediately hinge on getting married. I, however, did not have a plan and I felt immense pressure. I was riddled with well-meaning questioners every day, asking me what my plans were. If I was dating anyone. If I planned on serving a mission. If I was concerned about my future.

The truth is, we were all concerned about our futures; the next step in our lives would be a crucial juncture. I was walking away from the biggest pool of eligible Mormon singles in the world. I was aging out of BYU and stepping out into the unknown. I had a budding business, a great job, and a community of friends in Provo, but I couldn't stay there after graduation. I was done. My era had ended.

Serving a mission was the next logical choice, but it was expensive. All missionaries fund their own missions independently, and when you are earning your keep volunteering eighteen months of your life, five hundred dollars a month can be a pretty big deterrent. Plus, I wasn't sure Steelhead Designs would continue to succeed without me.

"I'm serious," Regina persisted. "She said if you've ever considered serving a mission, you are exactly the type of person she would want to support financially."

I knew the stigma associated with being a woman and a returned missionary, but I was also intrigued by the gift Regina's mom was laying at my feet.

I told our friend Gretchen about the offer. She, too, was turning twenty-one and the mission option was becoming increasingly attractive. She looked me straight in the eyes and said, "I'll go if you go." Our fate was sealed.

When I received my missionary call, everyone gathered around for the big announcement. I told my family I wanted to read it privately so that I could have a spiritual confirmation of the calling and its truthfulness before I shared it.

That was a lie.

The previous week Gretchen had opened her mission call in front of family and friends and read that she had been assigned to Anaheim, California. I'm sure many missionaries would be thrilled to spend eighteen months in Anaheim, but not me. The thought of going somewhere mundane and in a neighboring state was horrifying. I wanted a language and a culture and preferably an ocean to hide behind while I went proselytizing door-to-door preaching the good word of God. I never opened my door for the Jehovah's Witnesses that dutifully dropped by with pamphlets and I didn't want to have that same experience stateside and be rejected by my very own.

I asked to read my calling in private because I wanted to make sure that it was something or somewhere that I could stomach. I couldn't risk reading "Boise, Idaho" in front of my family when someone would inevitably volunteer some obscure affirmation: "That's where your great-aunt was born," or "Last night I had a dream I was watching you open your mission call and you were eating a big plate of potatoes." I didn't want to hear all the reasons Idaho was God's promised land. If I got a shitty calling, I was going to front-load.

Before I read this aloud, I just want to say that I'm not positive this is the right calling for me. I've been really filled with doubt and a stupor of thought lately. I think I'm supposed to stay home and get married. The love of my life is out there waiting for me and I don't want to waste a minute of baby-making time in Idaho. I know in my heart the Lord wants me to stay home and get married, and opening my call right now just confirmed it.

I was not going to the Fresno, De La Habra, or North Las Vegas mission. It had to be foreign. I didn't care where, but it had to require a passport.

Alone behind a closed door, as my family waited with anticipation in the next room, I opened the envelope:

You are hereby called to serve as a missionary of the Church of Jesus Christ of Latter-day Saints. You are assigned to labor in the France-Marseille mission. It is anticipated that you will serve for a period of eighteen months.

The South of France.

Full-body chills.

At that moment, I knew the church was true. God knew me. He knew that I would struggle if it was somewhere lame, and he gave me the Côte d'Azur, the French Riviera. *God is good. The church is true. You made the right choice.*

In that moment, I was grateful that I had never done anything to take me away from the church. It was true, and I had chosen wisely.

I was deeply grateful that I had let James Barnes's Drambuie-laced phone calls go unanswered, that I had put down my Pop-Tart and accepted Regina's mom's invitation, that I had stifled my laughter during the Hosanna Shout and instead raised the white flag of surrender, that I had recited the Young Women Values and strived to live them, that I had chosen BYU, that I had chosen chastity, that I had chosen faith over doubt, that I had clung to the iron rod and followed the Plan of Happiness.

The backyard gate had been flung open. But with the church on my side, no speeding cars or unfound badger dens could deter me from my mission.

PART TWO

BAD
MISSIONARY

CHAPTER 8

LOVE IS A TEMPLE

Once I had received a mission call to the South of France, I was queued up for the next essential rite of passage: the temple ceremony. Before leaving for the MTC, the Missionary Training Center, every missionary must go through the temple to be washed, anointed, and endowed.

I had always assumed I'd wait until I got married to go to the temple. I was hesitant about fast-forwarding to this milestone, because once I went to the temple, I'd be obligated to wear garments. I wasn't sure how a full polyester suit under my clothes would affect my ability to date, and I was worried about it. I struggled enough with one waistband, and now I'd be fighting against elastic binding not only around my waist but around my arms and knees as well. How could I seduce the man of my dreams if my body was always partitioned like a centipede? I told myself that any man *I'd* want to marry would be impressed by my dedication to the gospel, centipede segmentation or otherwise.

I had been singing the primary song "I Love to See the Temple" in

Sunday school since I was three years old, and I assumed that every time I sang it, it was preparing me for what the temple experience was going to be like. The lyrics were simple, sweet, and straight forward: *I love to see the temple, I'm going there someday.* The words promised that I would feel the Holy Spirit, listen, and pray. I assumed that the experience would be like a deluxe sacrament meeting in a more beautiful environment with everyone dressed in white.

Despite the fact that I had been born in the covenant, attended church weekly my entire life, graduated from the seminary program, and graduated from the Lord's university, I knew absolutely nothing about what actually happened inside the temple. I knew that we changed into white robes at some point and that the white represented heaven, and I also knew that once I went through the temple for the first time, I would be considered "endowed" and would have to wear garments, clothing underneath my clothing, for the rest of my life. That was it.

When I was nine, I stumbled on what I assumed to be temple clothes in my mom's closet. It was around Christmastime, and my second favorite activity after chipping stale Red Hots off the gingerbread houses was rummaging for hidden Christmas presents.

I still wholeheartedly believed in Santa Claus—his lore was nothing compared with the leap of logic needed to justify Joseph Smith's first vision—but there were still presents to be found. My mom was the master of the big reveal. She hid all the presents, from Santa or otherwise, until Christmas morning, when our living room exploded into our own version of FAO Schwarz. It was always magical and overwhelming, and the anticipation was so intense that uncovering a few gifts in advance abated my anxiety. Plus, I saw myself as a more feminine version of Harriet the Spy, and there was a case to crack.

My parents had a walk-in closet, and their clothes were separated just like their roles and duties in heaven. When I was on all fours crawling behind the dresses and skirts, I saw a little navy blue suitcase. I pulled it out and unzipped it. There was a pile of white gauzy fabric and some shapeless satin slippers on top. I started to pull everything out to investigate, but something stopped me in my tracks. A strange, physical feeling washed over me. I quickly zipped up the bag and shoved it against the wall concealed by all the dress hems and pretended it never happened.

A few years later, we were visiting our cousins in Wanship, Utah, for the Pioneer Day Parade—my dad never missed an opportunity to attend a parade—when I saw two protesters, a man and a woman, walking through the crowd dressed in similar fabric to what I had seen in the hidden suitcase. The man was wearing a little baker's cap, and the woman wore a short, heavy veil tied under her chin with a bow. They both had on bright green, shiny, square aprons at their waist, embroidered with leaf patterns that tied in the back with a thick white ribbon. They had layers of white tunics and then swaths of the same pleated white fabric diagonally draped across their chests and tucked into sashes tied around their waists. The mass of white and shocking green stood out from all the red, white, blue, and denim of the crowd.

Their path cut through the parade like a hot knife through butter. A hush fell over the masses. People avoided them in force, peeling off from the sidewalk and turning their children's faces into their legs or shielding their view by stepping in front of the children with their bodies. No adult seemed interested in the pamphlets they were handing out. No adult seemed surprised that they were dressed like Freemasons. No adult seemed interested by anything they had to say or stand for.

The children, however, were *very* intrigued by all of the above. Not only because their outfits were absurd, unlike anything we had ever seen, but also because of the pallor their appearance cast over an entire crowd that only minutes before had been jubilant and cheerful, full of Pioneer Day pride.

I stopped dead in my tracks, craning my neck to get a better look. "Dad, what are those people doing?" He looked over and paused for just a beat. I saw a ripple of horror pass through his countenance.

"They should not be doing that," he said sternly. "Just ignore them."

Doing what? I thought. *Dressing like that?* I didn't even know how to categorize what they were dressed like. It had Grecian toga overtones, but the cap and veil were rudimentary and looked more Mennonite than Mount Olympus. The bright green was out of left field. When did that color ever become part of God's heavenly palette of pastels?

"Who are they?" I innocently asked. My stomach was turning in knots, and I was starting to get scared.

"Don't look at them," my dad answered.

I turned my back and didn't question. *That's terrible*, I thought, but I wasn't sure why I felt the familiar tickle of tears approaching, and I felt bad for my dad. His pain was palpable, and I knew how much he loved parades and Pioneer Day. I hated these people for hurting my dad, and I hated the costumes they were wearing. I had a vague idea that what I was looking at had something to do with the temple and the clothes my mom kept secret, but the connection was still too disjointed to fully understand.

It would've been a completely different experience if my Dad had crouched down and simply explained that the protesters were wearing sacred temple clothing. "It looks weird outside the temple but it's actually sacred and symbolic. In fact, it's exactly what you and your future husband will be wearing when you are sealed in marriage." But he said nothing of the sort.

He did not mention the sacred priesthood robes, the fig leaf apron, or the bakers cap. The only instruction he gave me that day was to look away. It was sacred and never to be revealed, not even at the expense of Pioneer Day, a parade, or peace of mind for his daughter. He had made blood oaths and gestured that he would rather slit his own throat and be disemboweled rather than reveal the temple rituals. He knew the penalties for breaking the code of silence and he wasn't going to chance it for two disgruntled, ex-Mormon protesters.

I must have understood on some level that the ridiculousness of their clothes mocked something we believed in, but I assumed their outfits were an exaggeration. A parody. Never did I entertain the thought that they were dressed exactly like I would be every time I went through the temple.

Now that I was qualified to enter the temple, the church required me to take a temple preparation class and pass two rounds of worthiness interviews with my local leaders before they would issue me a temple recommend. A temple recommend is a bar-coded license that is scanned at the entrance of every temple around the world. It is only valid for two years and must be renewed through the same rounds of worthiness interviews every time. I was excited about being apart of this new elite spirituality, to strengthen my relationship with God and get answers to the questions that had been circling unanswered in my head since childhood.

My temple prep class was supposed to last for six weeks, but when I arrived at the church to meet with my volunteer instructors, the married couple explained that if we were efficient, we could cover all the material that very day.

"As long as I learn what the green aprons are all about, I'm good," I said jokingly.

It was the first time I had ever openly acknowledged the clothes I had seen that day at the parade and the possibility that they were connected to the temple. The two volunteers looked directly at each other and then directly through me. They were not pleased.

"We won't be getting into anything like that," the man said. "The temple clothing is symbolic and sacred and not to be discussed outside of the temple. It's deeply offensive."

I felt so sheepish I wanted to crawl under the card table we were seated at.

His wife sighed and clasped her hands in front of her. I could hear her thinking, *This is exactly why women should wait until marriage to go through the temple. Girls going on missions don't know their place.*

So far, the only thing temple prep was preparing me for was getting used to feeling shame oozing from every pore. In that way, the class really hit the mark. In only that way.

"In this class, you will be learning everything you need to know in order to return to live with your Heavenly Father. Celestial glory is reserved for those who obey the commandments and receive the ordinances, overcome all things by faith in Jesus Christ, and become pure in heart. You will be making covenants with the Lord to allow you to pass by the sentinels and angels that guard the gates of heaven. This is the only way you can dwell with God. God lives in the celestial kingdom. It is like the glory of the sun. Terrestrial glory is the glory of the moon, and telestial glory is the glory of the stars. For those who receive these blessings and turn away, there is no glory, only Outer Darkness."

The volunteer flipped on a TV on a rollaway cart that had been set up earlier. The screen buzzed to life, and a familiar song trilled, "Together Forever." A twenty-nine-minute film began to play about children and spouses dying only to be comforted with the promise of being reunited for eternity because of the blessings of the temple.

The rest of the class dragged on with a slow, methodical lecture about the plan of salvation at its most basic level. Adam and Eve? I'd mastered that concept, but it didn't matter, because we went through the creation story with each page-turning plot twist, from Eve's fruit of choice up to Christ's triumph over death to save us all.

The instructor paused the lecture.

He pulled out the lesson manual, flipped it around, and asked me to read aloud the following questions: "How important are the temple ordinances to us as members of the church? Can you be happy, can you be redeemed, can you be exalted without them?"

I looked up. Did he want me to answer? I still didn't know what the ordinances were! It seemed rhetorical. He leaned forward and pressed his pointer finger onto the manual emphatically. "Read the answer."

"Answer: They are more than advisable or desirable, or even more than necessary. More even than essential or vital. They are *crucial* to each of us."

OK, so great. What are they? If they're so crucial, *why can I only talk about them in the temple and why aren't you teaching me about them now?*

"The things you will learn when you receive your endowment in the temple will be the only way to return and live with your family forever," the instructor continued.

Obviously, the answer was "go through the temple." But never once did they ever tell me what "go through the temple" even meant.

They didn't mention Masonic rituals. They didn't mention anything about unison oaths or green aprons. They didn't say there'd be locker rooms. They didn't say anything about taking off your slippers halfway through the ritual and switching your robes to the other side of your shoulder. They didn't say anything about the loudspeakers, automated instructions, or thumb blade death penalties.

Instead, they went back to the basics. Adam and Eve. I knew more about my parents' sex life than I knew about anything that happened inside the temple. Which is to say, absolutely nothing.

Before I went into the temple, my mother told me, "You're so smart, Heather. I bet you're going to get it on your first try."

I thought, *Oh, geez, what do I need to get?*

She would not give me one word of what was to come. Then she said to make sure I had breath mints. She was frantic about the breath mints, which caused my thoughts to race like mad. I told all my friends about my mom's insistence. "Oh, yeah," they said. "That's probably a good idea."

In my head, I thought, *What? Like, why? What am I going to put in my mouth? Like, am I going to have to take a sacramental cup of fake blood and gargle it or something?*

I obsessed about the mints and my mouth the entire ride to the temple.

Why do I need breath mints?

What is going to happen?

I walked in blind, with no knowledge of what was to come. Just an understanding that if I wanted to be let into the tree house where all my friends and family were hanging out with Heavenly Father, I had to know the passwords and the handshakes. And if I didn't know them now, I'd learn them soon enough.

✳ ✳ ✳

In order to be worthy to receive your endowment, you must first be washed and anointed. Naked, I emerged from the locker room into a beige and white room with upholstered walls, chairs, and an altar. A female volunteer, dressed in white, shielded my nudity with an open drape. She dabbed a droplet of sacred oil from a dram shaped like a ram's horn onto her fingers and then she darted in and out of the draping shield like a mouse in a maze.

The volunteer touched my forehead and the pulse points on my face. "I wash your head, that your brain and your intellect may be clear and active; your ears, that you may hear the word of the Lord; your eyes, that you may see clearly and discern between truth and error; your nose, that you may smell; your lips, that you may never speak guile."

Then she progressed underneath the drape and touched my body. Each area received a droplet of oil and a new blessing.

"Your neck, that it may bear up your head properly; your shoulders, that they may bear the burdens that shall be placed thereon; your back, that there may be marrow in the bones and in the spine; your breast, that it may be the receptacle of pure and virtuous principles (*oops, she touched the nips on that one*); your vitals and bowels, that they may be healthy and perform their proper functions."

A functional drop of oil on each hip bone, a dot right by the Big V for eVe, Mother of All Living.

"Your arms and hands, that they may be strong and wield the sword of justice in defense of truth and virtue; your loins, that you may be fruitful and multiply and replenish the earth, that you might have joy in your posterity; your legs and feet, that you might run and not be weary, and walk and not faint."

As the blessings progressed, I began to feel the warmth of the Spirit's glow fill my body and make me feel warm and safe and cared for. Any weirdness I felt about being naked with strangers dissipated. It seemed sacred and divine. When she finished anointing my body, she was joined by another woman, a temple worker, also clothed in white. They placed their hands gently on my head and pronounced the blessings with no specific authority but with enough love and sincerity that they filled the beige room with a blinding bright.

During the course of these blessings, I didn't feel fear or shame. I felt protected. I felt seen. I felt like I belonged. In that room, I was enveloped by God's love. These blessings spoke to me like words straight from His mouth to my ear. Silently, I wept through the entire blessing, tears streaming down my face, overcome with the love that God felt for me. The pageantry, the weirdness, the nakedness, just confirmed that it came from the divine. What humans would come up with this on their own?

I had received plenty of priesthood blessings from men throughout my life, but the washings and anointings I received from these women felt different. I didn't question their authority or lack of priesthood power, I didn't feel less than or oppressed. I felt important. I felt valued. I felt fortified with the strength of God.

The volunteers told me to open the packages of garments I had brought with me and then they helped me put them on underneath the drape. I had purchased my sizes based on tips and tricks I had heard discreetly mentioned over the years. For the garment bottoms, you always wanted to buy the smallest size possible, otherwise they dangled past your knees when you were wearing shorts or skirts. For the garment tops, you wanted to buy them at least a size bigger so you could pull the neckline down and tuck the fabric underneath your bra. The straps and band keep the fabric from creeping up and completely covering your cleavage. Garments were always to be worn but never to be seen, and modern fashion choices did not accommodate clothes of the sacred covenant.

I had overestimated my size ranges and ended up with shorts that were way too small and a top that was way too big, but it was all I had. You can't try garments on before purchasing. This was one area where the church actually DID want you to learn from experience, I guess.

The shirt slipped on easily underneath the open drape but I had to put my hands on the temple worker's shoulders to balance as she threaded each leg through the constricting, silky, skintight white shorts.

Now dressed in my temple garments, they directed me back into the locker room to prepare for the next phase, the endowment ceremony. I was reunited with my mom. "What do I put on now?" I asked.

She whispered back to me, "Take the drape off, put on your temple dress, then the nylons, then the slippers."

I reached up onto the shelf of my locker and began to pull down my bra. It was black. Through the little slits in the changing stall, my mom spotted the offensive color like a piece of old coal in the new-fallen snow. "Do you have a different bra? You can't wear that one," she explained. "You can only wear white during the temple session."

A white bra? I didn't even own a purely white bra, and I definitely didn't have one with me. I was still freaking out about the breath mints! Why was this the first time I was hearing this? This apparently crucial detail had not been covered in my temple prep class nor by my friends. Was this all so sacred that no one dared tell me I had to wear a white bra? Was I the first girl in the history of time to show up with the wrong color of underwear?

I put my black bra back on the shelf next to my black panties. Panties that I might as well throw away now because I'd never need them again. All of my old underwear was obsolete. I would be wearing garment bottoms that looked and felt like biker shorts instead of thongs for the rest of my life. My future bras, black or otherwise, would also have to fit over the neckline and breast cups of my new garment tops. The weight of it all was suffocating. I was twenty-one, I was a virgin, and now I was endowed, clothed in the garments of the Holy Priesthood.

My single sexy days of matching underwear sets were over. Leaving my bra and panties abandoned on the shelf of the temple locker made me feel sad. Still, I resigned myself to walking commando through the temple, rather than offend God with my fashion choices. I offered a silent prayer that the temperature outside of the locker room remained comfortable and controlled.

I followed my mom into a nearby room where a volunteer organist quietly played hymns. The room was filled with men and women all dressed in white just like me. Everyone we had invited to the temple that day was sitting patiently on benches and they looked up at me and smiled when I walked in. The women were in simple white dresses with varying styles and details. The men were wearing white shirts, white ties, white ill-fitting pants, white knee-high stockings, and a masculine version of my same shapeless white slippers. I saw my dad, my former youth leaders, my parents' best friends, my bishop, my best friends. Was this what heaven would look like? The room was filled with strangers, too. Random temple patrons that had also come to the five o'clock session at the Denver temple that day, unaware that it was my maiden voyage.

There were complimentary copies of the Book of Mormon that a few people were thumbing through, but the majority just sat peacefully listening to the music. Everyone had a white fabric envelope or packet clutched on their lap, containing the priesthood robes, sashes, and aprons that we would be putting on throughout the endowment session. I slid onto an available bench and took a few deep breaths. I desperately wanted to feel the spiritual high that everyone said that temple ritual would bring. I was trembling with anticipation of what might be coming next, but I felt surprisingly calm.

A few minutes later, an elderly temple worker, dressed in white, appeared at the doorway and silently motioned for us to rise. We began filing out of the room row-by-row. Without speaking, we walked across a lobby and onto an escalator. This was my first time back inside the temple since the dedication ceremony. I marveled at how much I had forgotten and how beautiful everything looked. When I had been inside the temple before it was dedicated, everyone was dressed in their normal street clothes, but now, everyone was dressed in white, bustling about with soundless activity. It had always been described to me as a sacred and special place where God himself was present. But there was so much administrative activity it seemed more like a beehive than a blissful nirvana. I couldn't wait to get to the spiritual part.

I admired the crystal chandeliers, the beige furniture, the creamy white carpet, and crown moldings. The walls had occasional paintings framed in gold depicting scenes from the Savior's life and Joseph Smith's first vision in the Sacred Grove, but I could only quickly glance at them in passing as we made our way to the auditorium. Temple sessions start on the hour and are run like clockwork. There was no time for navel-gazing.

A temple worker stood outside the doorway nodding and smiling as we approached. I noticed a box of Kleenex on a little table and reached down to grab a few. I tended to cry when I felt spiritual, and based on the tears that flowed during the washing and anointing ceremony, I was convinced the endowment session would make me cry as well. I stuffed the tissues into the pocket of my temple dress next to my locker room key and beloved breath mints.

The auditorium had rows and rows of upholstered built-in chairs facing a simple altar and a giant ruched curtain. The set up was similar to a movie theatre, except the seating was parted with a giant aisle right down the middle. Women filed into the seats on the left separated from the men who were seated together on the right. I was flanked to my right and left by my mom and friends, grateful that I didn't have to sit next to strangers.

The temple workers stood patiently as the final patrons found their seats. The doors at the back of the auditorium clicked shut. Showtime. It was five p.m. exactly, no leeway for previews or snacks. A male worker at the front of the room surveyed the scene and discreetly pressed a button on the backside of the altar. Immediately, a pre-recorded track echoed throughout the room, welcoming us to the temple that day and directing our attention to the screen above the curtain.

The lights dimmed and the film flickered to life in front of us, reenacting scenes from the creation of the earth. It involved aerial shots of lava hitting the ocean, mountain scapes, jungle scenes, and sandy beaches. It reminded me a lot of the Soarin' Over California ride at California Adventure. White-haired actors in tunics and bare feet played the roles of God the Father and his son, Jehovah.

In the film, Elohim (God) instructs Jehovah to create an earth and place man upon it. Then Elohim instructs Jehovah to take a rib from Adam and make him a helpmeet and partner, Eve. *For it is not good that man should be alone.*

Jehovah lets Adam and Eve live peacefully in the garden until Eve does the unthinkable. Breaks the *only* rule they have given her, which is to not eat the fruit of the Tree of Knowledge of Good and Evil. *Oh,*

Eve. Eve knows the rules but is deceived by Satan, who convinces her that partaking of the fruit is the only way she can progress with Adam. It is the only way she can bear children; it is the only way civilization can come to pass. A 7–10 split, snake eyes, right there in the Garden of Eden. *The serpent beguiled me, and I did partake.*

I knew this story. I knew the outcome. But I still didn't know why we were learning about it again in the temple. I was here to commune with the Lord and to advance spiritually, not go back to the basics. I wanted to understand why we wore garments, why we needed green aprons, and why I couldn't wear my black bra. I hoped the answers to my questions would be in the second half of the movie.

Once Adam and Eve were driven out of paradise, they were left to roam the lone and dreary world. Their path was littered with noxious weeds and thorny bristles. They were forced to cover their nakedness now that they knew that they were, in fact, naked.

The lights came on. The voice on the loudspeaker interrupted the action on the screen. "All rise. You should now place your aprons to cover your nakedness as Adam and Eve did." *Ah. Intermission.*

The worker at the front of the auditorium stood passively, waiting for the participants to stand up, find their aprons in their personal packets, tie them around their waists, and sit back down. The thought of hiding our nakedness in these outfits made me smirk. I wasn't even wearing a bra. But under all the layers—the apron, the dress, and my new skintight sacred garments—I'd be lucky to find anything. It was like the princess and the pea. I knew my nakedness was down there somewhere, but I couldn't quite put my finger on it.

The movie resumed. There were no white robes or aprons on the screen, but it was implied that in order to pray in a way that God intended, you need to be wearing all of the priesthood robes and sashes.

"We desire all to receive it," the voice boomed over the loud-speaker. Suddenly, everyone around me began shuffling about. I took note and fell in line. I began to take the sashes and one-armed tunics and put them on the best I knew how. I looked to the people next to me for advice or assistance, but it's hard to help someone get dressed in layers of robes when you're not allowed to speak. A lot of head nods and eye gestures and follow the leader has to suffice.

As soon as the temple worker saw the last slow-dressing straggler place his robes on correctly, the loudspeaker voice announced, "That will do." The movie began again with Adam kneeling at an altar in the lone and dreary world, offering up a prayer in the way God prefers.

"Oh, God, hear the words of my mouth."

This was not a prayer structure I'd ever heard before. No Heavenly Father; no folded arms; no thee, thy, thou; and no mention of "In the name of Jesus Christ, Amen." *Welp, that's new, at least.*

The movie ended with a stern warning from the actor playing Luci-fer, looking straight into the camera and telling us if we did not live up to the covenants and promises we made in the temple that day, we would forever be in his power. The lights came back on.

"We would like to invite an equal number of brothers and sisters to join us in the prayer circle at this time. A few of you, including couples, please come forward and form a circle around the altar."

I kept my face cast down, hoping there were other eager beavers in the group anxious to participate in the true order of prayer with a captive audience. It was my first endowment session, and I could feel all eyes on me. My friends stood up and gestured for me to follow. Smiling like Cheshire cats, they walked me to the front of the auditorium, where we stood around the altar.

The voice returned over the loudspeaker: "Only the best of feelings should exist in the circle. If any of you have unkind feelings toward any member of this circle, you are invited to withdraw so that the Spirit of the Lord may be unrestrained."

I hadn't had any feelings of contention or unkindness toward them before they pulled me up there, but now I wasn't so sure.

We did the gestures for each sign and token of the priesthood, flipping and folding our hands into different shapes and different combinations as we somberly faced each other. It's not the easiest group prayer to master, and what adds to the difficulty is not just the involved hand actions, but the opposing tempos. We raised our hands high above our heads and chanted in unison while slowly lowering them. And just like in life, everyone had their own pace and rhythm. Once the chant was completed, we were instructed to take the hand of the person next to us in the Patriarchal Grip. I had not learned this handshake yet, so I wasn't sure what to do. I nervously clasped the man's outstretched hand next to me and went limp as he shuffled my fingers into the correct formation. We weren't allowed to speak, but we maintained eye contact throughout.

There was no way to avoid the awkwardness, and I was grateful when they asked the women to veil our faces. I didn't want to have to pretend this felt spiritual or normal or godlike. Because it didn't. It felt fucking weird. And I'm sure my face would have given it away. I didn't even know the men on either side of me, and yet my right hand was clasped in their's while my left arm was raised to the square, elbow resting on the other's shoulder.

I believed this had all come directly from God through the prophet Joseph Smith. Yes, it was kooky, but who was I to question God and His elaborate hand gestures? It was his tree house after all. He makes the rules.

I focused on the people pressed against me and how they were breathing hard or their hands were trembly and sweaty. Every part of my normal brain was saying, *Uhhhhh, what in the world?*

But then, as if on cue, my Mormon brain responded: *But we are not of the world. We are of the divine, and this prayer circle is evidence that God's ways will never align with our ways.*

After our synchronized chant, we were dismissed back to our original seats. I sat in the temple auditorium and I realized there was no going back now. Everything felt absolutely absurd, but I figured it was just because I wasn't spiritual enough. If I was going to survive, I was going to need to learn to swim in these waters. In order to call myself Eve, Mother of All Living, the single, unburdened girl would have to die. *But whosoever shall be willing to lose his life for my sake, and the gospel, the same shall save it.*

Scanning the crowd, I looked across the aisle and found my dad. He was dressed as instructed in all his temple clothing. I silently willed him to look over at me. I was certain that if we'd made eye contact I'd see something in his eyes that indicated we were on the same page, that all of this seemed crazy but that it would all be OK. But no. His eyes remained straight ahead, looking at the temple worker. He sat there not thinking about me, but thinking about his own oaths and promises to God. His gaze fixed in a death stare. A poker face. Based on his expression, it wasn't weird, it was just Wednesday.

I knew in that moment that mocking any of this was futile. There was no inside joke to get in on. If I wanted to belong, if I wanted to progress, I had to straighten up. So I snapped out of my fear and doubts and I leaned in. I leaned into the weirdness, because as far as I knew, it was true. It had to be. It was all too absurd to be made up. And more than that, it had to be true because there in the crowd believing it was true, were the people who meant the most to me. The people who loved me. There was my dad. There was my mom. My teachers, my youth leaders, my very best friends. When I asked the unspoken question, they were all there raising their hands to the square, bowing their heads, and saying, "Yes."

The temple worker removed a retractable metal pointer from his breast pocket and extended it to its limit. Meanwhile, a motor began to whir, and the curtain behind him slowly parted, revealing the veil separated into several stations with individual tapping mallets, temple volunteers, and personal pretend Lords hidden from our view.

The voice on the loudspeaker asked us all to rise. We stood and formed single file lines behind the curtained stations, waiting silently until it was our turn to go through the veil. A few minutes later, for the second time in my life, I stood awkwardly in front of a curtain with a hole in it.

This curtain was thicker, dingier, and had pre-stitched holes in varied shapes. Far too advanced for a robot pincer. These holes represented the sacred symbols on our garments and would serve as portals that we would have to reach through in order to break on through to the other side.

A female temple volunteer made eye contact with me, and I nodded to gesture that I was ready to begin. She smiled and fumbled behind the curtain for a rubber mallet attached to a rope dangling from the scaffolding. She flipped the mallet around in her hand so it was right-side up and pinged the metal bar deliberately and somberly with three distinct taps.

Tap. Tap. Tap.

On cue, a hand emerged from behind the curtain, and a man's voice spoke out.

"What is wanted?"

The volunteer cleared her throat and replied clearly but quietly to the floating hand, "Eve, having been true and faithful, has come to the Lord to request further light and knowledge, and to receive that further light and knowledge through the veil."

The man, still hidden behind the curtain, spoke out with authority, "She shall receive it through the veil."

This was my cue. The temple worker gestured with her head that I should approach, and I bellied up to the bar, so to speak. My body flanked the curtain as I positioned myself to line up with the out-stretched hands. My right hand grasped his at the waist, and my left hand slid through the curtain to rest on his shoulder behind the veil; his left hand responded in kind, landing on my right shoulder. We were intertwined like an awkward junior high school dance, concealed and separated. Our bodies were millimeters apart, and if either one of us so much as twitched, our knees and hips and chests would collide in a flurry of fabric and quivering flesh. It was uncomfortably intimate, but the second my mind went there, I snapped out of it. This was a sacred, treasured temple ceremony, and if my mind was wandering, there must be something wrong with me.

The tokens were the same, word for word, every time. True to form, all the answers were given to us right before we took the test. The man with the retractable pointer painstakingly explained the covenant and obligation associated with each token, its secret name, and its accom-panying sign. I remembered my mom's hope that I'd be able to 'get it on my first try' and I finally understood what she meant. No one likes a stumbler or a straggler at the veil. With an auditorium of enthusiastic Mormons on my heels, I didn't want to freeze up and forget my lines. I wanted to be fast, and I wanted to be precise. I wanted to make Jesus proud.

The first two tokens were simple, straightforward. *Scoop of choco-late, scoop of vanilla.*

Then it started getting tricky.

He clasped my hand in the secret handshake with his pointer finger pressed firmly on the pulse point on my wrist.

"What is that?" he asked.

"The Second Token of the Melchizedek Priesthood, or Sure Sign of the Nail."

He didn't pull his hand away. He didn't move at all. *I must've messed something up.* I looked over at the temple worker/script supervisor. She shook her head to indicate I was wrong, and leaned in to whisper the words I had forgotten: "The second token."

She nodded toward the curtain.

I whispered, "The second token."

She nodded affirmatively and guided me through the rest of the phrases in three word spurts.

"The second token, (Pause. Whisper. Repeat.), of the Melchezidek priesthood, (Pause. Whisper. Repeat.), the Patriarchal Grip, (Pause. Whisper. Repeat.), or Sure Sign of the Nail."

I'm holding up the line. I'm not getting it on the first try. I could tell the people behind me were getting irritated.

The voice behind the curtain asked, "Has it a name?"

"It has."

"Will you give it to me?"

"I cannot. I have not yet received it. For this purpose I have come to converse with the Lord through the Veil."

His somber voice shifted and he responded, "You shall receive it through the veil."

We placed our left arms upon each other's right shoulders through the curtain. His lips pressed up against the curtain by my ear and he whispered the sacred secret name that was never to be repeated.

"Health in the navel, marrow in the bones, strength in the loins and in the sinews. Power in the priesthood be upon me and upon my posterity through all generations of time and throughout all eternity." I repeated the phrase dutifully, word for word. When I finished, he unclasped my hand and parted the curtain.

"Let her enter."

I was pulled through the curtain into the celestial room. They timed it so that I was presented at the veil near the end of the session, allowing my family and friends time to have performed their signs and tokens, ensuring that they would be waiting to receive me in the celestial room, our reunion symbolizing eternity with my loving family forever.

I saw everyone's smiling faces and bated breath to see my reaction to the craziness. Was I freaked out? Was I skeptical? I wanted to be. I felt like I had the right to be. But I had long ago resolved to feel none of these things. I had made the decision a long time ago to believe, to absorb, and to love the gospel in all of its peculiarities. The more fantastical it seemed, the more it had to be true. I was too far in to back out now. After I hugged everyone I had cherished most in my life, they had me turn around and look at myself in the mirror.

"Look at how you can see eternity with the reflections mirrored back to each other. They go on forever."

I tried to change my focus to see the endless repeated reflections, but I couldn't take my eyes off my own reflection in the mirror. I assumed I would look ridiculous, but I had never looked so beautiful. I scanned my outfit, several layers of gauzy detergent-pungent fabric with a flash of bright green satin fig leaves and soft, shapeless white

Dearfoam slippers. I looked weird, but I felt radiant. What was it? My skin? My weight? My countenance? I had never looked that beautiful to myself ever before.

Despite the stillness I felt while looking at my reflection, my mind couldn't keep from racing.

"Do you have any questions?" they asked.

Yeah, I have questions, I thought. *For starters, will asking this question mean I will have to slit my own throat with my thumb blade, or does one of God's sentinel's at the gate handle that for me? What did I just sign up for? How am I supposed to remember it all? What about the covenant to avoid loud laughter and light-mindedness? How am I supposed to only laugh quietly? What does heavy-minded look like?*

Despite all these thoughts, I still had one question that was weighing on me. It had not left my mind all day, and had still not been answered during the temple ceremony. If I didn't ask it now, it would go unanswered until the next time we were in the temple together. "Mom, why did I need to have breath mints?"

She replied casually, "Oh, just because I always feel self-conscious about my breath when I'm whispering to the men through the veil."

That was it. That was the reason. Because we whispered into a man's ear through a hole in a curtain. And there, my perfectly beautiful, normal mother was saying, "I like to have minty-fresh breath for my sacred ritual recitations. What nice girl doesn't?"

My mom wanted me to be smart enough to go through the veil unprompted. She wanted me to not have bad breath for the nice man volunteering to give me permission to enter pretend heaven.

Every part of my humanity was astounded by how weird it was, but beyond that I couldn't stop thinking about how colossal a secret my friends and family were capable of keeping. *You have known about this and believed it. You have all embraced it and kept it secret from me and from each other for your entire life.*

I felt like I had discussed every single detail of every single novel and poem and song and scripture I liked with my friends, and the only warning I got from Gretchen before entering the temple was, "Try not to think about Chef Boyardee."

Everyone was in on this secret, and not just my family and friends I knew and trusted. But every. Single. Member. Of. The. Church. The fresh-faced missionary. The sweet older couple who brought Bundt cake to the potluck. The frazzled mom who arranged babysitters so she could spend three hours reciting rote phrases and going through the veil for dead strangers. Even the delinquent apostates who had left the church managed to keep these oaths a secret. Was I the only one who thought it was shocking?

The rest of my friends and relatives and ward members had walked through those doors as unaware as me and had said nothing afterward. As if ancient blood oaths and rituals were as commonplace as blessing the food at dinnertime. Had anyone seen *Indiana Jones and the Temple of Doom?* Were we one incantation away from human sacrifice and holding a beating heart in our hands?

Everyone I knew and trusted had been through the temple and accepted the rituals and rites of passage as not only a sacred secret but something beautiful, eternal, and divine. They put bright green satin aprons on and still thought the church was true. Who was I to question?

This was the only faith I had ever known. This was my church since I was born. These were the people who raised me, who taught me everything I knew. You don't question when you see your bishop, your neighbor, or the cool kid's parents at temple night. The beliefs aren't reinforced by strangers, they're reinforced by the people who love you most.

And it's in that moment that you don't really have a choice. You believe. You fall in line. You commit.

Nothing was out of the scope of expectation. It wouldn't have mattered if they'd asked me to castrate a baby lamb or lay myself down on an altar. I was going to do whatever they told me to do. I had signed up at that point. I had forgotten sex, Starbucks, two-piece swimsuits. All so that I could be considered righteous enough to enter the temple. It was the castle on a cloud. Once the fairy tale was a reality, they could have me do just about anything, and I would have done it with an open heart and mind. I was willing to suspend my disbelief because the promises were so great.

After we completed the temple ceremony, we changed back into our normal clothes without even a mention of the rituals. Instead, we were focused on leaving behind the three-hour session we'd just endured without snacks, water, or entertainment—unless, you're a fan of regional theater. The last thing we wanted to do was sit together and commiserate.

We left the temple, carrying our clothes in little suitcases, only to shove them in the back of the closet when we got home, never to be spoken of outside the temple. We talked about the errands we still needed to run or the shows we were excited to watch. We never acknowledged the oaths and covenants we had just made. We never mentioned how good it felt to be out of priesthood robes. We never uttered a word about how we had just spent the last three hours repeating primitive phrases, signs, and tokens that we would someday need in order to get past the angels that guard the gates of heaven.

But that's exactly what I did every time I went through the temple for close to fifteen years. Every single time. Locker room, movie, true order of prayer, tokens and signs, handshakes and rituals, walk through the veil, wash, rinse, repeat.

The only evidence that we had been to the temple was occasionally an indentation along our forehead made by the elastic of a too-tight cap or veil. With the exception of that physical reminder, everything else about the temple was secret, even to our own.

CHAPTER 9

CALLED TO SERVE HIM, HEAVENLY KING OF GLORY

For my mission, I tried to remove myself from the life I'd been living before. Friends, family, home, business, all of that was left by the wayside. I walked into the MTC and shut the door on all of the chaos and noise of college, boys, bills, and adulthood. I walked into a new identity, new constructs, where the bumpers were high and the rules were clear; I was going to bowl a perfect game.

The MTC is the Mormon West Point, dogmatically churning out missionaries to honorably spread the gospel from sea to shining sea. Every Mormon missionary must cross its threshold before being flung to the far reaches of the world with a black name tag and a Book of Mormon.

My first French instructor was a return missionary named Frère Beaufort—his last name translated to "handsome and strong"—and from the get-go, I adored him. He was like his name suggested, not only good looking and strong, but also witty and fun. His personality comforted me. He was proof that you could go on a mission, turn yourself and your life over to the Lord, and still come home and be a normal person. I loved the gospel, but I didn't want to become a religious fiend and lose all sense of self. After seeing the temple rituals and learning about some of our Mormon history, I wasn't sure how close we all were to being considered zealots. I wanted to keep one foot firmly planted in self-divination.

My MTC district consisted of three other sister missionaries all called to serve in Marseille with me and four elders called to serve in Haiti. They quickly became my very best friends, especially my companion, Soeur Brown. I adored her and she made me feel excited to be a missionary and excited to share the gospel even when it seemed overwhelming.

We loved to ask Frère Beaufort the questions about missionary life that we were afraid to ask people on the outside. A missionary who is too preoccupied with the country, the language, or the experience looks like a missionary who doesn't have a testimony of the work. We wanted to have an eye single to the glory of God, and God doesn't bother himself with questions like, "Is it true they don't refrigerate their milk?" or, "Will we actually be forced to eat frog legs?"

And the darker, more charged questions: "Is it fun at all? Is it worth it?"

But we trusted Frère Beaufort, and we knew he wouldn't doubt our dedication just because we gave voice to our deepest fears. We were leaving our lives at the height of young-adult development. Putting education, careers, fishhook earrings, dating, family, and friends on the back burner to work from six a.m. to ten p.m., seven days a week, for the next eighteen to twenty-four months. There was fear and apprehension, but we were called to put our personal feelings aside. Our duty as missionaries was to be joyful, to open our mouths, to proclaim the truth, and to encourage others to do the same.

Frère Beaufort was *just* different enough to draw the attention of the administrators at the MTC. I assumed it was because he was extra amused by our district: we laughed too loud, we joked too much, we seemed to be having too much fun. I assumed he was madly in love with me and that the administrators could clearly see the infatuation. They needed to separate us before an innocent friendship turned into a torrid love affair, dragging us both into *les profondeurs de l'enfer.*

Routine was at the heart of everything at the MTC, so when the administrators announced that we were abruptly switching classrooms, our alarm bells went off. What was happening? Had someone sinned? Were we being demoted?

All of us were on high alert. However, I, the girl in the midst of a torrid, secret, laugh-filled relationship with her instructor, was made to feel even more alert than most. Our new classroom came with a two-way mirror for observational purposes, but we were young and foolish and didn't pick up on what the darkened glass indicated. Frère Beaufort clearly knew what was at stake and hoped he could change the outcome.

"Today we are going to work on reflexive verbs and how they are used," he announced. He walked to the chalkboard opposite the observation portal and painstakingly wrote *Ils nous regardent* on the chalkboard.

"Can anyone tell me which verb we are using?"

"*Regarder?*" someone meekly attempted.

"Yes. That's right."

He seemed noticeably reserved, and when I looked at him, I could see it in his face. This was no ordinary reflexive verb. I studied the sentence he had written on the chalkboard again, *Ils nous regardent*, and translated it in my head: "They are watching us."

I didn't know exactly who or exactly why, but I knew exactly *what* the sentence meant. I instinctively straightened up at my desk and then scribbled a note for my companion to warn her. We knew what it meant to be watched. To be observed. To be judged on our 100 percent obedience. On our perfection in following the rules, in believing the doctrine, in dedicating our heart, might, and mind to missionary work. There was no way we were anywhere near perfect, and as soon as we knew we were being observed, we immediately turned inward and started doing a personal inventory on the thousands of ways we had shirked our sacred duties as missionaries. I thought about the late nights we had stayed up laughing about the way the cafeteria food produced stomach-exploding gas, the times I had danced around in my garments and black knee-high nylons calling myself George Washington, the letters I had written to my friend running Steelhead Designs with instructions about vendors and pricing and bead shortages. We had been instructed to leave all business dealings and things of the world behind. But it was difficult. We were far from perfect, and now we were in trouble.

And so, too, was Frère Beaufort. There was no laughing or bonding or below-the-surface questions asked that day. "They are watching us" was all it took to remind us that if you dabble in the gray, the Lord always knows, and he immediately informs his priesthood leaders so that they can help you get back in line.

This was my fault. I had laughed too loudly at his jokes, I had asked too many leading questions, I had displayed too much affection and desire, I had made it unsafe for him to be the French instructor God wanted him to be. I was impeding the work. I was a stumbling block. I needed to be less of a strumpet and more of a saint.

The following day, we returned to our regular classroom with a renewed desire to be 100 percent obedient in all things. We were committed to be better. To be perfect. To be pure. But we were too late. The classroom was the same, but the teacher was different. Frère Beaufort had been fired without so much as a simple *Adieu*. There was no explanation, no discussion, no opportunity to prove our worthiness. Our new teacher just introduced himself, and we got to work. *No unhallowed hand can stop the work from progressing.*

Years later, I looked Frère Beaufort up on Facebook and saw that he was married to another man. I couldn't help but laugh about the fairy tale I had constructed about our student–teacher relationship. Just because Frere Beaufort laughed at my jokes didn't mean he liked me in a way that would cost him his job. His firing had absolutely nothing to do with me.

The possibility that I wasn't the source of Frère Beaufort's woes never once crossed my mind. With an adult perspective, it all seems glaringly obvious, but at the time, I had the ability to fit every random circumstance into my paradigm of binary logic.

I was steeped in a patriarchal, heteronormative, cisgender world, and the only logical explanation for the firing was that Frère Beaufort couldn't hide his affection for *me*. I never once considered that perhaps the powers that be were observing him for entirely different reasons. And when I finally realized what likely caused his firing, it broke my heart and my pride.

It can be a hit to the ego when you realize that a bunch of older church leaders have better gaydar than you do.

CHAPTER 10

LE CHALEUR HUMAINE

I don't know what I expected my mission experience to be when I boarded my flight to France, but I knew I expected to love it. I wanted to immerse myself in the language, the culture, the people, and the purposes of God. I had dreams that I would speak so fluently people would mistake me for a native Parisian. I dreamed of cooking coq au vin and eating cheese for dessert. I wanted to transform my life into something special by turning it over to the Lord and the refiner's fire of service. I planned on being 100 percent obedient because they had beaten it into our brains at the MTC that without obedience to the commandments, ye have no promise. I wanted to do it all, and I wanted to do it well.

When I first arrived from the mission home at the train station in Marseille I met all the missionaries in my new area, including my companion and trainer, Soeur Slade. Within minutes of introducing ourselves, I noticed a man out of the corner of my eye keenly observing us. He seemed especially intrigued by the black name tag perched upon my perky *poitrine*. I walked toward him with an excited air of conviction, my companion trailing closely behind me. I was ready to show her how prepared I was to open my mouth and share the good news of the gospel of the Church of Jesus Christ of Latter-day Saints. As I approached him, I pulled the front of my dress down to proudly display my tag.

Salut!

He leaned in like he was trying to take a closer look and instead grabbed a handful of my left breast. I had never had my boob grabbed like that in my life. My companion, Soeur Slade, immediately windmill-slapped the guy's arm off my chest and pulled me back to the safety of the group.

Terrifying. But . . . thrilling.

Laissez les bons temps rouler!

Soeur Slade was an English-speaking Canadian, but because she shared her native country with French-speaking Montreal, she esteemed herself as more French than any of us American rubes. She was my trainer, so she taught me all about the rules and regulations of the France Marseille mission. She also gave me a few other made-up rules that I had not read in the missionary handbook, but that she still expected me to follow.

The first rule was no English ever. I had only been in the country a day or two and my French was limited to my memorized testimony of the truthfulness of the gospel and any French food word that crossed over into English. Not speaking any English ever was going to be difficult unless we limited our discussions to the gospel or crepes and croissants.

Turns out, talking about anything else isn't really a missionary's thing.

Occasionally I tried to sneak a question in English if I was desperate for a quick translation, but she never fell for it. The second an English word escaped my lips, she would purse her lips, wag her pointer finger back and forth, and make a tsk tsk tsk sound with her tongue and teeth. It bugged the hell out of me. "Hey, Soeur Slade, why did that man keep saying *Il me bete*? What does it mean?"

"Tsk tsk tsk. *En Francais s'il vous plaît.*"

"Oh, OK, um sorry, I mean, *Je suis desolee, qu'est ce que c'est* . . . never mind."

By the time I figured out how to ask the question I was no longer interested in the answer.

Her second made-up rule was the law of consecration when it came to planning all of our meals. We went to the grocery store and she threw things in a basket, explaining over her shoulder in stilted forced French that it was just easier if she did all the shopping and I paid her for half of the bill. At least I think that's what she said, neither of us spoke the language well enough to accurately discuss a budget or grocery shopping. Regardless, I didn't want to start off on *le mauvais pied* so I went along with everything even if I didn't like it.

I wanted to experience France through the food. I was desperate to shop on my own and sample all of the dense yogurts in little glass jars and the rows of frothy desserts on display in the patisseries. Soeur Slade had a bit of a different palette. Our first shared lunch was a delicacy she prepared in less than four minutes called *truc*. It was a combination of boiled rice, canned tuna, canned corn, and vinaigrette dressing mashed together in a giant bowl. It was warm and cold and disgusting. *C'etait dégueulasse*. My vocabulary improved with each communal meal.

Her third and final painful rule was more of a quirk. She liked to answer questions affirmatively not by saying "Oui" or "Yes" but with a sharp intake of breath. "Whay." It sounded like she was gasping in shock but she assured me that it was an old-school French method for saying "yes." She seemed a little too young and a little too Canadian to speak in old-school French, so every time she gasped her breathy "Whay" I wanted to reply with a resounding "Non."

These were not the types of hardships I had imagined I'd experience in France but they were my initiation to missionary life. A lot of it was about the work we were doing. But an equal part of it was about the people we were doing the work with. *Women.*

Everything about the mission was harder than I thought. The language, the schedule, the routine, the rejection, the poverty, and the endless workload that was always waiting. Twelve hour days on a hamster wheel of contacting strangers with no success. I had to dig deep to survive. There was no fear that I would fail, only fear that it wouldn't be what I had hoped.

I knew that I needed to be all in, because having one foot in and one foot out as a missionary was just too painful and too grueling. To do work like this as myself, as Heather, would be impossible. I had too much social anxiety, too much empathy, and too much of a cringe trigger to survive. In order to cope I imagined myself as Glinda the Good Witch, descending in a pink protective bubble of the gospel. Nothing could get to me if I surrendered everything I had to the work. The spirit would create an impenetrable globe that shielded me from the stares and taunts of the world while I was in France. It was the only way I could get through it.

* * *

My next companion was what they would probably describe in the corporate world as a demotion. Soeur Bueller was a *specific* kind of missionary. The specific kind I really couldn't stand. Prior to serving, she had been a nanny outside of Paris for three months living with an American family and she thought this experience made her God's gift to the French language. She would physically shudder whenever I spoke French and when I pointed it out to her she'd sigh dramatically and say "Your accent just grates on my ears." Oh really? My accent? *You're American, too, sweetie.*

I worked tirelessly to make Soeur Bueller like me. Every morning at six o'clock, per her request, I would sing her awake with one of her favorite preselected hymns. A capella. My devotion was deep. We prayed six or seven times a day. We read her favorite scriptures, ate her favorite foods. I tried everything, and I had been taught that the only solution for trying too hard was to try even harder. Still, no matter what I did, I simply could not win over Carol Bueller.

My next and favorite companion was Bethany Campbell from Manhattan Beach. Bethany was a rosy-cheeked redhead obsessed with hip-hop and her boyfriend (also a missionary). She knew everything about Tupac—knew every song and every lyric. She slept in a Tupac nightshirt, and she believed he'd live forever. I loved her like she loved Tupac: unconditionally.

We'd rise before dawn and go on a run through the streets of Montpellier. Jogging along the esplanade on those early mornings felt like a wrinkle in time. We were not sister missionaries with responsibilities or agendas. We were two best friends living in France and loving it. I felt free when I ran, like I was living a normal life again. I wasn't wearing a T-shirt underneath a sundress and a full set of sacred garments, I was a twenty-one year old in a tank top and running shorts, feeling the French air on my American thighs. It made me forget for just a moment that I was a missionary responsible for the salvation of the South of France.

Soeur Campbell and I spent most of our time ringing doorbells, or ringing *sonners*, in the large, subsidized apartment complexes on the outskirts of the city. If we encountered a locked apartment building, we would push the *sonner* button on the intercom trying to get an invitation. If that didn't work, we'd press all the buttons one-by-one, going down each row until we hit every single apartment. If someone buzzed us in, it was a gift.

At our first-zone conference we were introduced to a new, radical approach in our proselytizing. We called it the one-minute rule. Instead of focusing on conversation starters or prepared missionary discussions, we were instructed to get inside and kneel in prayer within the first minute of meeting them.

We'd walk in the door. We'd open our mouths. And then we would immediately kneel down. The reactions were varied but usually out of embarrassment and shock, the unsuspecting French hosts would see us kneeling in their foyer and kneel down with us. We were thrilled and terrified. Thrilled by the challenge but also terrified because it was so weird. What we said wasn't important. How we spoke French wasn't important. All that mattered was that if we got through the door, we knelt down, and we got them to feel *something*.

Most of the men and women in the wards we served in had only been to the temple once or twice in their lives. The nearest temple was in Bern, Switzerland, which prevented even the most valiant members from attending endowment sessions regularly. Over the years, many of the members had adopted their own practices for wearing garments and had forgotten a lot of the rules and instructions taught in the temple. There was no crib sheet or synopsis to study once you got home. Without regular temple attendance to remind you of all the rules, it was easy to slip into noncompliance.

That's where we came in. Lucky for them we were well-versed in not only how to wear the sacred garments, but also how to handle them appropriately (they are never to touch the floor, just like the American flag), and how to dispose of them properly (they must either be burned or the sacred symbols must be cut out). When we discovered that many members were wearing their garment tops over their bras and not underneath as instructed, we were horrified.

We were twenty-one-year-old girls only a few months into being endowed, letting lifelong members in France know that they were not being protected by God because they were wearing their garments wrong.

It was an intimate switch. Lovingly, and with all the patience in the world, we would explain, "The garment is a sacred thing meant to always touch the skin. It's more important for your garment to be against your skin first. The bra goes over the garment top."

They would protest and shake their heads: *Non. Non. Non.*

And we would respond, "*Oui. Oui. Oui.* This is how we have been instructed in the temple to wear our garments. And it's beautiful this way. It's sacred this way. It's the only way it will protect you."

The women would then come back to us with their sacred white garment top underneath their purple bra, and we would breathe a sigh of relief: all was right and true. We were fixing the church in France.

God *cares* how you layer. God wants the bra over the shirt over the boobs. We were truly engaged in the work of the Lord.

CHAPTER 11

I GOT SO HIGH THAT
I SAW JESUS

In every missionary apartment in every mission around the world, there is a sacred binder that contains records of all the missionary work being done in the area. We had a tiny info sheet for every French person who had been contacted by a missionary, even if it was just a notation that we had met them on the subway or in a park. Every investigator interested in learning about the church had a file, or a *dossier*, if we were feeling French and fancy. We called them our *amis d'eglise*, friends of the church, and we tracked them all. We recorded who'd been interested in baptism, who'd been excommunicated for sin, who hadn't been to church for six months. These were God's lost sheep, and we had the sacred responsibility to seek them out and serve them and then send our reports up the ladder to our mission president at his estate in Aix-en-Provence.

We were not only required to preach the gospel, but to also find ways to serve the community. The service we did was completely self-directed and usually dictated by whatever was written in the binder.

We had the opportunity to choose how we spent our service hours and we had been given the directive to set aside four to six hours a week where we focused on doing secular service in the community with no mention of our faith. Usually I was happy to pick up where the previous missionaries had left off. We only spent two to three months in one city so it was often easier to do what had always been done rather than reinvent the wheel. If it were a task I couldn't stand, I would give it a chance before switching to something else two weeks later. I wasn't going to be an asshole; I had to play the game. You don't get the promotion and immediately change the protocol. You ease in.

One of our first service assignments was to help a single mother with her severely challenged neurodivergent child who had grown too big for her to manage physical therapy alone. He was fifteen years old and lived with autism spectrum disorder and cerebral palsy. She sought eager Mormon missionaries willing to wrangle him and someone somewhere thought this was a great idea.

Was she in need? Absolutely.

Was it appropriate for twentysomethings with no clinical experience to do rudimentary bilateral patterning on a fifteen-year-old man child as a means of trauma response? Absolutely not.

Every week, we would assist this mother as she tried to manage her son, a grown man for all intents and purposes, who moaned and flailed and resisted. He didn't want us restraining him, but his mother insisted that we conduct his therapy with a series of alternating hot and cold towels in a type of Swedish horror massage. She believed that these towels would shock his brain into symbiosis and that he would snap out of his cerebral palsy and be magically healed. Who were we to question the magic of ritual?

As we covered the boy with wet towels, we would recite poetry in

English, because she believed that he could hear and absorb everything we were saying. She believed that one day, the Swedish towel system would work, his brain would click into gear, and he would wake up speaking English with a perfect American accent. As Mormons, this logic tracked for us. She wouldn't allow us to speak his native French for fear that he would pick up on any of our mispronounced words. And so we stuck to English and the classics.

Whose woods these are I think I know. (hot towel on the chest, semicircle clockwise)
His house is in the village though; (arm to chest, left to right)
He will not see me stopping here (neck to thigh, counterclockwise rotation)
To watch his woods fill up with snow. (cold towel on stomach, brace for recoil)

It wasn't appropriate that we were doing physical therapy on her teenage son, much less therapy that clearly wasn't helping and honestly seemed abusive. And then she added the layer of reciting poetry while keeping him confined to a ping-pong table with a blanket. It was all too much. If we messed up once, we would stop and restart the pattern from the beginning. She would immediately reprimand us, because she believed that only through the precise rhythm of this ritual would his brain snap back into functioning. It was horrifying. This was not the kind of missionary service I envisioned.

I could see the mother's futile efforts. I understood her hope and belief, but I still cast judgment. She was a single mother doing this alone. But from my perspective at the time, single mothers weren't women who were doing it all without a man. It was the worst of the worst. Not only did you have the responsibility of a child, but you had no one to help shoulder the burden. You had no accolades, no money, no esteem, no safety. I would have rather wandered the earth barefoot and begging than be a single mother.

Single motherhood was something to be feared. I had no positive examples of single mothers in the church. No thriving, independent women raising their children on their own. There was no example to cling to, no idol to look up to, no model to direct questions to. It was the opposite of the future I pictured for myself where my husband doted on me and where most of my kids got good grades and *maybe* told the occasional hot dog joke. That I could handle. This I could not.

I could see wasted effort in other people, but I had no mirror with which to see it in myself. As I looked at this boy and his mother who so desperately believed in this exercise of towel whipping, I knew that he would never snap out of it. Only in retrospect do I realize that her unflinching belief in the impossible was a sort of foil for my own recognition.

I, too, was never going to snap out of it. I was always going to be me: the girl who loved Drambuie and read *Mandarin Orange Sunday* no matter how many hot and cold towels you slapped on my chest, no matter how many trips to the temple you encouraged me to take.

After two weeks, we found a way to make it clear that the work was no longer appropriate, when, in truth, it hurt us too much. It felt wrong. This woman trusted us to do therapy on her child because we were the only ones who were willing and hopeful enough to try. We understood the importance of repeated patterns and rituals. That performing these things with exactness held the keys to salvation. Just as in the temple, if we missed a word, we had to start from the beginning until we got it right. But even in the precision, we eventually lost hope.

I set out to find a task that would be easier and less wrenching, both physically and emotionally. I knew just the thing: drugs.

Doctors without Borders was looking for volunteers to handle controlled substances with no chaperons in Toulon. *C'est parfait!* It was a service opportunity I had been born to render. Our job was to take paper sample boxes of narcotics and prescription medication and sort through the used cartons to make sure that the blister packs weren't opened. We needed to verify that the drugs weren't past their expiration date, and that the pills hadn't been contaminated in any way. All of those that passed inspection were returned to the organization we were serving, Les Medecins sans Frontieres (Doctors without Borders). The compromised packets, still full of usable pills, were thrown into a garbage bag and then tossed into a medical waste bin.

In a vacant medical office with zero supervision, we sorted every discarded drug and controlled substance that the hospital dispensed, and it was our job to make sure that only pills that passed inspection were packaged and donated.

The volunteer coordinator would arrange to have us pick up boxes full of illicit drugs and have our way with them. They were banking on the fact that we were too straitlaced to be interested and too American to understand the complicated small-print French labels. The volunteer coordinator underestimated us. *Imovane. What could that mean? Sounds interesting to me.* I would memorize certain words and then go back to the apartment to look the terms up in my French/English dictionary.

I had no intention of using drugs from Doctors without Borders, but I had every intention of learning both the street value and purpose for the expired pills that we were tossing in the incinerator. Even though I was a missionary I was still an entrepreneur at heart and there seemed to be lucrative business lessons to be learned. It was a victimless crime, so *pourquoi pas?* I became a mastermind of the trade, sorting through compromised blister packs at a blistering pace and hiding the interesting packets to take home for further research in the sacred space between my garments and my bra.

Doctors without Borders welcomed our American selves into their volunteer circle with open arms, but the rest of France did not. Our doughy white upper arms coupled with our little black name-tags signaled to all the locals that we were interlopers. And we were not welcome. We chalked up their disdain to downright sin. *Go ahead, make fun of us now, we will see who's laughing when you are burning in hell!* Most people ignored us but some had severe reactions to our presence.

Once, a man stopped on his bike to scream and pound his fist at us, two twenty-two-year old American girls, "C'est vraiment horrible ce que tu fais. Retournez dans votre pays. Nous ne voulons pas de vous ici." *It's really horrible what you're doing. Go back to your country. We don't want you here.*

It was a miracle if a week went by without a pointed jab or a direct affront. On especially hard days, like when we rode our bikes through dog poop or made it to the patisserie a minute after closing, we would recite the Standard of Truth as a way to pump ourselves up.

The Standard of Truth was an excerpt taken from a letter written by the Prophet Joseph Smith to Mr. John Wentworth, editor and proprietor of the *Chicago Democrat*, and it was written to explain the goals of the Church of Jesus Christ of Latter-day Saints. We memorized it in French and in English, and it motivated us and made us feel powerful and a part of something great.

The Standard of Truth has been erected; no unhallowed hand can stop the work from progressing; persecutions may rage, mobs may combine, armies may assemble, calumny may defame, but the truth of God will go forth boldly, nobly, and independent, till it has penetrated every continent, visited every clime, swept every country, and sounded in every ear, till the purposes of God shall be accomplished, and the Great Jehovah shall say the work is done.

The Standard of Truth flowed through my veins. Nothing could stand in my way, because I was called to serve. And God's words justified as much.

We tried to live by the missionary motto, "Quiet Dignity," but oftentimes the scenarios we found ourselves in were too absurd to be dignified at all. In many of the apartment buildings we visited there were always children running around half naked. But not the half that you would expect. We'd politely avert our eyes and try not to physically recoil when they offered us the same metal chair they'd just persuaded their bare-assed son to get out of. It got even more quietly dignified when, with no available chairs in sight, that same child asked if he could sit on your lap. My prayer came out suddenly and silently as I prayed for the sanctity of his soul and the sanctity of my thigh. *Dear Heavenly Father, please bless sweet Yacine. Bless him with hope, and faith, and spatial awareness. Please bless him to keep the tip of his dangling penis from grazing the top of my thigh.*

Nothing could deter us from the work. We taught the gospel to anyone who would listen. Rich, poor, happy, sad, pants-wearing, pants-free. Our Good News did not discriminate. We did our best to build on common beliefs, on the foundation already laid. Occasionally, we'd play the minute-to-win-it, kneel-down-and-pray routine and hope for the best.

One of our lucky contestants was an unassuming teenage boy. As soon as we finished praying and said "Amen," we asked him what he was feeling.

"I feel good," he replied. "I feel warm, I feel happy."

We jumped right in: "That's God, that's the Spirit."

His eyes lit up, and he said, "Yes, it is! I'm Muslim, and it's just like the stories Muhammad told. Like the feelings Muhammad had when he was fifteen and prayed and received the Quran."

"Yes, yes, it's exactly the same," I said. "But Muhammad didn't have the full story. God still had more to say. Take all of your faith, all of your diligence, all of your dedication to Islam and let us add to it a new and restored gospel. I'm sure your parents will understand."

I would build on the story of Muhammad and I'd build on the Quran and how he was a fifteen-year-old boy and how Joseph Smith was a fifteen-year-old boy and how God absolutely loves fifteen-year-old boys. I didn't know anything about the Quran at the time. I genuinely thought Mormonism informed Islam—my world religion professor at BYU seemed to agree. "God wants this for you. Do you feel happiness when we're here? Do you feel joy? Would you like to experience more of that same joy?"

We'd read verses of scripture from the book of Mosiah in French:

And it came to pass that he said unto them: Behold, here are the waters of Mormon (for thus were they called) and now, as ye are desirous to come into the fold of God, and to be called his people, and are willing to bear one another's burdens, that they may be light;

Yea, and are willing to mourn with those that mourn; yea, and comfort those that stand in need of comfort, and to stand as witnesses of God at all times and in all things, and in all places that

*ye may be in, even until death, that ye may be redeemed of God,
and be numbered with those of the first resurrection, that ye may
have eternal life—*

*Now I say unto you, if this be the desire of your hearts, what
have you against being baptized in the name of the Lord, as a
witness before him that ye have entered into a covenant with him,
that ye will serve him and keep his commandments, that he may
pour out his Spirit more abundantly upon you?*

*And now when the people had heard these words, they clapped
their hands for joy, and exclaimed: This is the desire of our hearts.*

After reading the scripture we'd close the Book of Mormon, look at
them intently and ask, "Is this the desire of your heart?"

And they would often say, "Yes. That sounds wonderful. What do
I need to do?"

"Nothing," we'd reply. "That's why we're here. Sit down. Let's get
started."

Once they committed to baptism, we'd set a date to return, and
we'd teach them all the rules they'd need to start following. They had
to give up drinking all alcohol (yes, even wine), they had to give up
smoking (yes, even if its only one cigarette on the weekend), they had
to give up sex (yes, even if he's been living with you for three years),
they had to give up ten percent of their income for tithing (yes, you
can choose to pay off your gross or net), and finally, they had to give
up any affiliations with any other churches (yes, even if you're baptized
Catholic). They had to promise to consecrate their time, talent, and
money to the building up of the kingdom of God on the Earth. Nothing
too major. Just the big and fine print of an eternal contract that makes
religion both beautiful and nefarious.

If they were still open to baptism after hearing all the rules we'd say, "Great, wonderful. We're so glad. In order to prepare for your baptism, there are a few things we need to teach you. But let's set a date, because what we've found is as soon as you make this wonderful commitment to the Lord, Satan and all his forces will come out, and everything in your life is going to start going wrong. But don't think it's because of the church. It's because you're *choosing* the church that Satan is upping the ante. So when your family tells you you're crazy and your boss fires you and your landlord kicks you out because he doesn't want the weird Mormons around, it's because the gospel is so important and so true. You're going to be filled with doubt, and you're going to be filled with fear. We need you to be strong."

They just had to believe in the principle, and that was enough.

The devil was in the details.

One night, I heard a wailing noise coming from the other missionaries' room. The sounds of a crying missionary were commonplace, but these cries seemed different. More primal. I needed to make sure she at least wasn't bleeding. I walked into her bedroom and saw her with her knees bunched up to her chest and her arms cradling her legs as she rocked back and forth and back and forth.

"They're all going to hell!" she cried. "They're all going to hell!"

I looked at her and thought to myself, "She's lost it. She's completely lost it! She's batshit crazy. But if I really believe the same things she does, she's right. They are all going to hell."

The sinners on the Côte d'Azur weren't as keen on our stop drinking, stop indulging, stop sexing, stop smoking message as we had hoped.

It felt like we were Americanizing them. And to be fair, we were trying our hardest to; it just wasn't taking. The church seemed to run
so much better in the United States compared with what we saw in
France. Leadership was spotty, there weren't enough priesthood hold-
ers to maintain the organization. Women converts outnumbered the
men four to one. Gems of the gospel were getting lost in translation,
and the people we encountered on the street were rejecting us at every
turn. "Get out of our country. You're a cult."

If the church was true, she was right. They were all going to hell.

As much as I didn't want to see myself in this missionary, I did.
When you're surrounded by your community and the tropes are reinforced at every turn, it's hard to remain immune. When you see a missionary rocking on her bunk lamenting the corruption of the people
you serve, it's hard not to think, "Do I really believe this? Why am I
wasting my time?"

I distinctly remember waking up the following morning, feeling
overwhelmed and exhausted, and placing my feet on the cold tile floor.
I sat there for a moment, looking down at my toes and dreading the
thought of standing up and starting my day.

How am I going to do this? *The hill I'm walking up is getting good
and steep.*

All I have to do is wake up at six every morning, roll out of bed, put
my feet on the floor, stand up, and show up.

I couldn't continue to serve with full energy of heart and spirit like
I had been anymore, but I could certainly do the work. I could put my
feet on the floor, put on my tag, and *sonner, sonner, sonner*, over and
over again everyday until my mission was over. And for the next four
hundred days, that would have to be enough.

I look back on my ability to relentlessly preach the Word of God and attribute it almost entirely to the Glinda bubble that kept me shut off from the world and shut off from the most natural parts of myself. My bubble kept me safe, but it also kept me separated. I wasn't loving the people of France like I wanted to. I always had an agenda. I couldn't just accept and enjoy them where they were in their lives. I felt compelled to push for baptisms, to push for reactivation, to push for them to pay tithing when I never should have pushed them to do anything at all. I couldn't be their friend without always having a wonderful surprise.

The capacity to shut off an entire part of yourself is a terrifying thing.

Even more thrilling and terrifying is the capacity to do it well.

There's something to be said about preaching eternal life while slowly dying inside. As it turns out, saving souls can be soulless work. It was painful. It was hard. It wore us down. It more than pulled on our heartstrings, it strung us out wholeheartedly.

CHAPTER 12

MY HEART WILL GO ON

Despite my blackening soul, or perhaps because of it, I was a very effective missionary. I could get butts in seats, or bodies in the font, if you know what I mean. I held the record for most baptisms in our mission: sixteen dunked in eighteen months. The average for other missionaries was one or less. My mission president asked me to train seven other sister missionaries while I served in France. I'd heard of other missionaries having the opportunity to be a trainer once, maybe twice, but for me, the hits just kept on coming. Being a trainer: Mormon flex.

Because of my impressive track record, the president granted me a few indulgences not available to the other missionaries. Normally, missionaries were expected to be within sight or sound of their companion at all times. If for any reason your companion became unavailable, the president would assign you as a third wheel to an existing companionship until you're able to pair off again.

On my next to last transfer day as a missionary I was supposed to send my latest companion on a train to Perpignan at eleven a.m., but my replacement companion would not be arriving until five that afternoon. That gave me a six-hour window where I would need to be supervised or assigned as a third wheel. I explained my dilemma to the president, and instead of shuffling schedules to find a way to keep me tethered, he unlocked the leash and set me free. "Just go home to your apartment and wait until her train arrives," he suggested. "I'm not worried about you getting into any trouble."

And it was in that moment I realized that if you give a mouse a cookie, she takes the whole damn *gâteau*. I promptly repaid my mission president's trust by immediately betraying it.

I dropped my companion off at the train station, bid her *au revoir*, and headed straight to the theater where the marquee was lighting my path brighter than the noonday sun. *Titanic.*

I slipped my name tag into my pocket, walked up to the theater counter, and squeaked out a timid, "*Un billet, s'il vous plaît.*" Before Bill Paxton in all his frosted-tip glory could say, "*C'est le jour de payer les enfants,*" I was safely enveloped in the weighted blanket of the darkened theater. A real girl, really living in France, really watching a movie.

Rose talked about the *Titanic* being a ship of dreams for most, but she felt imprisoned. The well-brought-up girl screaming inside to everyone's inattention, willing to fling herself off the top of the ship to avoid living a life as the wife of the arrogant Cal.

I was so mesmerized by the sweet relief of anonymity and darkness, that I failed to see the connection.

The movie was in French with no subtitles. I didn't fully catch every word, but I did not care.

I was the king of the world.

I felt peace. I felt calm. I felt more like myself and closer to God in that theater than I had felt over the past sixteen months of prayer-filled, scripture-filled missionary service. No prior feeling in France compared to the tranquility I had while cloaked in the sanctity of the theater watching the iceberg sink the ship.

After the movie, I snuck out and didn't put on my name tag until I was a safe distance from the theater and in my own neighborhood. I waited for my new companion to arrive, shadowed with shame about what I had just done. I vowed never to tell a soul. *Loose lips sink ships.* But still I was paranoid that the mission president would somehow find out and send me home. I feared that one movie would undermine all the good I had done on my mission and in my life. I would lose the crown and kingdom I had sacrificed so much for. *It's all there, black and white, clear as crystal! You stole fizzy lifting drinks! You bumped into the ceiling, which now has to be washed and sterilized, so you get nothing! You lose! Good day, sir!*

I buried the truth. A woman's heart is a deep ocean of secrets.

On a flight back from Norway recently, I discovered my seat was separated from my friends. Rather than spend the thirteen-hour flight next to a stranger, we considered asking the young man across the aisle to switch seats. Before we could summon the courage, he looked over and volunteered to swap places.

"Are you guys together?" He eagerly jumped up, moved his bags, and helped us get settled. He was young and cute and chivalrous. A throwback from a forgotten era. We were both impressed.

My friend whispered that she thought he was a missionary. I shrugged her off because he wasn't wearing a tag. Later, as we waited in baggage claim, I saw him reach into his pocket and pull out a little black placard and affix it to his shirt.

I approached him.

"You're a missionary?"

Immediately, he launched into an explanation.

"Yeah, we aren't allowed to wear our name tags in Amsterdam." He was so apologetic, worried that I might rat him out to the authorities or his mission president. He wanted to let me know that he was a good missionary, not one that broke the rules or snuck off to movies.

"No, no, no," I reassured him. "It's not about your name tag. There was something different about you, and now I know what it was. Thank you for switching seats."

He smiled, and we parted ways.

What I really wanted to do at that moment was hug him.

I wanted to say, "I know you, because I was you. I know I don't look Mormon, and I know that I'm hanging out with these obvious rule breakers, but I know you. And what you hold sacred I held sacred. And if one day you realize that you want to leave all of this, you can. And you can come find me and I'll still know you. And I'll help you. I don't want you to ever think that I'm not on your side."

Despite everything, when that missionary put on that little black name tag, there was no one in that airport I wanted to talk to more.

Returning to the states as a return missionary, I needed a new chapter. I wanted to live with some friends in Washington, D.C. I'd pursued a humanities degree because I wanted to be a well-informed, well-rounded mother and docent on my future children's field trips. But of course that isn't what I told everyone. Instead, I said my degree would help me get into law school if I ever decided to attend. During a mock debate in grade school, four-fingered Mr. Poole had told me that I'd make a great lawyer and I had clung to it. "He's badgering the witness" just flowed like honey from my fifth-grade tongue.

He was the only adult who had ever suggested that I be anything other than a mother and wife, so I took his suggestion to heart.

My dad said nervously, "I don't think that's a great plan for you. In D.C., everyone's kind of single and career-minded, and you really need to focus on finding a guy and getting married and, you know, settling down."

This was my dad, and I wanted to make him proud. I wanted to make him happy and prove to him that I could be trusted. I knew that what he was saying was a little backward, but he was smart, and he loved me enough to say what he and the church knew to be true. He wasn't afraid to say what he knew was unpopular. So I listened. *Of course, it's unfair. We're women. Our choices are never easy.*

I eschewed the idea of being around career-minded women and instead moved to Huntington Beach, California, where, according to my dad, people apparently were more interested in furthering their relationships than they were in furthering their careers. Huntington Beach had one of the largest singles ward in the nation, and it seemed like a target-rich environment in a place where I could still fly free while simultaneously yearning for someone to tie me down.

And so I went west, young man. West.

PART THREE

BAD
WIFE

Heather's parents outside the SLC Temple on their wedding day.

Heather coming home from the hospital in Carmel-by-the-Sea.

Heather at two years old.

Heather watching football with her dad.

Heather (center) with her family on a Sunday morning before church.

Heather (second from left) on a camping trip with her cousins.

Heather (center, in blue) with her relatives on her baptism day.

Heather (second from right) with her family at the Denver temple dedication.

Heather during her hot-dog-joke phase.

Heather (far left) with her friends on the San Juan River.

Heather (center) with friends in high school.

Heather and her brother at BYU graduation.

Heather (left) with Soeur Campbell in Montpellier, France.

Heather (center) and other missionaries at the Missionary Training Center (MTC).

Heather and
Billy dating, on
their first trip
to Hawaii.

Heather and Billy dating, on
New Year's Day.

Heather and Billy
on their wedding
day outside the
Laie Hawaii
Temple.

Heather on her wedding
day outside the Turtle
Bay Resort.

Ashley's first Christmas.

Heather in Huntington Beach.

Heather with
Billy, Georgia,
Ashley, and
Annabelle,
posing for the
Christmas card.

Heather at Ashley's baptism.

Ashley's baptism.

Ashley and Billy at her baptism.

Heather with Ashley, Georgia, and Annabelle on her first trip as a single mom.

Ashley, Georgia, and Annabelle posing for the Christmas card.

Heather with Meredith, Whitney, and Lisa while filming the sizzle reel in Little Cottonwood Canyon.

Heather (right) with Whitney Rose.

Heather with Meredith Marks.

Heather (far left) with Meredith, Lisa, and Whitney while doing press at Beauty Lab + Laser.

Heather with Jen Shah having a Hot Girl Summer in New York City.

Tim, Dre's brother.

Dre and Heather.

Heather filming a confessional for Season 1 of *The Real Housewives of Salt Lake City* (RHOSLC).

Heather with Lisa and Jen while promoting Season 1 of RHOSLC.

Heather behind the scenes of the RHOSLC Season 1 reunion.

Heather with Mary, Jen, and Andy Cohen at the Season 1 reunion.

Heather with Kristen Chenoweth at Beauty Lab + Laser.

Heather with Ashley, Georgia, and Annabelle while skiing in Utah.

CHAPTER 13

LOST ON YOU

Imet Billy Gay the day he moved to Huntington Beach. And that chance meeting changed both of our lives forever.

Billy was, for all intents and purposes, unlike any Mormon man I'd ever known: more than six feet tall, born of a wealthy family, and interested in pursuing me. He was handsome and straight, a descendant of good stock, and undeniably the first actual matrimonial candidate who seemed remotely attainable. He was a man with a lust for adventure, and I was a woman with a lust, period. He was my Goldilocks guy: not too hot, not too cold, but just right.

I felt my heart flutter the first time I saw him. He had a natural ease and confidence that I found alluring. He was quick to laugh and smart and accomplished. He had graduated from BYU and then gotten his master's at Northwestern. He had worked at his dad's company but eschewed the easy fast track of nepotism and the corporate ladder. He was an artist, a creative, and he didn't want an office job; he wanted to be an entrepreneur. It curled my toes to hear him talk about business.

His blue eyes and bright smile were irresistible. He was *the* guy, and I wanted desperately to be *the* girl.

My roommate knew his roommate, and we went over to their apartment to welcome them to the neighborhood. He began flirting with me immediately. Because he was so new to the area, he hadn't had time to assess the dating landscape of SoCal, and that worked to my advantage. He'd come from a singles ward in Park City where the ratio of single men to single women was fairly even, so I had the pleasure of him taking the lead right out of the gate. I was smitten by the effort.

Billy was a Benson scholar, one of a select group of esteemed students that were given full-ride academic scholarships to BYU. His résumé was already impressive, but he sold me on his grit and ambition and adventurous spirit. He had walked away from a six-figure corporate job to pursue his dream of being a filmmaker. He produced extreme action sports videos and had just returned from premiering his latest snowmobiling stunt movie in Las Vegas the night I met him. He was the real deal, humble and unassuming but still opinionated and strong. All the guys I knew were sputtering to get their careers started or they were permanently stuck in a pattern of failure to thrive, but not Billy Gay. He was living the dream. His films were doing so well that he could afford to take a year off to travel and surf the world. Huntington Beach was his first stop, and he was planning on using it as a home base while he ventured around the globe in search of the best longboard waves possible.

"Where do you think you'll go next?" I asked him.

"I'm not sure," he said. "Probably Costa Rica, but HB has the best waves in the world, so I'm in no rush to leave."

He smiled. I blushed. The vibe was palpable. *It's all happening.*

He didn't hesitate. "What are you doing tomorrow night?"

Tomorrow night? I wasn't ready! We made plans to go to a church singles event in nearby Irvine. It was all so seamless and smooth and grown-up that I began to question it once I got back home with my roommate.

"Do you think he thinks it's a *date* date or just a hangout?" I asked her.

"A *date* date," she replied flatly. "There's no question."

Guys in Huntington Beach were not known for asking girls out on actual dates. Everyone just hung out and hooked up and avoided show-ing too much interest in any one person. I was turned on by Billy's savoir faire and chivalry. This was a man who went after what he wanted, and if he wanted me, then I wanted to make sure I didn't mess it up.

Our first date was fun and flirty, but we kept it friendly and made plans to meet up with our friends the following week when we were both in Salt Lake City. We had our first kiss on November first in Gretchen's driveway. It was a quick peck on the lips, because his friends were in the car waiting and watching, but it still felt significant. I was into him. He was older, smarter, funnier, and taller than any of the guys I had dated previously. And the chemistry between us was undeniable. He left for Minnesota the next day to promote his latest snowmobiling film, but we talked on the phone every night, and when we were both back in Huntington Beach, we didn't even bother with the premise of dinner or a date. He came straight over to my apartment, and we made out for hours on the couch in my living room, oblivious to my room-mates walking in and out of the adjoining kitchen.

We were falling in love fast. The next morning, I found a little folded note under my windshield wiper asking me out to dinner. We went to the Surf and Sand in Laguna Beach and ate Chilean sea bass while we watched the sunset over the water. On the way home, he called his mom just to check in and say hi. His affection for her was endearing. I had always heard you could tell how a man will treat his wife by the way he treats his mother. He was wooing me, and it was working.

Meanwhile, I was *actually* working as a tech writer and business analyst for a software company in Tustin, and it was a nine-to-five job with a thirty-minute commute each way. I became an efficient sleeper, thriving on less than four hours a night. I never even noticed a deficit; when I was with Billy, time seemed to stand still. He'd stay at my house until two or three in the morning, then slink home and sleep in.

While I was at work, he would plot and plan cute little dates and excursions. He would buy me flowers and write love notes. He would wait anxiously for me to return home from work so that our adventures together could begin as soon as possible. He was currently self-employed, so he made courting me his nine-to-five, and I loved it.

About six weeks after we started hanging out daily, he surprised me with a trip to Hawaii. His cousins lived in Laie, and he had spent summers living with them and working at the Polynesian Cultural Center adjacent to the BYU Hawaii campus. I had never been to Hawaii, and I couldn't wait. He greeted me at the airport with a plumeria lei and a red Jeep for our rental car.

We drove straight to Waikiki Beach, where he had booked me my first surf lesson. He held up a towel for me to change into my suit in the parking lot and walked me over to my surf instructor.

"Take good care of her," he said tenderly, as he sauntered off to catch his own bigger waves.

I paddled out into the Pacific on a surfboard for my private lesson and marveled at the moment. The water looked like liquid silver and felt silky on my skin. My instructor pushed me into a slow-cresting wave and coached me first onto my knees and then into a standing position. I was catching waves and catching feelings.

The next few days were filled with lush hikes, magical waterfalls, and secret coves. Billy knew all the hidden hideaways and tucked-away treasures usually exclusive to locals. We drove the Jeep around the island until we reached the end of the road. We got out and sat down in the sand and started making out.

"I think I'm falling for you," he said quietly between kisses.

"I think I've already fallen," I replied.

And we both felt it. It was tangible. *I want to know what love is. I want you to show me.*

I was having the time of my life with who I hoped would be the love of my life. When we got back home to Huntington Beach, we met up with one of his old work friends. During dinner, I heard his friend mention something about the stock price of Billy's dad's company. My mind started racing.

"Your family has a public company?" I asked. "Traded on the NAS-DAQ?" *Ticker symbol say what?*

This here was a jumbo popcorn with extra butter, Jujubes, Skittles, Milk Duds, *and* Red Vines kinda movie date. *He's rich, honey. He's rich.*

Billy's family business was called Nutraceutical, a vitamin and mineral brand worth more than $400 million. It had offices around the globe and employed thousands of people, especially in the state of Utah where it was headquartered. The Gay name was one that had found favor among the Salt Lake City saints and Silicon Valley and had historical weight as well. Mormon Royalty. If you are wealthy, famous, or related to a general authority, you earn the crown, and Billy had all three.

Bill Gay, Billy's grandfather, was famous for forming the Mormon Mafia that ran Las Vegas and worked for Howard Hughes, the eccentric billionaire, in the 1970s. He was a diligent servant, waking up early to drive Hughes to the airport or to the Cottontail Ranch. All the while, never once did he expose Hughes. *What happens in Vegas stays in Vegas.*

And the benefits of Bill Gay's network and net worth were passed down through the generations. When it rains, everyone gets wet.

The tales of Howard Hughes and his Mormon Mafia are many, and they have been recorded in scores of Hughes biographies. Everyone has their own theories about the Hughes–Gay connection, but one fact remains undisputed: Howard Hughes loved Mormons, and he loved Mormons because he loved Bill Gay. Bill Gay was not only an excellent Mormon, but he was also an excellent employee and friend. *Therefore, if ye have desires to serve God ye are called to the work.*

Mormons are comfortable living with secrets. Church members go into temples all over the world and conduct complicated and elaborate rituals that they keep secret from their friends, their children, their employers, even their own spouses. When you get married in the temple, the woman reveals her new temple name to her husband when he takes her through the veil, but he does not ever reveal his name to her.

Mormons are as devout as the men and women in Borough Park or on Bedford Avenue with their yarmulkes, their payos, their wigs to cover their hair. We just hide it from the world. We are zealots on the inside, masquerading as good old-fashioned, "God bless America," go-with-the-flow soccer moms and dads.

When I started dating Billy, I was in such a love fog that I almost forgot how desperate I was to get married. For the first time in my life, I was falling in love with a man who was an actual *candidate*. A man who could take me to the temple and be sealed for time and all eternity. He was the goose that would lay gold eggs for Easter. *At least one hundred a day.* And I happened to cross his path. There was no moral dilemma to wrestle with. No real decision to be made.

When an opportunity like this comes along, you grab it with both hands, kid. You grab it with both hands.

CHAPTER 14

SECURE YOURSELF
TO HEAVEN

Billy didn't seem to have a dark side. He wasn't a man about his own appetites. He had money but lived frugally, he had status but was humble, he was entitled but he was kind.

The sexual tension surrounding our relationship was so thick it was like walking through sheets of cobwebs. I couldn't think straight, I couldn't focus, I just wanted to be with Billy. To scratch the itch, to clear our heads. One night, I begged him just to run away and have sex with me. We could travel the world and never look back. But he was unflinching: "If we are going to do this, we're going to do it the right way."

When I pushed back, he replied, "Trust me, do it the right way. Once we are married, you'll be having more sex than all your single friends combined."

Billy was the answer key to the test. His devotion to the faith was admirable, and I hoped it would elevate my game. I could already envision our life as a married couple. We would vacation in Hawaii and South Florida, own a mountain home in Midway, sit courtside at the Jazz, spend summers in Newport Beach and Lake Powell. We were going to have the brass rings that every successful family in Utah so proudly displayed.

Take all the money away, all I wanted was a home where the man presided and provided and where the woman cared and prepared. I didn't want the entire setup, I didn't want to be in charge of the food or drinks. I just wanted my corner of heaven here on earth.

Billy proposed on Saint Patrick's Day, March 17. We had been officially dating since December. Three and a half months. And we were getting married.

The night of our engagement, Billy took me camping in Malibu at Sycamore Cove. There was a full moon, and we were walking along the beach when he dropped to one knee and said, "The only way to make this night more perfect is if you say you'll marry me." And he opened up a little black box with a not-so-little round ring. I dropped to my knees in the sand across from him and kissed him. "Yes. Yes. A thousand times yes."

I felt happy, I felt heady, I felt horny. The motivation to get married was slowly changing from eternal salvation to eternal satisfaction. I needed to *be* with this man, and if it required my oath to obey him for time and all eternity, so be it.

I knew that I would never say no, but I also knew that the muffled white noise screaming from deep within was desperately trying to say something I was unwilling to hear. I pushed that feeling down into the same place I pushed the thrill of running a business or the dream of Drambuie. *Sayonara, Sweetheart!*

For the first few weeks following the engagement, I didn't wear the ring—in part because I didn't believe this was it. It didn't seem monumental enough to be real.

But my sacred little secret didn't last long, because my roommate found my ring and forced it onto my finger. "You've got him. Now, don't lose him."

My roommate had converted when she was eighteen years old. She had a full life before coming to the church, giving her a perspective that was different from anyone else I had ever been friends with. She'd been out in the world and had slept with the tattooed Huntington Beach surfers we ogled daily. But in the end, she turned her back on all of it to be with the Dick Van Pattens. She wanted Dick because she had been out among the dregs of society, and it wasn't good. She came home and clung to the safety of the 99. And if she endorsed the soft dad bod, the generous, affectionate guys—who was I to long for the latter?

In the faith, I knew there were only enough lifeboats to take half the women and children after all the men were rescued. Billy was my shot, he was my life preserver. And no matter how I felt, no matter the little, tiny voice and the muffled white noise, I wasn't going to say no. I wasn't going to drown.

Looking around, I tried desperately to find someone, anyone, to check me. No one said, "You really shouldn't marry anyone without seeing how they act in all four seasons. How do they spend Christmas? How do they spend Mother's Day? A pack of cigarettes and a walk around the block or breakfast in bed with croissants and orange juice? How do they react when it's snowing outside and the car battery's dead? How are they hungry? How are they tired? Maybe you should know that before you commit to time and all eternity."

No one asked these questions because we already knew the answers. We had both been following the same exact script from the day we were born. There was no line straddling. No Mormon 2.0. No deviation from the Plan. Instead, they stood there with a death stare, a poker face. Nobody said anything different from what had always been affirmed to me: now that you have a man, your life can actually begin. *You don't have to go home, but you can't stay here.*

I started preparing for the wedding, with the intention to make it as spiritual and significant as possible. I wanted small and sacred. There were no bridesmaids or flower girls. Billy's grandmother took the photos. My mom prepared poignant quotes and scriptures for the guests to read. I asked my friends Regina and Amy to sing.

On July 7, in the two-thousandth year of our Lord, Billy and I were dressed in all our priesthood robes and aprons in a tiny room inside the Laie Temple on the North Shore of Hawaii. No vows were made, no rings exchanged. We knelt across an altar, he held my hand in the Patriarchal Grip, and when the temple officiant asked if I was willing to submit to my husband for time and all eternity, I bowed my head and said, "Yes."

Our wedding reception, following the temple ceremony, was at Turtle Bay Resort. We filled the glass gazebo overlooking the crashing waves of the Pacific with our closest friends and family. We ate mahi-mahi and fed each other cake with smooth coconut fondant. We draped ourselves in traditional Hawaiian wedding leis and slow-danced to Andrea Bocelli. It was tender, it was trite, it was true.

CHAPTER 15

GOD GAVE ME YOU

I sold Billy on the tip of the iceberg and hoped the depth and neediness under the surface would be a wonderful surprise.

Little by little, as I exposed more and more of myself, I wanted him to be amazed by the magnitude of the woman he had married. I was going to fill his home with music and laughter and fun facts about art and literature. I was going to raise his children with love and faith and matching pajamas. I was going to build a shelter with a toothpick and some duct tape. *I'm gonna treat you so nice you're never gonna let me go.*

At our wedding, Billy's uncle Ron gave a toast: "You know, Billy, they say to keep your eyes wide open before you get married and then your eyes half closed after. But Heather is such a beauty, I say keep your eyes wide open."

It was funny and sweet and I appreciated it. But I took the original adage and committed it to memory, dedicating myself to being in my marriage with one eye closed.

My life was beginning! I did it! Now what? *And now when the people had heard these words, they clapped their hands for joy, and exclaimed: This is the desire of our hearts.*

I had to make it work.

Billy and I stayed in Hawaii for our honeymoon. As a wedding gift, his aunt gave me a used book, dog-eared and annotated. The book was called *Man and Wife*, and it gave newlywed women tangible, prescriptive steps to making their husbands happy.

My value in the community was tied to my purity. It was based in keeping something that I was about to give away. Overnight, I went from safeguarding my virginity as my most sacred treasure to highlighting passages out of a book about faking an orgasm so that my husband never felt inadequate.

This gift was commonplace and normal. It was as if Billy received fist bumps and back pats while I received advice from the church's clucking hens: *Just take a breath. It'll all be over before you know it.*

Our wedding night was everything I needed it to be. Under the blanket of stars, we swam for hours, floating and wading through the deep indigo waters of the lagoon outside the Ihilani Hotel. Accompanied only by the warm summer wind, we made out in our swimsuits and lay together in the sand. We traipsed upstairs to our suite, and flung ourselves onto the bed scattered with rose petals. The soft strumming of a ukulele filled the air, balancing the natural buzz of anticipation, anxiety, and excitement that emanated from both of us.

I loved being with Billy. It felt natural, it felt right. As lovers, we were compatible enough. It was just in every other department we'd discover edges. I was in love, and he was my husband, so whatever happened, I was going to work with it. I was going to turn it into a fairy tale. I had heard horror stories from friends who thought they were marrying a vanilla sex guy but discovered on their wedding night that they had actually married rum raisin. I had gotten past the gatekeepers, the sentinels, the morality checks, the background questions, the barcoded temple recommend, the mission, the engagement, and the wedding. All my dreams were coming true, and I wasn't going to mess it up by having an opinion.

I had already made oaths in the temple and had sworn never to reveal any of the secrets I had learned. Billy could've asked me to do just about anything sexually and I would've done it without ever shaming him for asking. In the temple, men make covenants that bestow them with "dominion over all the earth and the inhabitants therein," and women make covenants to obey them. I was taught to say "no" to a lot of things outside of our faith. But inside the faith, I was taught only to bow my head and say "yes."

For most of my life I found that concept to be unbelievably romantic and noble and safe. I thought being cherished and protected was better than being respected and heard. But when I actually had to live this way, the reality of being just a helpmeet was much different in practice than it was in theory.

Billy was raised in the same systems of power that I was. He'd always pushed up against expectation—rebelled against the demand—by moving to Huntington Beach to surf, by quitting his family's company to start his own. But with a healthy mix of his bad luck and my desperation, he came into my orbit and I snared him, pulling him back into the magnet he'd been so tirelessly working to repel.

For the second part of our honeymoon, we went to Molokai. Molokai was a smart choice for a couple who had nothing in common. It was a leper colony abandoned by everyone except the lepers and the dutiful priests who helped them. We felt the energy of the island, and it became a prison. Our wedded bliss lasted three days, and then somewhere on Molokai, before the honeymoon vouchers had even been fully redeemed, I already wanted out.

There's a reason nobody goes to a leper colony for their honeymoon, although visiting one was our big excursion. Since I'd quickly learned that sex didn't take more than twenty to thirty minutes, we found ourselves with time on our hands. It wasn't long before we were driving through our one-stoplight town in order to find a movie theater showing *Scary Movie* in the middle of July.

We thought going to the movies would be fun. Something safe and anonymous. However, when the lights dimmed, *Scary Movie* turned out to be a stag film with a dildo and a glory hole. Suddenly, my adventurous, not-afraid-to-be-uncool-as-long-as-he's-doing-the-right-thing husband rose to the occasion. He forced us to stand up in the middle of the movie and walk out of the empty theater in a far-reaching attempt to honor our righteous indignation.

He marched to the box office and demanded our money back. His open protestation at something as innocuous as a scene in a movie made me want to die inside. I was embarrassed. I'd rather have been murdered with a dildo through a glory hole than be humiliated in front of the teenage theater clerk.

I hadn't thought past the wedding day. I'd gotten the big commitment, I'd clapped my hands for joy and exclaimed that it was the desire of my heart, and here I was, feet planted firmly in a leper colony, arguing about the righteousness, or lack thereof, of *Scary Movie*.

I sat there for the next two days making the most of my time. *Don't let God down with a frown.* I listened to Hawaiian radio so that

Billy could relax undisturbed. I did puzzles, and I went to the Marriott timeshare clubhouse to find books to read and old magazines to thumb through. I found ways to remind myself of who I was and what I loved doing, trying desperately not to think about the fact that I was alone on Scary Island with no friends.

Upon our return, we attended marriage counseling pretending to be a cool, progressive, evolved couple, when in reality, we were both freaking out, terrified that we had made a horrible mistake. The best counseling we could have received should have happened before we got married. We could've solved all our problems with a weekend in Atlantic City where we had sex and realized that it was all we had in common. But instead, our therapist was a Mormon man who'd written a book called *How to Hug a Porcupine*. There simply was no way that a young, faithful couple who checked every box the way we did would receive any other advice other than, "Love the Lord, love each other. You're halfway there."

In my journal, I wrote down my questions and doubts. *Do I believe in God this much? Is the gospel true? Will he fortify and sanctify this marriage? Because if so, I will give 100 percent.*

However, it was clear that I had just married a man who was already giving 100 percent when I thought he was only giving 30. And he wasn't ever going to be able to do the math. He couldn't see the differential, and that was terrifying.

As we unpacked the events of Hawaii, the counselor congratulated us on passing the first milestone of marriage: getting over the unmet expectations of the honeymoon. "We build up the honeymoons for you kids, and guess what? You're devastated," he said. "You're sad. It wasn't all you wanted it to be. It wasn't the knight in shining armor and the fairy-tale castle. Every kid is set up to fail. All the hoopla creates unrealistic expectations, and it's a normal response to be disappointed. But all those doubts and all those fears are just a normal rite of passage."

I had not only heard his sermon before, I had preached it. *In order to progress you in the new and everlasting covenant, there are a few things we need to teach you. We've found that as soon as you make this wonderful commitment to the Lord and your husband, Satan and all his forces will come out, and everything in your life is going to start going wrong. But don't think it's because of your marriage. It's because you're choosing marriage that Satan is upping the ante. So when your husband storms out of an empty theater or belittles your feelings or denounces your advances, it's because the gospel is so important and so true. You're going to be filled with doubt, and you're going to be filled with fear. We need you to be strong.*

I just had to believe in the principle, and that was enough.

The devil was truly in the details.

CHAPTER 16

WHICH PART IS MINE?

Back in Huntington Beach, we got over our disappointments and settled into life as newlyweds. Billy bought me a red Porsche, and suddenly all my other concerns took a back seat.

I, the aspiring homemaker, set to work. *Trading Spaces* was in its prime, and Paige Davis made me feel confident enough to paint the walls periwinkle and cover the couch with cranberry throw pillows. I bought Picasso prints from IKEA and hung them on the wall. I put contact paper over the dark, wooden wet bar and made it white and bright and beautiful. I painted our kitchen cornflower-blue and persimmon orange and buttery yellow. I made magic salad with caramelized walnuts and cranberries and homemade balsamic vinaigrette. I had myself a man, a home, a job, and a new car.

I was living the life I had been bred for, and I loved it.

For so long, I'd been caught up in this holding pattern, living single in search of the next step: a man. And here he was. The fact that I kinda hated him and he kinda hated me was small potatoes. The chains had been lifted, the drudgery of spinsterhood erased, and the promise of a lifetime role as the cool aunt at the kids' table was no longer.

My life was beginning, and even though Billy and I discovered our deep incompatibility on a leper colony, it was the smallest part of the plan. It was the fine print, and I just signed on the dotted line, vowing to look at the details when the bill collector came calling, when the layaway program kicked in. But for now, I was enjoying my six-month's of subscription free service.

I knew what was expected of me, and I figured the more I fulfilled my role, the better our marriage would be and the more that Billy would like me. A good wife is a companion and helpmeet to her husband, meaning she helps him meet all of his goals and dreams. She cooks the meals, decorates the home, keeps herself in shape, loves sex and never refuses. She blesses the home with music and flowers and decorative pillows. She loves babies and she loves rendering service. The only way I could progress as a woman and as a Mormon was to get married and be a wife so I needed to dig in. But it wasn't working.

Three months into the subscription, once the excitement of the new home died down, I called my mom. I told her that I had started to sense that *my* joy and *my* life beginning was somehow creating the demise of Billy's. He wasn't working on his entrepreneurial pursuits. He wasn't surfing the world. Instead, he now had to preside and provide. I was working and bringing home my own money, but that was like play money to him. He took no joy in being provided for by me.

"Mom, I hate it. I'm miserable. We're completely incompatible. What should I do?"

"Well," she responded. "There's nothing you can do about it now."

I pushed back. "I can get a divorce."

I said it to test her. It wasn't a word my family uttered: divorce. No one in my family had been divorced. I had fifty cousins, and nary one had been divorced. I knew the reaction its mention would elicit.

I was looking around for someone to make eye contact with and give me a nod of recognition. But no one was attentive. Instead, they stared straight ahead with their hands to the square.

"Join the club and figure it out. It's too late now. You can't get a divorce. This is just how it is."

I was throwing it out there to see how she'd respond, hoping for an escape plan or at least some mutual commiseration. Instead, she just laughed. She told me that it didn't matter how I felt, it was better to just bow my head and say, "Yes."

I began to regret ever pretending I wasn't a gold digger when Billy declared that despite having access to a private jet and first-class travel, his airline of choice was Southwest.

These were the days of the big, empty planes, blue-sky flights, and plenty of legroom. But whenever Billy booked our travel, he booked with Southwest. I hated everything about the airline. It felt like I had married a cheapskate, and I took it personally. He had the money, he just refused to spend it—a pitiable result of Mormon frugality's dark underbelly.

I did what I had done on my mission and flipped the script. For our one-year anniversary, I bought him a single share of Southwest stock. I took the stock certificate and had it matted, framed, and inscribed with the words, "I'd fly anywhere with you." Fortuitously, the NASDAQ ticker symbol for Southwest was LUV.

I wasn't going to argue with my husband or be a bitch about Southwest Airlines. I wasn't going to give an airline that much stock. But having my opinion disregarded stung, and I took note. I didn't want him to think I was down to fly Southwest because it was economical or because it was somehow more exciting to fight over the unassigned window seat. I wanted him to know that I was down to fly Southwest because I was his wife and he was my husband. I loved him, and I'd fly anywhere with him, even if it meant sacrificing a little part of myself for the principle of marriage.

He unwrapped the gift, but of course, he didn't really understand. He said thank you and made some pithy comment: "What are we going to do with one share of stock?" And of course, because we were celebrating our anniversary with family, everyone in the room just laughed at the silly little wife who didn't understand finances, who wasted her money on one useless share of stock.

CHAPTER 17

I'M HARBORING A FUGITIVE, DEFECTOR OF A KIND

I knew that as soon as I became a mother, I would be all in. And despite my feigned commitment to the corporate world, God knew, my coworkers knew, and my family knew that as soon I left for maternity leave, I wasn't coming back. It didn't matter how much I loved working or how much purpose I found in my job. Once I had a child, none of that mattered. I was going to stay home, raise my children, and fulfill the role I had dreamed of for a lifetime.

In Huntington Beach, I had mastered managing Billy with kid gloves. Just like with Soeur Bueller, I let him do his thing, molding and shifting into whatever needless, brainless form was required of me. We fell into an easy, reassuring routine. I sat with him on the couch and watched hours of *Survivor* and *The Amazing Race*. I biked with him to the beach and walked along the boardwalk. I went to Wahoo's and graciously shared one plate of two fish tacos and asked for a complimentary cup for water.

It was soul-crushing, but it wasn't *terrible*.

You know, it's not like anyone plans this, it's not your childhood dream. I was married. I had a man. I made it. This is what I had worked for all my life. All that was expected of me was already floating on the surface. I could forget about the fathoms of future goals and abandoned aspirations that lurked underneath. I didn't need to worry about my own life anymore, because I didn't really have my own life anymore. I was a wife. A plus-one to the patriarchy that ruled and reigned. I was his problem now. And the thought was thrilling and terrifying.

Less savvy single girls were struggling by the sweat of their brow and forced to fend for themselves among the noxious weeds and thorns of the dreary world. Meanwhile, I could sit around on silk pillows and start trying for babies if I wanted. So long as I didn't get fat, turn frigid, or fuck around, I'd be taken care of for the rest of my life. And even if I did do those things, I'd probably still be able to work it out. I didn't know anyone who had ever gotten divorced, even when the circumstances were horrendous. We had signed with our souls, there was no going back. Certainly not for something as selfish as self-fulfillment or personal destiny. If my cup didn't runneth over, I needed to find a smaller cup. *Sit down, Sister Gay. You should be grateful.*

Despite our comfortable routine, Billy was still not thriving. But as Eve, Mother of All Living, I knew what needed to be done. I wasn't sure whether our marriage could handle it, but I knew what would force his hand and cause him to step up: we needed a baby.

I wanted Ashley before she was even a twinkle in my eye.

Mid-pregnancy, once my twenty-four-hour nausea abated, I traded in the Porsche and drove my new-mom-car four-door BMW to the

L.A. fashion district. I parked on Maple and 9th right behind Michael LeVine, Inc. I bought yards and yards of blush-pink dupioni silk fabric. I didn't bother cutting patterns or measuring with a ruler. I rushed straight in, laboring for hours over her bedding, stitching together crib bunting and a cascading sash to hang above her bed. I wanted the cradle to look like Princess Aurora's from *Sleeping Beauty*. I reveled in the tiny stacked diapers and miniature bundles of folded onesies. My nesting tendencies were unleashed, and I was surprised at my ability to lavish so much unmitigated love on something that wasn't feral. Being a mother wasn't only my duty, it was my destiny, and one I couldn't wait to meet.

For her very first Christmas, I dressed Ashley in a hand-knitted four-piece white footed bunting with a bonnet. I balanced her with a few stacked books and a blanket at the base of the Christmas tree and handed her a white-ribboned Tiffany-blue box to hold. She clutched the gift with her pudgy baby hands and gave a toothless smile to the camera and my. Joy. Was. Full. It didn't matter who I was married to or how he treated me, he had given me this child and that eclipsed everything else in my life. Inside the little blue box was the first gift of Christmas: a silver rattle inscribed with the words, "We had each other, then we had you, and then we had everything."

CHAPTER 18

SOMEWHERE THAT'S GREEN

When you are a woman entrenched in a system where only men have power, the message, implied or otherwise, is "keep sweet, pray, and obey." There is no way around it. You are no longer captain of your own ship. You are destined to be Gilligan; you may become the star of the show, but you always report to the Skipper. And eternity is longer than a three-hour tour.

I was embodying the unique paradox of being an overachiever and a Mormon woman who finally got her man. I had clawed my way to the top only to be told to sit on my hands and be satisfied. Your former life is over. Your future is contingent on your ability to make your husband's dreams come true while keeping him on the straight and narrow. If you are lucky, his dreams will become your dreams, too, and you will share in making them come true for your children. If your dreams and goals don't align, then you will just have to pretend that they do.

My second pregnancy was planned to the day. At Ashley's second birthday party, she opened a tiny T-shirt on which I had ironed the letters, "I'm going to be a big sister!" It was the last present she opened, and everyone was gathered around her as she sat wide-eyed in her white embroidered Strasburg dress with pink smocking ribbons and her wispy blond hair. Everyone gasped and cried and cheered when they realized what her shirt was announcing. They hugged Billy and congratulated us endlessly.

Adding a second baby to the family only doubled my ambition to be a good mom. I dressed them in matching clothes and had their names embroidered on their Pottery Barn pajama sets. *Ashley Rose* and *Georgia McLean*.

To everyone on the outside looking in, our marriage was flourishing. We had courtside tickets to the Jazz, we got invites to corporate dinners and fundraisers. Our friends invited us to stay at their vacation homes in Newport Beach and Lake Powell.

I didn't know what Billy did at his job all day, but it didn't matter. I never really knew what my dad did, either. I assumed because he was paid well and didn't seem overworked that his career was secondary to his duties as a husband and father. We had money, free time, and two healthy children. I had no reason not to be deliriously happy.

When I got pregnant with my third child, I didn't even realize it had happened.

At first, I thought it was just a cold or the flu. My friend came over and encouraged me to take a pregnancy test. I had been hoarding pregnancy tests from the Dollar Store and had about fifteen stored in the bathroom drawer. Lo and behold, two lines.

Georgia was still a baby, only nine months old, and now Annabelle was on her way. It became a little too much too fast for Billy, and it started to expose the cracks. *I'm in this alone. I have to think of everything, I have to do everything, I have to be everything, and I have to give you all the credit.*

✳ ✳ ✳

The more comfortable I got with juggling the tasks of motherhood, the more industrious I became. I had creative juices to squeeze. I wanted to find ways to bless my family and feel fulfilled. Billy's parents had given him a Canon 5D Mark II professional camera for Christmas, and I intended to take it for a spin. I stayed up late at night watching YouTube tutorials on raw exposure and white balance. I learned about aperture and shutter speed. I was going to save us thousands of dollars in professional photography fees and outsource my skills to the masses. I started out taking pictures of our kids, and then it advanced to taking pictures of local models for their portfolios. I joined Instagram and a few other online photography groups and spent hours and hours learning Photoshop while the girls slept. My dedication to the hobby was liberating, and I became passionate about the craft.

At the time, the living prophet had declared that everyone should have a picture of the temple in their home. And so I took a picture of the Salt Lake Temple and made it look less Gothic. I turned its outline into a white, princess-like castle and put it on a pink background. In cursive font along the bottom, I wrote a lyric from the primary song that had taught me about the temple, "I'm going there someday." I hung the prints above my daughters' beds.

Eventually, I started making them for friends and family as baptism gifts and blessing gifts, because everyone freaking loved my priestcraft ingenuity. I started selling them to friends of friends because I just couldn't help but monetize. Once Billy started to take note of the profitability of artistic temple prints, he decided to turn it into an official company.

He named it Old Nauvoo and wrote up a business plan, designed a website, and found a framer and distributor who would cut us a deal. Billy handled the business end, and I handled the art. I'd take photos of the temple and give it a Tuscan flair: sepia tones, grainy sandpaper grit, papyrus font with each individual temple name featured in the bottom right corner. They were an instant hit.

We had become a team. And then one day, Billy came home and said that the framer had hired an in-house graphic designer. The new artist basically copied what I'd been doing for two years and offered the same product for half the price. By this point, Photoshop wasn't a niche skill. Photography and filters had become more accessible, more democratized, and, tired of negotiating with Billy, the framer decided to work him out of the deal.

I felt powerless. I had been deeply invested in Old Nauvoo because it was something we built together. I felt like I was supporting him and he was supporting me, and what we couldn't figure out as married partners we could figure out in business. But now it had gotten messed up, and I had no say in how we handled it. Instead of trying to persuade Billy otherwise, I swallowed my advice. I was supposed to be his doting wife, not his business partner.

Billy kept all the laws and covenants of the gospel; there was no gaping hole in his behavior that I could patch up and plug. It was through the little gaps that the water got in, and our ship started to sink. We said we loved each other. But there was no joining of souls. We didn't cleave unto each other with all our heart. To him, I wasn't Eve, Mother of All Living. I was just his little buddy. And even if I could steer the ship to safety, it wouldn't matter. That's not the chain of command.

I knew that our marriage was performative, but I didn't care. I just assumed that, as with all things, there was a time and a season. I thought that eventually he would come back around, or something would happen and we'd fall back into step. After all, I knew how to endure, and I knew how to be resilient. It didn't matter what I had to do, I was never going to leave.

There was no fear that the marriage would fail, only fear that it wouldn't be what I had hoped.

I was married with one eye closed.

It was draining and exhausting. But when you have the key to the test, there's no excuse not to get an A. The harder I tried to flex, the more Billy retreated. And just as the roteness of our performance forced me to become smaller and smaller until finally I had reached a bearable size, so, too did it wear on Billy.

CHAPTER 19

PUT YOUR SHOULDER TO THE WHEEL, PUSH ALONG

We'd been married for nearly ten years, living in Utah for close to five, and coasting with one eye closed since perhaps the beginning.

Somewhere along the way, our marriage hit the iceberg. I had sold Billy on what he could see on the surface, and as the ship drove slowly closer and closer, it unknowingly struck the bottom. But by the time either of us noticed, it was a little too late. I pivoted and adapted and steered in the opposite direction. But the more I tried to fix the problem, the deeper and wider the gash became, tearing away at the base of the boat, slowly filling it with water while we lay heedless on the deck.

And then in the distance, a signal flare, a sign from God in response to our mayday. I needed something, anything, to shift my focus from the discontent of my marriage to the delight of the gospel. The Plan of Happiness wasn't unfolding like I had expected it to and I needed a course correction before I wandered too far off the path.

The bishop called me in and told me that I had been on his mind.

"We'd like to call you to be our next Relief Society president," he explained. "It's a big job but I know you can do it."

As Relief Society president, I would be the leader of all the women in my ward. I'd be assigning lessons, selecting teachers, conducting meetings, and doing my part to run the largest women's organization in the church. This was the answer to my prayers. A chance to pull out from my inward struggles and focus on serving others. I had to believe that God knew the contents of my heart, he knew that I was struggling in marriage, and so he reached down, spoke to our bishop, and told him that Heather Gay needed something, anything, and this was as good as it gets.

I wanted to contribute in a way that mattered. I wanted to mourn with those who mourned. I wanted to comfort those who stood in need of comfort. I wanted to stand as a witness of God at all times and in all things. I wanted to grow in stature and knowledge and gain the friendships, trust, and confidence of the women in the ward. I clapped my hands for joy and exclaimed, "This is the desire of my heart."

The role fulfilled me, so much so that I didn't even notice that I was donating twenty or thirty hours of my week to the church. Instead, I believed that I was being cradled in the hollow of God's hand because he knew what I needed; he had looked down from his heavenly throne and seen his beloved daughter twisting on the vine.

I knew it was a diversion. But it was a diversion that kept me within the safety of my own backyard.

I had been dying on the inside, hiding from the state of my marriage behind the curtain of motherhood and homemaking. Through the Relief Society, I could find purpose in my life again. After years of wilting, years of loneliness in my partnership, I could find companionship and community in the structure of the church. I embraced the systematic organization and sanctity of the institution. And just as missionary service came naturally to me, so too did serving the Relief Society.

At times, I felt like the prophet Joseph Smith: charismatic, charming, and self-deprecating, all the while leading with grace but scrambling to figure out my next move. My days were planned out, I had responsibility, I had purpose. And just like before, by losing myself in the service of others, I found the strength to continue. I was filled with industry and integrity, all while my marriage was falling apart.

I was embarrassed and hurt by what I perceived as Billy's lack of support. If he had been called to serve as bishop, I would have been bursting with joy. I'd put it in my Facebook profile and drop that flex at every party, every potluck, every priesthood blessing. And yet, instead of rising to the occasion with my position, Billy shrank.

On some level, I wanted to be a good Relief Society president because I wanted the accolades and validation. I wanted to look across the room and make eye contact with someone, anyone, who would say, "Marriage is hard, but you're doing great. Keep showing up. It will get better." But no one did. I had more than most women hoped for, and my complaints made me sound like a spoiled child.

"Oh, you're so lucky to get to go to Hawaii. Oh, you're so lucky to have a husband. You should be grateful. No one wants to hear you complain about flying Southwest. This is what you've always wanted, and you wouldn't have any of this if it weren't for Billy. You wouldn't be able to raise your daughters in matching pajamas. You wouldn't have the overflowing Easter baskets or the scavenger hunts on Christmas."

"Just sit down, Sister Gay. Sit down. You don't have to do the most. You don't have to be the most. Just sit down and be still."

But I didn't get it. I thought I was just rolling up my sleeves and getting in there to help. I was a good Mormon, and if ye have desires to serve God ye are called to the work.

To think that my service would have saved us was naive. For even though it was a faith-affirming thing, it was the *wrong* faith-affirming thing. Ambitious women aren't rewarded for their drive and ingenuity. Pig-bladder balloons aren't of this world but are instead fictitious pipe dreams sold to prairie girls in storybooks. No one cares if you can turn a corncob into a baby doll in the twenty-first century. Do what you want, but make sure dinner is on the table by five.

CHAPTER 20

IF YOU LOVED ME,
WHY'D YOU LEAVE ME?

My marriage was failing. The warning signs were clear; water was flooding the deck. But with one eye closed, I pretended not to notice when the drips became leaks and the leaks became floods.

We were checked out. There was no comfort in the roteness. No pleasure in the security. The magic that drew us to each other all those years ago in Huntington Beach had been lost to time, exposed by our own frailty, and shattered by the unmet expectations we had both for ourselves and for each other. I always thought that one common goal and one common Spirit paired with 100 percent obedience would be our saving grace. *If ye keep my commandments, ye will be blessed in all things.* That was the promise. We didn't have to like each other, we didn't have to spend time together, but with the principles of the gospel no unhallowed hand could stop the work from progressing. I assumed we could weather any storm.

And so I pressed on. No matter how I felt inside, time was still marching forward. *The ground thaws, the rain falls, the grass grows. The seeds root, the flowers bloom, the children play.* I still had to register the kids for school, coach the soccer games, and plan the birthdays. Ashley was turning eight, and it was a big one.

At eight years old, a child is not only wise enough to bake a green bean casserole, prepare the baby formula, and sit in the front seat, they can also discern between good and evil.

The Age of Accountability is not an era in the history books, it is the age at which the prophet Joseph Smith decreed children know right from wrong. Eight is great, unless you don't want your sins to start counting. It is at this age that the church asks children to make their first covenant with the Lord and participate in their first saving ordinance: baptism.

I remember every part of my baptism down to my first lie. The first mark of sin on your perfect clean slate is a milestone a Mormon never forgets. You come out of the font as clean as the white towel you're wrapped in. And you want to stay that way. But as it turns out, it's really hard to stay perfect.

A few hours after my own baptism, I was using the bathroom, and my dad accidentally opened the door.

"Lock the door next time." he scolded.

"I did," I retorted too quickly and without thinking.

Silence.

His response pierced my eight-year-old heart: "You just told your first lie."

I ruined it. Two hours in, and I ruined it.

My stomach fell to my toes as I sulked in the quiet solitude of the unlocked bathroom, too afraid even to lift my head and face my reflection in the mirror.

I wanted Ashley to remember more than her first lie at her baptism. I wanted her to remember how much I loved her. I wanted to create enough happiness around her and the event to distract from the holes in my own heart. And so I made it a white party, modeled after Kyle Richards herself. *White everything.*

I served white lemon bars, white jicama and celery sticks with ranch dressing, and white popcorn. There was a giant candy buffet with glass jars full of white gumballs, clear rock-candy lollipops, powdered-sugar donuts, and peppermint Life Savers. Custom cotton candy with white monogrammed labels dangled from white string with white clothes pins. I bought Ashley a tiered Rapunzel-style dress with a high-low hem and fluted sleeves. I timed everything down to the second with precision and love.

I talked Billy into wearing his white suit and tie for the baptism rather than the complimentary zip-up jumpsuit everyone else wore that screamed Warren Jeffs. I didn't want Ashley wearing the canvas jumpsuit either. So, for the actual baptism, I had her walk into the water wearing a custom circle-skirt dress with flutter sleeves. It floated in the font like a jellyfish in slow motion. For my baptism, I had worn a cotton eyelet dress that my mother had made, and I remembered how the layers and ruffles made me feel luxurious and celebrated, and I wanted the same for Ashley. It was decadent and divine. I imitated the gravitas to the very last mark.

I wanted Ashley's baptism to feel like a bat mitzvah, a quinceañera, a celebration, but Billy did not seem to share the same enthusiasm. He didn't see that I was so deeply invested in every little detail, from the white-paper covered tables to the ribboned sash around her waist. Instead, he thought it was yet another example of me going overboard, blowing something up too big, making the day about me. *Sit down, Sister Gay.*

He would have been happy to wear the white zip-up jumpsuit instead of a shirt and tie. He would have been happy to have a group baptism where the program and the refreshments were provided potluck-style. He would have been happy to have a baptism that didn't cost money, cost time, or cost his peace of mind. And I was planning on spending all three. It was no longer about balance. Instead, it was about power.

So, in an attempt to undermine my absolute investment, at the eleventh hour, he asked to change the time.

Billy's sister was flying to Utah from Tacoma with her kids and dogs on the day of the baptism. Grandma Rose, Billy's mother, wanted to be at the airport to pick them up. The time of the baptism had been advertised well in advance on the personalized, didn't-use-a-template invitations that I edited and framed with decorative accents and original vector art.

"We can't just change the time, Billy," I pleaded. "I've rented the building, I've arranged the pianists, the speakers. I've scheduled the ward missionaries to start filling the font at nine a.m. so the font will be full and still warm when the baptism begins. I've thought of everything." *You don't have to help me. You don't have to care. You just have to be there.*

Believe me, Billy, I'd baptize her myself if I could but I can't. I don't have the priesthood and this is where the beautiful division of roles is supposed to take place as God intended. I'm passing the baton and asking you not to drop it and not to hit me over the head with it. You just have to show up. *Death stare. Poker face.*

My dad gently suggested that I make a flyer and take it around to all the friends in the neighborhood announcing the time change.

"Billy's really upset. Is it really that big of a deal to change the time? Just change the time."

But instead, I doubled down and dug in my heels.

The following day, Billy texted me asking one last time about the time change. The never-say-no girl had found her voice. And he responded by announcing his departure.

"Do the baptism when you want. I'll move out next week."

I had no fight in me. We never officially changed the time like he requested. Billy ended up running late anyways and we didn't begin until his mom and sister had arrived. I don't remember anything beautiful or spiritual about the event like I had imagined I would. Instead, it was clouded with too much resentment, shame, and pure despair.

Billy sat on the front row with Ashley proudly next to him, his arm casually draped on the back of her chair. I was late to find an available seat, lingering and greeting the stragglers, and found a random empty chair on the second row a little to the left of center. I was not second in command; I was steerage. I plastered a frozen smile on my face and tried to feign the joy I so desperately wanted to create.

My role had become abundantly clear. I served at the pleasure of the King. My worth was wrapped up in my ability to not only plan a perfect baptism, to be a devoted mother, but to love doing it and to feel fulfilled regardless of any external validation. It was what was expected of me. But there I sat alone on a throne far unlike the one I had dreamed of for so long. I had believed it was my role as a mother to make sure my daughter was baptized, to make sure her father was worthy, to make sure the baptism was perfect. *This is what I was born to do, born to be. This is what God has asked of me.* And in trying to do all of those things, I sabotaged everything. My kingdom for a white party.

Watching from the side of the church, I saw my firstborn daughter, in her delicate little white dress, walk into the waist-deep water of the font and be immersed by her father as he baptized her. She was eight years old, the Age of Accountability, and yet I was the only one accountable for putting her on this path. So little did she know of what lay before her. She didn't choose the faith, she was born into it. It didn't matter if she wanted to get baptized or not, the dress was ordered and the invitations were sent. This was the life for which she was assigned. Choice, autonomy, independence were all secondary to the throne and the kingdom she was inheriting. And I was willing to abdicate my throne for just a singular moment of true sovereignty and recognition. The absurdity of it all had me spinning.

I suppose it's unsurprising how little you see through an opaque veil, but it is a bit of a shock when, outside of the temple, you remain blind.

Despite everything, the day progressed quickly, and I continued to hope that someone in the room would take notice of all the effort and details and mention it in front of Billy. Out of all the people there, I craved his validation the most, and hoped that seeing all my effort would somehow change his heart. I wanted recognition, some sort of eye contact or head nod, some social cue of connection. But the weight of his threatening text cast a shadow over the entire event. He laughed and joked with friends and family as I played the role of the happy, newly-baptized daughter's proud mother.

The baptism broke me.

We had hit the iceberg, and no amount of readjustment or course correction would save us now. I had nothing left to give. No energy to jump. No energy to fight for a lifeboat. And so I stayed on deck, dancing along to the haunting dirge of the string quartet. I was going down with the ship.

※ ※ ※

Never did I think Billy would actually leave. I believed he thought he was as miserably locked-in as I was. He had hurt me so badly that I put him to the test. *Fine, put your money where your mouth is. Move out.* I wasn't going to stop him. I wasn't going to sing a hymn, find a way to bond, pretend to like another stupid-ass action movie. I was done.

I was running on fumes. I didn't want to keep going. I wanted to give up, to give in. But what I wanted didn't matter. I was bound to this family, and my duty to them and to God outweighed any personal desire I might've fostered. If I could so easily die inside and just do the work, why then was it so impossible for Billy?

I didn't want us to pretend to be anything anymore. I had cared and prepared for ten long years. God gave us families to help us become what he wants us to be, but all I was becoming was a ghost of my former self. We hadn't been a family for a really long while, and it was finally time to face it.

Billy lived with us for the rest of the summer. We didn't talk, just danced around each other the very same way we had done for the last decade. I still had three kids to care for, a Relief Society to run, friends to see, photographs to take. Billy became a roommate I couldn't stand living with but couldn't pay the mortgage without, and we avoided each other at all costs. I disengaged.

Around mid-July, he asked to talk.

"What is there to talk about?" I asked, cold as an iceberg. "You said you were going to move out."

We sat there in silence as the words fell heavy on our shoulders. I was testing him the same way I had all those years before. He hadn't faltered then, and I doubted that he'd falter now. It had been more than a month since the baptism, and he still hadn't left. His presence imbued me with the strength to brazenly confront him.

"You really want me to move out?" he asked, looking right through me.

I retorted quickly and without thinking, "I'm just waiting for you to leave."

Silence.

By the end of the summer, he left. Billy was gone.

PART FOUR

BAD
MORMON

CHAPTER 21

I CAN BREATHE FOR
THE FIRST TIME

That summer ended just the same as every summer before it: the days began to shorten, the light began to fade, and the air in the Salt Lake Valley grew heavy with the impending onset of winter's icy chill.

As the girls prepared to return to school, I made sure their outfits matched, their lunches were packed, and their school supplies were plentiful. I kept their life as normal as possible, performing a reality for not just my daughters, their friends, and all the other class moms, but also for myself.

Billy had moved out. And no amount of masquerading would distract me from the reality that was simply too enormous to fathom.

I did what I always did, and I played the tried-and-true game of mental gymnastics. I pretended that our impending doom was only a dream from which I'd quickly awaken. Sure, Billy was gone for now, but there was no way he was gone forever. It was an impossibility. I had married Billy for the specific reason that guys like Billy don't leave. They stay steadfast in their commitments, even if only half-heartedly. Divorce and separation weren't options for me, and I couldn't believe that they were options for Billy. If there was *one* thing we were both committed to, I was absolutely certain that it was the promise we'd made across the altar in fig-leaf aprons, held together in the Patriarchal Grip.

In the first few days after Billy's departure, I assumed he was using the move as leverage—strategy, the art of war, we duel at dawn. He had simply left to amass his strength and resources, enlisting an army of foot soldiers to back him up in our inevitable squabble.

He didn't tell me where he was staying, but I heard through the grapevine that he was crashing at his single friend's house in Midway. "He took the boat out with his friends and a bunch of single girls," my friend reported. "They called to ask me if he was still married to you." I felt the hot shame flood my cheeks. I was livid. He was boating? I was raising his three little girls and crying in the shower so they wouldn't hear me and he was . . . boating? I wanted to Betty Broderick him, but instead I just laughed it off. "Everything is fine. There's nothing going on. He's just letting off steam." *The lies! The lies! The lies!*

I made my husband disappear.

"Heather, you're completely helpless."

"You know Heather, you're what the French call *les incompétentes*."

"There are fifteen bridesmaids in spaghetti straps, and you're the only one who has to wear a bolero jacket."

"Sit down, Sister Gay."

"Do the baptism when you want. I'll move out next week."

Silence.

I made my husband disappear.

I MADE MY HUSBAND DISAPPEAR!

* * *

If Billy was gone, I was going to be like Frederick the mouse from Leo Lionni's storybook. I was determined to store the sights, sounds, and sun of my single summer in order to survive the dark, cold winter of marriage that I was certain would return. Billy was coming back, there was no doubt about it. *Summer should be fun!*

When the cat's away . . . the mouse will *play*.

And so began what I later learned was the inevitable whore-phase of my post-separation.

Dinner didn't have to be on the table at five o'clock. Laundry could pile up. Beds didn't need to be made, dishes could sit in the sink. My photography equipment didn't have to be stored away each night. Garments didn't have to be worn. This was halftime. No one was keeping score. No one was watching my game on replay. I didn't have to love Billy; I didn't have to sing to him or serve him. I had my first whiff of sovereignty, and it smelt like early morning boulangeries along the esplanade in Montpellier.

Water, water everywhere, but not a drop to drink. What was I going to do with all this newfound freedom? All of my friends were true, believing, married Mormons. They still had homes to keep up and husbands to keep happy. But then Diana moved into my neighborhood. She was immediately and identifiably different from the other moms I knew. She was separating from her husband and was totally open about it. She loved being free and independent and she wanted me to love it too.

The TV show *The Bachelor* was in its prime, and Diana had been recommended by mutual friends to apply. I took her photos and helped her fill out the application. When she got the announcement that she was in the running for Season 10 with Sean Lowe, we couldn't believe it. Good things were happening for her even when she was so clearly sinning. We shopped together for her outfits and fast-tracked her divorce to avoid any potential bigamy.

The night before she left, we had a big going away party at her house to wish her well. The house was decorated extravagantly with red roses and *Bachelor*-themed cupcakes. We made her practice her limo walk for the crowd.

That night, I met a lot of her friends, some single, some married, mostly all Mormon but no longer practicing. It was a new crowd, and I felt less conspicuous and more accepted than usual. I immediately made friends with a young couple who asked me about my current status. I felt safe enough to tell them the truth.

"Well, I was raised Mormon, served a mission, and I've been married for ten years, but my husband just moved out and I don't know what I'm going to do."

They understood my plight and offered me advice.

"We're gay and we're Mormon and we're trying to figure it all out, too. It's really difficult when you've lived your whole life trying to fit into an idea of who you are supposed to be even when that idea rejects the best parts of who you are. It's ok to walk away from beliefs that no longer serve you. It takes a long time to retrain your brain, but if we can do it, you can do it. And we will help you."

It was exactly what I needed to hear. Their friendship allowed me to celebrate everything I loved about my faith and my heritage, but also to openly reject the beliefs that caused me shame and dissonance. We hung out constantly, traveling all over the world and laughing about the ways we had been traumatized the same and the ways we had been traumatized differently. Their friendship was the life raft I needed in the stormiest time of my life.

Diana's stint on *The Bachelor* was not as successful as my night at her going away party. She got sent home a mere two weeks after the show started.

I was sitting in church when I saw her text my phone. I knew enough about *Bachelor* protocol to know that contestants are sequestered while they are filming. If she had her phone, it meant she was no longer in the game. I was devastated. How could she let me down like this?

Publicly, Sean said he withheld her rose because he knew she had a career in Salt Lake City and wouldn't be open to relocating. Privately, we heard that she was actually sent home because one of the producers, Elan Gale, had heard that she had hooked up with Jef with one F from the previous season's *Bachelorette*. It was not the crossover they were looking for. A premonition to the fickle world of reality TV. Diana was shaping up to be more than just a mentor in life after Mormonism.

CHAPTER 22

THERE MUST BE FIFTY WAYS
TO LEAVE YOUR LOVER

I n Billy's absence, I felt empowered to pursue everything that I had previously sidelined. Things like laughing at my own jokes, eating late at night, and a growing passion for photography.

I loved taking photos, even before my days of Old Nauvoo. I have a photographic memory and a penchant for aesthetics, so much so that Tuscan temple prints barely scratched the surface of my talent and intrigue. I once Photoshopped a larger woman in a red and white polka-dot A-line dress out of a group photo of my friend with Van Halen. I was not only a master editor but also a good-ass friend. I had a creative vision; I had dreams. I'd photograph newborn babies with flower crowns nestled inside wooden bowls and flower pots just like Anne Geddes. I'd spray-paint couches red and take photos of my friends lounging on them in open fields. I'd make family photos editorial.

After putting the girls to bed each night, I'd avoid thinking about my failing marriage and lose myself at the computer, spending hours studying camera settings and joining online photography groups.

I threw myself into my side gigs and can-do make-did. Despite the growing dread and despair I felt, I was bound and determined to survive and make the most of this precious independence.

Even though I was juggling three babies, a newly imposed tighter-than-necessary budget, and the emotional despair of a life unlived, I focused on what really mattered: the Christmas Card.

Every December, Christmas cards would adorn my kitchen walls like seasonal wallpaper. Billy and I always fought over the spectacle of the Christmas card. He complained that it was a lot of unnecessary work and disruption for something that only fed my ego. And he was absolutely right. I wanted our Christmas card taped up in every home in the Salt Lake Valley. And I didn't want to stop doing them. So every December, as we hauled out the holly, we put up our mitts for the same scripted fight. Once Billy left, I refused to let the Christmas card serve as collateral damage.

I'd be damned if any member of the ward's yuletide wasn't Gay.

I'd be damned if any member of the ward didn't receive a holiday greeting or a Gay happy meeting.

And so I doubled down on the card—Mormon flex, family flex, Photoshop flex.

Instead of a family photo since I was currently single with no husband in sight, I included just a photo of the girls. They were always posed like little dolls, dressed to the nines with bells on, black leather boots in front of a patisserie with Christmas cookies, their hair curled and ornamented with bows and feather headbands. The girls were great; the photos were great; the editing was great. Each card would simply be signed with innocuous greetings: *From Our Family to Yours*. I never wanted to give any indication that something was amiss. I just pretended I was a married housewife, performing reality better than

I ever had. Through the camera's lens, I presented what I wanted my world to be.

I secretly wished I could've Photoshopped Billy, not only into our Christmas card photos, but also into my life. I didn't want the current version of who he was, it was too difficult, too incompatible, too dismissive, but I wanted to stay married and I wanted to grow old with the father of my children. I just wanted the father of my children to be a different man. I wanted the Instagram version of what everyone else's husbands seemed to be.

Social media was in its infancy, and Instagram was the wild frontier and I, just like my pioneer ancestors, was trying to blaze a new trail. I was connecting with photographers all over the world, getting immediate feedback and validation. My profile name, @hdgpics, was an OG of the IG. A true groundbreaker ready to whoop it up. I was a fledgling photographer with zero official training, but I knew deep in my heart that I could be great. I knew it. *Throw me in. I'll swim.*

I worked hard at cultivating my content, laboring over each caption, scrolling through filters with breakneck speed, placing emojis with poignancy and purpose. My feed was a reflection of my outer shine and inner depths. Once, I saved a picture of Andy Cohen attending the *real* Met Gala—not in Salt Lake City and not across from a P. F. Chang's—and I used Instgram to publicly declare my devotion. I posted a picture of him wearing a tuxedo, smirking at the camera. For the caption, I simply put, "I love Andy Cohen." I didn't realize that I was buttering what would, in the next few years, become my bread of life.

During those early days, I connected through the app with some other photography pioneers of Instagram. One of my favorite photographers to follow was a young talent from Mexico, Santiago Perez-Grovas. His Instagram profile name was @santiagopgm, king of the three B's in boudoir photography: boobs, butts, and barenakeds.

His specialty was editorial and artistic images of hot girls; my specialty was being hot-girl adjacent.

Santiago crossed my path when he had a layover in Salt Lake. I immediately messaged him and offered up my friend Diana as a model willing to reveal all three B's if that was what it took. I wanted to see an Instagram artist out in the wild. It was so easy, so effortless. Santi magically replied to my message, and we made plans to meet.

Diana took the news of her sexual exploitation without protest; she was always up for anything. Sure she could model and was comfortable in lingerie, but she was also a celebrity. I wanted him to know that Salt Lake City was full of stars. I knew there was no one more worthy.

We picked Santi up at his hotel and brought him back to my house for the first photo shoot. On the drive, Diana and I both conveniently failed to mention that our five children (all under the age of eight) were also planning to participate in the pictures. Instead, that element would be a wonderful surprise.

He was this young artist, completely at ease with himself and his talent, traveling around the world, taking pictures, collaborating with strangers. Born and raised in Mexico, Santiago was a visitor to the United States and English was his second language. Suddenly, the tables had turned from my days as a missionary in France. Now I was being taught and inspired by a stranger I had met only minutes before. It felt like what I had always hoped my mission would be: making friends internationally, focusing on expanding my soul artistically and spiritually. This felt pure. I was building a relationship of trust with no ulterior motive of baptism or church attendance.

I remembered what it felt like to be recklessly confident and to make spontaneous creative plans without fear of reprisal or judgment from a husband. I was still in the salad days of separation, and the taste of new freedom shone like sugar on my lips.

At this point, Billy had yet to serve me divorce papers. We were separated, and sure, the ship was sinking, but with God at the helm, I had no fear that the marriage was anywhere near over.

Billy still had a key and was able to drop by the house unannounced whenever he wanted. Despite the fact that I assumed our separation was only temporary, his presence was always disturbing and intrusive. The girls and I were doing fine without Billy.

In and out of our lives, Billy would walk with the ease of someone who never has their steps questioned. He would come over casually and just walk into the house, not even knocking. It was frustrating, a reminder of the chain of command. I was still his wife, and even though I may not be working *with* him, I still worked *for* him. His casual attitude about his new role in our life grated on me. I was jealous that he was able to have a family at his leisure at what felt like my expense.

At the same time, it was also strangely comforting to know that he still considered it his home. I took his comings and goings as evidence that he wasn't really going to leave for good.

I was going to force a physical boundary whether he liked it or not, and I needed to change the locks to do it.

I was terrified, but I hyped myself up and looked at it as a wake-up call to remind him that we were separated and needed to figure things out. Maybe this would be the push he needed to come back home.

I didn't tell Billy when I changed the locks. Instead, that element would be a wonderful surprise.

Turns out surprises weren't really his thing.

On his first unannounced visit when he couldn't barge through the front door, he was pissed. He threatened to take legal action, because he had to have access to his kids at all times and in all things and in all places, and he was paying the mortgage, after all. He installed a garage code and ignored that he didn't have physical keys to the house. He made me feel like an interloper, a squatter. The rumble of the garage door opening unexpectedly created panic in my heart. He doubled down on his eminent domain and would stay longer and later with each passing visit. What was casual and unaware before now seemed sinister and brazen. A half-eaten sandwich on the kitchen counter. A use of the bathroom for an uncomfortable amount of time. A smear of mustard in the mayonnaise jar.

Message received.

CHAPTER 23

THE HILL I'M WALKING UP IS GETTING GOOD AND STEEP

After I changed the locks, there was a shift in power.

Despite the shift, I still believed in the patriarchal order of the family. I still believed in the promise that if we were doing the right things, if we had been married in the temple, and if we cared moderately enough about keeping our family together, then we could assuredly patch this sinking ship. *Yield to your husbands, as you do to the Lord.*

I found opportunties for him to come over and interact with the kids in hopes that, by being around us, he'd remember the commitments he had made. While conducting welfare visits for the Relief Society one night, I left Billy with the girls, half expecting to come home to performative parenting: the kids in pajamas, the house warm and inviting. I wanted him to make an effort and be a partner. I wanted him to just be my husband, or at least pretend.

Instead, I came home to an abrupt awakening.

While I was gone, he had gone through all his drawers and his closet in order to collect more things. He was preparing to leave, loading things into his car, as the girls ran around with their diapers full, bellies empty, and snot running down their cherubic faces. I was frustrated, disappointed, and reminded of exactly why Billy and I had never worked in the first place. The things I valued were of little worth to him. Our priorities were different, our lived experiences foreign.

After Billy left the house, I saw his wallet and a few other things had been left on the counter. *Serves you right.* It was late, and I went to lock the door. However, through the window, I could see Billy approaching. Instead of leaning in and submitting, I doubled down and dug in my heels. We made eye contact through the window. Challenge accepted. I watched as he ran around the corner straight into the garage.

Instinct and adrenaline kicked in as I, too, ran for the very same door—one of us inside, the other outside. Reaching it at the exact same time, I resisted and put my full strength into keeping him out. I didn't want Billy in our home or in our life, definitely not like this. I wanted to shut the gate and lock him outside with the speeding cars and angry badgers; I wanted to regain control of my kingdom. We got amped up, and eventually his strength won out. I fell to the floor as the door slammed open. Staggering up to my feet, I worked to defend myself as our worlds, our diametrically opposed realities, collided like a hull into a hidden iceberg.

For the last couple of months, I'd been left at home with the kids, all the while serving the church; pretending to be happy; and storing sights, sounds, and sun for winter. Meanwhile, Billy lived with another single friend in a Midway mansion, whistling his worries away as he filled his car with things he'd take back to his child-free, nag-free, responsibility-free home.

Now, as our worlds continued to collide, the scuffle moved into the house. I ran to the phone, and as my hands grabbed for the receiver, I stopped for the briefest of moments as the reality of the situation fell on me.

If I called 911, I could never take it back. It would be a blackspot, an unerasable mark on this season of our marriage. A mark for time and all eternity. I would have to explain it to my children. I would have to include it in our family history. Our separation would no longer be a secret. It would become real, not a field trip that I could ignore for the sake of Rumspringa. I felt so desperate for someone to hold Billy accountable, for someone to tell him that he was in the wrong. That he wasn't perfect, his steps weren't perfect, his life wasn't perfect.

So I called.

And Billy ran.

The police came and urged me to file charges. By this point, the girls were in their beds, and I had calmed down enough to reevaluate. Pressing charges was not an option. Despite my protestation, the officers pressed me to give a witness statement.

"Whether or not we press charges is not up to you," they insisted. "We are required by law to file a report regardless of your cooperation."

I tried calling Billy to give him a final warning, a flare shot at sea, but he failed to respond.

I left a voice mail.

"The police are here, and they want me to press charges and give a witness statement. What should I do?"

Silence.

It was my final distress call from the captain's deck. I wanted the masters at arms to hunt Billy down, rough him up, and throw him into the brig until he got his act together. Shape up or ship out, Billy. It was a far cry from the romantic notion of marriage that I had held just ten years earlier. *You jump, I jump*. There would be no swan dive into the sea for this marriage. Not tonight. Nothing was pulling Billy back into my orbit. Not the seriousness of the situation, not the long arm of the law, not even the Patriarchal Grip.

After he took off, Billy went straight to his parents. His family circled the wagons and protected their son. At the time, I still had access to his voice mail, and I listened privately as the calls came in from all of his family members expressing support, love, and acceptance. It was clear that he had told his family every last detail and that they were on his side. No matter the events of that evening, his family was always going to have his back.

Inversely, I didn't tell a soul. I was too ashamed, and I wanted to pretend it hadn't happened. Despite everything, I still believed Billy Gay would come home to his family and stay true to his covenants. Divorce was not an option, and if I resisted the urge to turn to the wall and hide beneath the covers while listening to Fleetwood Mac on a loop, there was no doubt that he, too, could make the sacrifice and step up.

Two weeks later, Billy barged into the house and handed me the court summons he'd received. He had been charged with domestic violence in the presence of a child. I tried to plead with him and convince him that I hadn't filed the report. But instead, he annihilated my character with little room for rebuttal. But what more was I to expect?

Misogyny runs deep. It was my fault he was unhappy in the first place. It was my fault he had left. It was my fault for trying to lock him out. It was my fault for calling the police. It was my fault he wasn't coming back.

For the past nine months, I'd been putting my feet on the cold tile floor, so lost in the roteness that I had failed to notice the water pooling now above my ankles. Distracted by the performance of keeping the faith, the performance of hiding the separation, I neglected the reality that lay numbingly at my feet.

There was no escaping the truth that our marriage was over. No filter or Photoshop, no obscured dark lens, no way to turn the camera away from the fact that we were drowning and the water was about to overtake us.

CHAPTER 24

LOOKING FOR HEAVEN, FOUND THE DEVIL IN ME

When a court officer pounded on my door, the last thing I expected to see was a divorce summons. He handed the papers directly to me and I smiled and thanked him. I didn't want him to think I was getting divorced because I was a bitch.

I called my friend in shock and told her what happened. She was surprised, but she was great in a crisis. She told me not to worry, but to get a babysitter because she was taking me out. A few hours later, I met her at the Maverick Center for front row seats to see Kelly Clarkson. If there was ever a time in my life that I needed music to buoy me up, it was a moment like this. Her setlist played like an anthem to my soul, and I couldn't hold back the tears as I swayed and cried and sang every word as loud as I could. *Since you've been gone. I can breathe for the first time.*

Billy was divorcing me. How was I going to do this? How was I going to face my friends, my family, myself, my kids and tell them that I had failed?

Kelly belted out her next to last song, "Stronger," and as she sang the words, I had my answer. *What doesn't kill you makes a fighter, footsteps even lighter, doesn't mean I'm over 'cause you're gone.*

The song ended. She looked me straight in the eyes and tossed me her guitar pick. The baton had been passed, and I knew that I could find the strength to finish the race.

I was going to be a single mom, I could not bring myself to say it out loud. I still had no idea what I was going to do and I had no one to turn to for support. And so I did what I had always done and I doubled down on my commitments to the church and to my role as Relief Society president. But my vulnerabilities and utter despair kept me in a fog of trauma.

I was easily tempted, drinking and dating whenever possible to fill the void. No amount of Sunday service or temple work would allow me to feel truly free from the tether that so easily transformed into a fetter. I was starving, and the fruit of the tree looked delicious to the taste and very desirable.

As Eden fell in shambles at my feet, I was welcomed into the netherworld of Mormon perfection. A few months after Billy filed for divorce, I went to Market Street Grill for a birthday dinner. After a round of oysters, we decided to stay downtown and Frederick it up. I made the colossal mistake of volunteering to drive. Our friend Britney was celebrating her birthday at Club One, so we decided we'd stop in for a bit to say hello and dip before things got a little too Outer Darkness-adjacent.

At the club, I never even ordered a single drink. I sipped from everyone else's drinks, esteeming myself to be above the fray and somehow unaffected. I was naive and I was numbing out, which turned out to be a dangerous and, in my case, criminal, combination.

We stayed at the club for probably no more than an hour, just long enough to meet two cute guys who wanted us to drop them off at the next venue, and long enough for me to get a BAC of 0.05.

We were happy to exit the club with the hotties. No one needed to know they were using us for a ride, we hoped everyone would assume we were using them for their bodies. I never considered that I had been drinking, I never considered that I was taking a risk. I never considered that I could be a danger to anyone else other than myself. I was self-destructive and self-absorbed. A dangerous combination.

The valet attendant pulled my car around to the front entrance and left it running. The AC was pumping, the music was blaring, but the headlights were not shining. Pulling out of the club's entrance, it felt as bright as midday, and I had barely gone half a block before I saw the flashing red and blue lights in my rearview mirror and realized that my headlights weren't on.

I immediately pulled the car over, extinguished the ignition, and turned on the interior lights. We had been blasting T.I. and Rihanna, "Live Your Life," and I fumbled with the controls to turn the music down. I had seen *Locked Up Abroad*, I knew not to fuck around. I fumbled to find my driver's license and nervously babbled an excuse about the valet and the music and the hot guys needing a ride. I was spinning out, concerned about pleading my case to avoid a ticket for no headlights, never considering the fact that I had been drinking and might be facing much more serious charges.

The officer asked me to step out of the car. He didn't buy my story, he didn't buy my piety, he didn't buy my bullshit. There was no mug shot, no jail cell, no walk of shame. But there were plenty of charges.

First they filed a charge of DUI metabolite, only to dismiss it and then refile a charge of DUI, which they then reduced to a charge of

Reckless Driving. In 2012, the legal limit for drinking and driving was 0.08 BAC, and even though I tested well underneath that at 0.05, filing charges was still at the officer's discretion. It felt like a horrible black mark on my soul. Maybe I truly was a bad seed. I didn't want to do terrible things, but here I was. I wanted to repent of it immediately.

The safety of the church and the gospel became a shelter in the storm. I didn't want this life, I didn't want to Frederick it up anymore. I didn't want to have to go to clubs or flirt with boys. I didn't want any part of this world I had been thrust into against my will. I wanted to be free of the shame and sting of all of it. Suddenly the chance to sit in my bishop's office and answer all his questions sounded like the safest, sweetest place to be.

I loved my bishop dearly and never wanted to disappoint him, but I was so broken that confessing came easy. I was no longer parsing words or experiences to keep up appearances. I was willing to expose all my failings if he could make the pain and humiliation go away. He listened and comforted me and I felt true compassion in his words and his guidance.

"I'm worried about you. I don't want you to define yourself by this one mistake. I don't want this to be the reason you leave your calling, or leave the church, or leave the standards you know you need to live by. Put this behind you and don't dwell on it. God knows you are struggling right now. He loves you. I love you. The ward loves you. You're forgiven. Go and sin no more."

He told no one about our conversation, and he encouraged me to tuck it away and not talk about it either. "Why be reminded of something that you've moved on from?" he offered. He began checking in on me, bringing treats by the house with his wife. He made sure I knew I was loved and that he was on my side, and I cherished our relationship. I was willing to give up my newfound freedom and fun in order to return to feel safe and secure. I knew how to navigate life with the church's standards. I didn't want to go off the rails if the consequences were so steep.

Finally, I grew brave enough to tell someone in my family that Billy had left. I told *no one* about my reckless driving. I was on the phone with my brother and he asked me point blank about how Billy was doing. Before the words could escape my tongue, I began to weep.

"Billy's moved out, and he wants a divorce."

Silence.

I braced myself for his response.

"Oh, no, Heather. Oh, no."

We wept together for a few minutes, and for a moment, I felt the sweet relief of unloading a burden. The secret of Billy leaving, the secret of my marriage ending, and the secret sins I had been ignoring had been a constant weight on my heart. Sitting there sobbing with my brother on the other end of the line, I thought I had found some comfort. I wanted him to break out of his trance and to affirm that we were on the same page. His tears were evidence that he had it in him. He could comfort me, bear my burdens, mourn alongside me.

For just the slightest of seconds, he broke the death stare, before once again raising his hand to the square.

"You have the capacity to fix this. You have the capacity to bridge the gap."

He wasn't afraid to say what he knew was unpopular. So I listened.

I responded through the tears. "What if I don't want to fix it? What if the cost is too high?"

I cried into the phone, baring my darkest fears. He was my brother, he knew me, he knew my heart, and I needed him to understand. I wanted to hear him say that this wasn't my fault. That my happiness was important. That I had tried my best and that this was not the end of the world. I could find love again. I could remarry. I could have more children with a man who saw me and loved me for exactly who I was. A marriage where we were both treasured, not just tolerated.

But he didn't say any of those things, and I can only assume he didn't say them because he didn't believe them. He believed in the Plan of Happiness and the promises of the new and everlasting covenant. He believed in duty to God over duty to self and duty to daughters. He believed in the doctrine. If two people love the Lord and love the gospel more than their own lives, they can make the marriage work. Choose the right. Choose martyrdom. Choose the church. *She who suffers most wins.*

Sit down, Sister Gay. You're not special. This is who God wants you to be. You may have to beg Billy back. You may have to apologize for being selfish and passive aggressive. You may have to paste a bigger smile on your face. You may have to lose twenty pounds. Get your priorities straight. Whatever it takes, figure it out, and help your husband thrive.

I asked him if I could fly out with the girls to spend Christmas with him and his family. I could not bear the thought of Christmas morning alone with the kids. He was living in Palo Alto at the time, and I knew the girls would love to be surrounded by their cousins and the sights and sounds of a different environment.

I felt vulnerable imposing on his family, but I was desperate. We flew out before Christmas and filled our days with the finest food and festivities San Francisco and the giant gingerbread house at the Fairmont Hotel had to offer. It was a welcome distraction until reality crept back in.

My brother informed me that he had invited Billy to fly in as well. He'd be coming by the house for an hour or two on Christmas Eve and then return the next morning to open presents with the girls. The selfish and insecure part of my heart felt an immediate slap of betrayal, but then my maternal brain immediately felt ashamed. I was their primary, and only, caregiver. There was no question that Billy would give me 100 percent custody of the children when we divorced, but I still felt guilty keeping the kids all to myself over the holidays. What I wanted or needed at that moment didn't matter. Billy was always going to be their father, and my family would forever facilitate his role in their lives.

As luck would have it, immediately after Billy left Christmas Eve, the girls began throwing up. I spent the better part of the night trying to contain both the sights and sounds of sick children and projectile puking. When Billy arrived at the house the next morning, the girls were feeling fine, but I was feeling frazzled. I excused myself and left for a nearby Laundromat with two vomit-soaked duvets and a garbage bag full of flu-infested jammies. I spent Christmas morning with a roll of quarters and a row of oversized washing machines, sleep-deprived and sobbing.

I thought of my mom and dad and all the magical Christmas mornings of my childhood. Opening presents lasted all day, we'd take turns opening gifts, youngest to oldest, pausing each round to try on the new clothes or build the Ewok village. I could feel my heart churning like the clothes in the washing machine as I slowly realized that I wouldn't be able to recreate those same types of memories with my daughters. That my Christmas mornings from here on out would be split, right down the middle. And the joy, and the magic, and the traditions would forever be divided and diminished. I felt sorry for myself, sorry for my children, sorry for this new reality and awareness that Christmas was happening without me, and that nobody seemed to notice. I didn't want this future but I couldn't figure out how to fix it.

The divorce filing loomed over me like a dark cloud of bad weather. In every room I entered, I tried to be the joyful Sister Gay who completed her roles with little complaint.

I had switched off the part of myself that put up a fight out of a need to survive.

I finally caved in a Relief Society meeting. I sat my counselors down and conducted business as usual, not a cloud on the horizon. As the meeting continued, the weight of Billy's absence and the recent filing became too much to bear.

Interrupting the flow of the meeting, I interjected, "Well, you guys, as concerned as I am about all of these things, it's really hard for me to be invested, because I think Billy has left me. I mean, he definitely left, and I don't think he's coming back."

I wanted to be honest with them. In my position, I felt safe enough to unfold my secret, but I still couldn't say the word divorce. I wanted my counselors to offer that coveted eye contact, that desired acknowledgment that said, "Yes, life is hard and seems unbearable, but you will get through this."

They listened, patiently waiting for a time to respond.

Eventually, my first counselor spoke. She looked me dead in the eyes and said simply, "Run. Run, and don't look back."

In response, my jaw fell open. *Run?* Was that an option? I absolutely wished I could have run, but there was too much at stake. I knew that, she knew that. This was a woman who had been through all the ups and downs of marriage, who had been in love and married for close to fifty years. And yet here she was, letting the doctrine fall to the side in order to be my friend. It felt like she was the first person to tell me it was OK to leave. The only one to indicate that our safety and wellbeing was more important than the covenant. That I had the capacity to survive without Billy. That I could make it on my own. That we would be OK.

CHAPTER 25

IN MY LIFE, I LOVE
YOU MORE

Word of Billy's absence escaped like the leak of a large balloon: glacially slow and painfully loud.

Georgia was in the first grade when I was forced to acknowledge that the girls had noticed Billy's absence more than I thought. Her class was doing an art project that required students to place little goldfish in a bowl, one for each member of their family. In Georgia's fishbowl, she placed only four fish: Ashley, Georgia, Annabelle, and Mom. A friend asked her where the fifth fish was, and in answering the question honestly, my sweet, innocent Georgia told Brynlee what I'd never had the courage to admit: "My dad doesn't live with us."

I could learn from her candid and forthright explanation.

Later that day, the second after the kids returned home from school, Brynlee's mother, Bonnie, came over and knocked at my door with a concerned urgency.

"I don't want to impose," she began. "Brynlee told me that Georgia said her dad doesn't live with you anymore."

She was fishing for goldfish in a glass bowl. There was nowhere to hide.

"Yes," I replied. "He's served me papers, but nothing more has happened. I don't really know."

I turned around, shut the door, and retreated. I accepted defeat. If Bonnie knew, it was only a matter of time before every house in Zion knew that Heather Gay was soon to be a divorcèe.

I was detaching from my feelings when my face began detaching from my body. It happened slowly at first, and then all at once. I was at dinner eating ramen with a friend when the soup began dribbling down my chin despite my careful spoonfuls and slurping.

"This ramen is really messy," I explained sheepishly. I asked for a to-go container and decided I'd finish the meal at home alone where I could slurp shame free.

The next morning when I was brushing my teeth, I struggled to spit out my toothpaste. What was wrong with me? I looked at myself in the mirror and tried to spit again. Only half of my reflection was moving. The left side of my face was contracted and pursed while the right side remained slack and still. I panicked. What was going on? Was I having a stroke? Did I have a brain tumor?

I immediately called Diana.

"Can you come over?" I asked, my speech slurring. "Something is wrong with me."

She drove me to urgent care where the doctors took me through a battery of tests. They diagnosed me with stress-induced Bell's palsy, a temporary but debilitating paralysis along the right side of my face.

My prognosis was grim. "We aren't sure what causes it, we aren't sure how long it will last, and we have no proven treatment to help you get better. The best advice is to relax and avoid stressful situations."

"Have you been experiencing anything stressful lately?" the doctor asked gently.

"Ummmmmm . . . nothing too major. Just a divorce, a reckless driving charge, a high-demand religion, and three kids under the age of eight. Nothing out of the ordinary."

For almost eight weeks, my face was paralyzed on one side. May my Costco card serve as evidence.

I continued as Relief Society President, conducted meetings, and taught lessons all through the one properly functioning side of my mouth. I sang hymns, volunteered at school, and never missed a Sunday service, all while the right side of my face tried ever so slowly to slip off.

My social life came to a screeching halt. This was a message from God. I knew exactly what was happening. I had read about it in the Book of Mormon.

In the book of Alma, a man named Korihor travels to Zarahemla, a city in the ancient Americas whose streets, according to illustrated Mormon children's books, are lined with red adobe clay houses with straw roofs right next door to ancient Mesoamerican temples. Korihor was preaching against the word of God. God had him thrown out of cities and arrested, but he still continued to disobey. In a last ditch effort to save Korihor from himself, God struck him down and made him dumb and mute. He was forced into a life of destitution, until he was eventually trampled to death by the Zoramites (Alma 30:59).

I couldn't move half my mouth or enunciate my words. There was no talking my way out of this one. In my heart, I knew that Bell's palsy was God's muzzle sent from His hand to my face. I was struck down, and it kept me small; it kept me safe. *And thus we see the end of him who perverteth the ways of the Lord; and thus we see that the devil will not support his children at the last day, but doth speedily drag them down to hell.*

My partial paralysis was a wake-up call. A bitch slap from a loving Heavenly Father to one specific side of my sloping face. Once again at a crossroads, I dove deeper into the faith. I was Korihor, struck dumb so as not to contribute to my own demise.

I was bowling with bumpers: Bell's palsy when you're trying to be Frederick, soaking up the sights, sounds, and sun of summer with other divorcèes? I was swept off the earth.

Sure, divorced men expect a little bit of baggage, but they don't expect that baggage to be a carry-on hanging off your jowl.

Truly, no part of me believed that Billy and I would get divorced. With papers on the table and the water continuing to rise, I was distracted by the newness of the life I was building apart from him. For an entire year after he served me, nothing happened. Instead, he would routinely transfer money to my bank account, keeping me on a strict budget. He was able to monitor all of my expenses, and yet I had no idea where any of our money was nor how he was spending it.

We never talked about the divorce. Exchanges were centered around the kids and nothing more. I chained myself to the tree of marriage and refused to leave. I didn't want to get divorced. I didn't know *how* to get divorced. And so I put the power in his hands: he had to either come up with the terms to negotiate me down or choose to leave the tree alone. To let it stand.

I wasn't actively trying to win Billy back. I wasn't trying to work on our relationship. My performative reality had its limits. We were at an impasse, both unwilling to budge. The process wasn't excessively emotional. True to his word as my Goldilocks guy from Huntington Beach, when we finally signed the divorce papers, it was not too amicable, not too contentious, but just right.

For a while, I had been building a life apart from Billy, outside of our pretend reality. I wasn't performing anymore, I was just living. The ship was lost to the ink-black depths of the Great Salt Lake. In the months since he had filed, I lay lifeless on the tiny remnants of what we had built together. I held on to Billy because there was no other hope. It was finally time to let go.

In order to reach the whistle and save myself, I had to drop the frozen, lifeless hand. I had been floating aimlessly and alone, numb to all around me. My lips an icy blue, my skin a ghostly white, I held on to life if only for the reason that my hand was frozen tight in the Patriarchal Grip. Dewy tears clung to my lashes like little particles of ice, weighing down my eyes and closing them to all in my peripheral sight.

My marriage was done. And if I had any chance of saving myself and my family, of starting fresh with my three beautiful girls, I had to let go of that which was dragging me down. The Standard of Truth had been newly erected in me—persecutions may rage, mobs may combine, armies may assemble, calumny may defame—but I was determined and destined to go forth boldly, nobly, and independently for the sake of Ashley, Georgia, and Annabelle.

You must do me this honor: promise me you will survive, that you will never give up, no matter what happens, no matter how hopeless, promise me now, and never let go of that promise.

I'll never let go, girls. I'll never let go.

PART FIVE

BAD
ASS

CHAPTER 26

ALL OF THESE LINES
ACROSS MY FACE

After the divorce was final, my new reality set in and life was bleak. It was the darkest time of my life. A black so dark I couldn't tell the sea from the horizon. There was no map, no compass, no ship to even steer. I was alone, floating along the surface of the water with nary a lifeboat in sight.

The dark was enveloping. But not in the way that once comforted me in the theater in France. No longer was I finding refuge in the solitude and anonymity of the back row. I wasn't watching Jack and Rose in a fictional tale of romance and loss. Instead, I, too, was on the screen. Destitute. Laid bare. In need of resuscitation.

After he left, Billy kept me on a pretty tight budget. Sure, the mortgage checks never bounced, but there was no room for discretionary spending on things like Botox. I had to get creative.

I was industrious. I understood the value of my work as a photographer. How best could I use my skills to get free, or at least discounted, services at local Salt Lake med spas? There had to be more benefit to the work than just staged Christmas cards and Tuscan temple prints. Who's to say you can't add a fourth B to Santiago's equation: boobs, butts, barenakeds, and Botox.

One week at church, I had a friend divinely intervene and stop me in the hallway.

"Where do you get your Botox done?" she asked. "They've spocked you."

"B-b-botox?" I stammered.

How did she know? If I was being "spocked," I figured I'd better find out.

She leaned in and pointed to my eyebrows, tracing one with her finger.

"You can tell you got Botox recently because your eyebrows look like the character Spock from *Star Trek*."

I gasped. I don't remember what I thought getting spocked meant at the time, but I know it definitely didn't involve Leonard Nimoy.

My friend was a nurse and explained to me how muscles and Botox work together and how they *do not*. My Vulcan look was not the look I was going for, and she could get me in on Monday with her doctor. He would inject more Botox to correct it, and I'd be unspocked in about a week.

Sounded sus, but sure.

She worked for a med spa called Visage MD, and the doctor was a kind but overwhelmed entrepreneur and father of six. He was an ophthalmologist and facial plastic surgeon with big dreams of operating a glam, high-end med spa for the Valley's rich and famous. He never missed a week of church, but he would never be a bishop. Less Dick Van Patten and more Josh Gad.

The doctor looked at my Instagram account and readily agreed to have me run his social media in exchange for free treatments. I couldn't wait to wow him with my full skill set. I had marketing campaigns and sales strategies in addition to access to models, influencers, and people in the community. I'd catch him with the bait of free Botox and seal him with the switch of my whole arsenal of skills. And since this wasn't a formal matrimonial courtship, ambition served me well.

The first event I threw was an influencer soiree catering to the city's young and glamorous. I knew all the influencers and had taken their pictures from Sundance to the Salt Flats.

Cara Loren, Amber Fillerup, and Christine Andrew—all of Utah's most elite influencers—were invited. The event featured signature cocktails and a bartender donated by Salt Lake's most noble and righteous supplier of spirits, Vida Tequila. Lisa Barlow represented the best of the best tequila, and she had been in my orbit ever since she crossed paths in college with one of my best friends. Lisa had introduced my friend to her husband, and her yenta prowess kept them forever intertwined. Long before she became Lisa Barlow, anyone within our insular radius had heard tale of Lisa Lee.

Our party was a huge success, the doctor couldn't help but kneel down to my businesswoman gravitas. I couldn't help but succeed. And if Bell's palsy had taught me anything, it was that a fully functioning face is the currency of a single, floundering mom of three.

My performance was so noteworthy that the doctor asked me if I wanted to buy the business. I was just trying to be a good photographer with a side hustle, but I was, after all, Entrepreneur Student of the Year Honorable Mention. I just couldn't help myself. Industry and enterprise were in my pioneer bones.

I was a throw-me-in type of gal; no matter the circumstance, I was going to thrive. After all, it was a business, and if Steelhead Designs, Old

Nauvoo, and @hdgpics meant anything, I would be fine. Besides, I had nothing to lose.

I handled his bills until, finally, his name was no longer on the ledger. It wasn't a loss for him, as he had already moved on to greener pastures. He's currently running a luxury vaginal rejuvenation clinic in Salt Lake City. For an ophthalmologist with one eye closed, it was a lateral move.

Three months into owning a med spa, I realized I was in over my head. That's when I ran into Andrea Robinson. I had known Dre peripherally since our daughters started elementary school. They were in the same class, and I would see Dre every morning dropping Elsha off at the school. She was the image of the hardworking single mother, who dropped off her daughter and immediately left to go to work. The stay-at-home mothers had a different routine. We would show up at drop-off with our strollers full of siblings and our giant Diet Cokes and linger and chitchat long after the kids were seated inside. Dre's daughter Elsha was Ashley's very best friend, and I wanted to be Dre's friend too, but I never imagined it was a possibility. We lived in two totally different worlds. I was a lady of leisure on the path to exaltation, and she was a single mother living by the sweat of her brow in the lone and dreary wilderness. *Two paths diverged in a yellow wood.*

The next time Dre and I crossed paths, things had changed dramatically since our daughters' kindergarten days. Dre had become a lady of leisure, settling down, remarrying, and having two more children. I found myself reeling from divorce, single and adrift in the world of luxury med spas.

"Dre, I hate it. I'm miserable. I don't know what I'm doing. What should I do?"

"Well," she replied, "let me help you. There's a lot of things you can do to make it successful."

"Would you be interested in coming in once or twice a week?"

I felt selfish even asking her. I assumed she'd immediately say no. She was busy raising two toddlers in addition to her now-tween daughter, Elsha. A side gig at a struggling med spa for commission cash seemed out of reach. What I didn't know was that she, too, was drowning. She was struggling in her role as a stay-at-home mom. She missed working and felt crushed and ground down by her scripted role as wife and mother. She, like me, was just putting her feet on the cold tile floor.

Dre was the first person I could be completely Mormon around *and* completely myself. I didn't have that ability with anyone, ever. She became my center pin, and if I could line it up with her, I was bound to get a strike every damn time.

Together, Dre and I set out to build a business that didn't exist. We knew exactly what we wanted: to know how much injections were going to cost and how long they were going to take. It was important for us to make sure that our customers knew we valued their money, their time, their experience, and their ability to determine their own outcomes. If an eighteen-year-old came in and said, "I want lips the size of two small pillows," who were we to say no?

Whatever you want within the medical guidelines, we will give you. I don't have anyone at Target telling me what to buy. When I'm putting boxes of Cocoa Pebbles into my cart, no one trails behind me saying, "You really should balance that out with some greens." No. It's my body, and I will put into it what I want to put into it. Our goal, from the start, has always been to put the power back in the hands of our customers. *Beauty by the people, for the people.*

Our clients are young and highly sensitive to customer service.

They don't like contracts, upsell, hidden tips, or price hikes. They value transparency and authenticity. We make it our mission to alleviate all the anxieties that come with self-care. It's already intimidating and expensive to get cosmetic treatment. You have no idea how much you're going to spend or how you're going to look. It's your appearance, the most sacred part of your identity.

I struggled adapting to a business within the medical sector. I hated everything about it. The regulations, the licensing, the limited vendors, the overhead, the liability, and the competition. Salt Lake City was a saturated market for plastic surgeons and med spas. We had as many med spas per capita as Beverly Hills and they all seemed to be run by rich white men who were not keen on allowing two novice stay-at-home moms to burst onto the stage. When the word got out about Beauty Lab + Laser and the ways it was disrupting the industry, the push back was intense and immediate.

With no experience, no investors, and no idea what we were doing, we turned a bankrupt plastic surgery practice into a booming Beauty Lab Business. In September, we launched the Mini Lip Plump, a new service never before created. The brainchild of Dreather. Before the Mini Lip Plump, if you wanted to inject your lips you were limited to a minimum purchase price of at least $600. This was the preassigned quantity and price decided by the manufacturers and the FDA. As business owners, we felt hamstrung, held to minimum prices and services that didn't work for us or our clients. There was no medical justification, just a forced upsell, and we refused to accept it. Back in my Steelhead Designs days, Charlie had challenged me to create a product within the customer's price point. I drew on my experience at Doctors without Borders and remembered that goods could be parsed out according to the customers' needs, not just according to big pharma's standard minimums.

We started buying filler in smaller quantities and then created an easy process so that customers could try injecting their lips for half the price and half the downtime. For girls who want a little, not a lot, the Mini Lip Plump at $350 was a hit and everyone wanted to get one. We tore down the mystery curtain that doctors loved to hide behind: the art of war when it comes to pricing, and units, and syringes, and specials. We trademarked all of our services, made our pricing transparent, eliminated tips, eliminated upsell, and sold skin-care products at cost plus shipping. Once customers realized what we were doing, the business took off. Our staff couldn't inject people fast enough.

When we look better, we do better, we feel better. And I knew *that* better than anyone from my days of partial facial paralysis and half-mouthed public prayers.

In January 2017, we incorporated Beauty Lab + Laser as the love child of your plastic surgeon and Sephora. We changed the name on the wall and pushed forward full steam. With business booming, I went to the celebrity-frequented Sundance Film Festival to promote our Mini Lip Plump. We gave away free vouchers and B_{12} shots in the swag bags of yet another Park City entrepreneur: Meredith Marks.

Meredith Marks has been there since the beginning, but she doesn't like to boast. Boasting is unbecoming, after all. We met through Lisa Barlow and were business associates before we became friends.

Our first project was a trunk show on Main Street in Park City featuring her fashion and jewelry. Vida Tequila provided alcohol to party, and Beauty Lab + Laser provided IVs to recover. Meredith Marks provided a little of both.

Nothing about Meredith or her life screamed Mormons or mountains. She was a big-city girl, an Eloise grown up and all about town. She was brunch at Jean Georges, lunch at Balthazar, and dinner at Le Bilboquet followed by drinks at the Regency: Belvedere up with a twist, ice on the side.

The last fancy drink she ordered on a girls' night out was called the Impossible Dream because it was impossible to choke down without retching. Mezcal, Grand Marnier, tequila, Belvedere, and bleccchhh. We all took one sip before Angie Harrington exclaimed that the atrocity Meredith had ordered tasted exactly like a Dollar Store smells. The Pic 'n Save Margarita was born. And by the end of the night, she had us all ordering them.

And even though Meredith and Seth lived and raised their kids in Park City, the hometown heartiness of the High West repelled off their backs the same way cheap fabric melts when you iron it.

Meredith is always couth, always measured, rarely frazzled, and never not sure. Of all the SLC Real Housewives, Meredith Marks has the most real education. A JD and an MBA from Northwestern University, a jewelry business, an apparel line, a coffee business, and housewares on the horizon. Add NFTs to her CV and she will be a TKO.

Our first independent event together was a family affair. Her friend had loaned us her store on Main Street for the evening, and we set up to ply her patrons with B_{12} shots and IV hydration bags. Meredith invited her two youngest children, Chloe and Brooks, to attend as well.

Brooks was barely sixteen and already breaking boundaries back in the day by wearing baby pink before it was gender-bending. Even as a teenager, he oozed star quality. The kind of kid who would be plucked from the audition to star in his own Disney series and then transition seamlessly to leading man before he was twenty-seven. He had the bone structure, the bankroll, and just the right amount of banal malaise that made both the girls and the boys swoon. If Meredith wasn't destined to be a Real Housewife, her youngest son was destined to be a real star.

Meredith's parties always featured her real-life friends, and they are everything you'd want the noshing and poshing Upper East Side crowd to be. Mind you, Meredith is neither exclusively New Yorker, Los Angelean, or Chicagoan. She's a mixture of all the major metropolises of the world, and she's making her mark on the Mountain West. It's rare to meet someone in your life who personifies a word, but Meredith does just that. She is the human embodiment of hobnob.

Any good sociologist would tell you it's important to study Meredith's migratory patterns in order to fully understand how she operates. If you can keep her up late enough and keep the drinks stiff enough, you may be lucky enough to witness Meredith Marks descend from her ivory tower and slowly slide into her alter ego: the Dread Pirate Mary Poppins. There is no spoonful of sugar for this sourpuss. Her accent will transport you like a pirate ship to a world where only Dorit Kemsley recognizes its exotic origin.

Above all things, Meredith is always a mother. She's deeply entrenched in her children's lives, and if they are anywhere in the vicinity, you can plan on being eclipsed by their immediate needs. It's rare to have a phone conversation without one of her children ringing through. And she always answers. I've pushed decline on my kids' calls one thousand times for every call that Meredith picks up on the first ring. She may be an empty nester with all her children away at school or beyond, but her brood is still nestled in her bosom. She is as dedicated and involved with her kids as any Mormon driving a minivan in the Midwest. With her, it's just harder to tell, because Meredith doesn't drive. In fact, she might not even have a driver's license. Her first car was a limousine, which is almost as cool as her first lasting love: the self-confident, schmoozing Seth.

Meredith was on the original group text with producers talking about a show in Salt Lake City, and she was also one of the first people, along with Lisa, to recommend me as a potential cast member. She saved all her receipts. Why doesn't MM pretend like she's in charge of production? Because Meredith Marks doesn't give a shit. Let the peasants squabble over scraps of bread.

We've shut down Sundance together. We've danced on tabletops at Tao. We've even shared an entree at the Cheesecake Factory—an act I forced her into at Fashion Place Mall in Murray, Utah, and one that I will never live down.

When we first began filming *The Real Housewives of Salt Lake City* and it became clear that Lisa might feel territorial, Meredith and I both gracefully retreated from our friendship to allow some space. It was just a matter of time before she had burned bridges with both of us, giving me and Meredith the chance to split as many SkinnyLicious tacos as we wanted.

Watching Meredith ride back from Zion in a Sprinter van surrounded by junk food and Jennie Nguyen's self-taught karaoke is an image burned in my brain. It was like looking at an oil painting of dogs playing poker: absolutely absurd yet totally believable.

When I heard that Meredith had fucked half of New York, I wasn't surprised, she doesn't do anything half-assed, unless it's her pants size. There are still a few tricks I can learn from this garbage whore.

✳ ✳ ✳

Collaborating with stars like Meredith and Lisa at Sundance only fueled the success of Beauty Lab + Laser back in Salt Lake City. Dre and I together were "getting butts in seats." The BeautyLabbers were rolling in one right after the other. It was amazing. We were two moms making the tables shake and surprising ourselves at every turn. We had spun straw into gold. Feeling supported in my business, I felt emboldened to continue pursuing my other hustles and hobbies.

My love for photography never faltered, and when I wasn't focusing on the fifth B, business, I was happy to photograph the original three.

Photography and my lust for all things led me into the art of boudoir. I knew sex. I had been a married woman, and I had been outside the backyard gates enough to learn a few things. I worked solely on referrals and denied more clients than I accepted. When Whitney Rose reached out, there was no doubt I wanted to take pics of her wild and untamed.

The first time I hung out one-on-one with Whitney was behind the camera lens. I was prepared to be the art director, the set director, and the boudoir stylist. Most boudoir shoots required a lot of hand-holding, confidence-boosting, and lingerie-coaxing.

"Try this leather harness, bra, and matching thong. I know it feels weird, but it photographs fantastic."

"Try getting on all fours and arching your back. Tilt your head toward me, chin down, relax your lips, booty pop."

Click.

"Nailed it."

Within five minutes of arriving at Whitney's shoot, I knew this was not going to be an ordinary session.

This wild rose was not scared to handle a little prick.

As soon as I arrived, she showed me the shopping bags she had brought, overflowing with thirst-trap thongs and thigh highs. She had enough stiletto heels to make a stripper pole jealous and just enough kink to make me feel like I might be in over my head.

It was clear that she knew all of Victoria's Secrets and I had things to *learn*!

The next few moments did not seem like the beginning of a boudoir photo shoot, they seemed more like a scene from *Titanic*, where Rose takes Jack back to her first-class cabin under the guise of pursuing art. I was clearly Jack, the eager artist, and the outspoken Whitney was, quite aptly, Rose.

I suggested she wear the black gauzy nightgown that swept romantically to the floor and opened in front all the way to the waist. I took note that the matching panties were microscopic and dangled off the hanger like a tiny pirate's eye patch.

When Whitney emerged from the bedroom in the outfit, all the lessons about boudoir photography that I had learned from Santiago years ago came sharply into focus. I was filled with what can only be described as *el espíritu de los tres B's*. This was the sign, the mantle shifting, the calling made sure. My time had come at last to sip from the Holy Grail of boudoir photography. I was to shoot the three B's, and I would glorify them through the chosen vessel: Whitney Rose.

We started out with a few pictures of her walking, the nightgown billowing behind her bronzed boobs and butt.

She was a natural model: playful and sexy, sweet and seductive. I could not take the photos fast enough. *I had the music in me.*

We went outside in the floaty black nightgown to get some natural wind and golden light. Whitney shone. There wasn't a second of cajoling or negotiating for a good shot. She was down for anything and everything and flipped through expert poses the way I flipped through Instagram filters.

In a town full of beauties and beasts, there is only one wild rose. And she was blooming.

We were wrapping up scene number one and getting ready for outfit number two when Whitney went straight for B number three.

Jack, I want you to draw me like one of your French girls. Wearing this. . . wearing only this.

She reached down and slowly removed her pirate-patch panties. *Ahoy, matey!*

My prayer came out instinctively, fervently, and surprisingly in Spanish.

Oh, espíritu de Santiago! I pray to thee, dime fuerte and guide mi mano that I may honor you and los tres B's, especially the barenaked part which is presented before me now.

I felt the answer to my prayer immediately after I offered it. Why was I panicking? I knew exactly what to do. Something about Whitney's panty-less attire was strangely familiar. I had seen this once before.

Yacine, in the city of Perpignan, in the South of France, sitting bare-assed on my lap, penis dangling, as I taught the sacred Law of Chastity. If he had taught me anything, it was to embrace the philosophy: no pants, no problem.

Whitney pulling a full Winnie the Pooh? Been there, done that, bought the T-shirt.

I proceeded with the photo shoot as calm as a summer's morn. I photographed her from belly button to backside without breaking a sweat.

As I was leaving later that night, I spotted the tiny black panties on the patio—once flung, now forgotten. I walked over, picked them up, and slipped them into my pocket as smoothly as a sleeve of French Imovane. You never know when an eye-patch might come in handy.

CHAPTER 27

ONLY GIRL
(IN THE WORLD)

Lisa Barlow had given me her fast-talking quick pitch—"I'm putting together a reality show"—but I had never given it much thought. Whenever I interacted with Lisa, I just smiled and nodded in awe and told the emperor how fabulous her new clothes were. The irony was that her actual clothes *were* fabulous. Her style impeccable.

Anyone who can relate to the "fake it till you make it" motto would absolutely relate to Lisa Barlow; her performative reality made mine look like a sock-puppet show. She enters a room and . . . *begin scene*.

"Hiiiiiiiiiiii."

The conversation is mostly one-sided but still scintillating.

The private plane is ready for her trips with her friends. Not you. Her *friends*. "It's a G6, not a Cessna. Anyone can own a Cessna."

The obscure villa on the Mediterranean she visited while yachting: "Marseille? I love that. You served your mission there? Amazing. I love that."

The multiple lots with multiple homes in the beginning stages of construction: "Most of our projects are *in media res*. That means 'right in the middle.'"

My favorite version of Lisa Barlow is when she is unhinged, enraged, and raw. She's tough and mean and scrappy. This is usually when she claims her "NYC" is showing. Lucky for Lisa, "New York is not a city, it's a world" . . . because she's from Schenectady. But that's the only thing small town about LB. She's bright lights, big-city energy. If you want to eat and drink well at a restaurant, you want to be sitting next to Lisa. She knows more about terroirs and oak barrels and soil acidity than the most seasoned sommelier. She will help you pronounce foreign fashion words and remind you not to fidget. She's unfettered and fancy, but she will still *throw down*. It's a peek behind the stage curtain that is terrifying and thrilling.

Lisa is an overachiever and, as such, takes the gold medal in many things, but especially in the art of the subtle name drop. "I'm friends with Denzel." This is one of the many events in the Mean Girls Olympics: the name drop, the disinvite, the Radar Online, the compliment sandwich, the naked wasted.

I never thought that Lisa was lying about being a mini-producer for her television show. She believed all the things she was saying were true because she wanted them to be. This is a coping mechanism that I'm more than familiar with. I'm sure people saw me parading around keeping dinner warm for Billy months after he had moved out and just nodded and smiled and told me how fabulous I looked in my new clothes. Performative reality works; let this be your cautionary tale.

Lisa had plugged her show enough that when a casting agent texted me out of the blue, I was not surprised. I figured it would be a one-and-done phone call, and I'd be able to give him a few names of my influencer friends and BeautyLabbers as potential participants. The stakes were not high; I felt zero pressure about being cast myself. I just didn't want to let Lisa down. I wanted her to be glad she had given them my name.

I responded immediately when I received a text message that, on the surface, seemed to be nothing significant. An ice floe on a calm sea.

"Hey Heather, it's Joey from InventTV. Let me know when you have a few minutes to chat."

"Hey, Joey! I'm free now or anytime this afternoon."

Freedom's just another word for nothing left to lose.

When Joey called me the next day, I laid it all on the line and answered every single one of his questions authentically from my heart rather than from the script I'd been given as a member of the Church of Jesus Christ of Latter-day Saints. It was scary, but it was easier than I thought it would be. *Sometimes the truth is like a second chance.*

The casting process was fascinating and arduous. It was a little bit like falling in love. . . it happened slowly and then all at once. It started with a phone call, less than forty-five minutes, just chatting with the casting director while he asked questions to gauge my interest level and basic stats.

"Tell me a little about yourself and your friends. Are you a Mormon?"

"Yes."

"Tell me a little bit about Mormons and the LDS Church."

"We are a worldwide church, worth more than $140 billion, run by men—specifically, twelve men we call the general apostles, who then report directly to our living prophet, seer, and revelator."

"Are you Christian?"

"Yes, we believe in God the Father, his son Jesus Christ, and in the Holy Ghost."

"What makes you special or different?"

"There are a lot of rules. We follow the Law of Tithing: 10 percent of our income goes directly to the church. We follow the Word of Wisdom: no coffee, tea, alcohol, or nicotine. We follow the Law of Chastity: no sexual relations outside of marriage. We do proxy work in the temples for people who have died. We volunteer as teachers, choir leaders, ministers, youth leaders, primary leaders. We wear sacred undergarments that we believe protect us from temptation and evil."

"Is that the magic underwear?"

"It is an outward expression of our inward commitment to follow the savior. But yeah, magic underwear."

"So are most of your friends Mormon?"

"Yes, for the most part. I would say they are all Mormon or Mormon-adjacent."

"So, do you drink?"

"Sometimes."

"Do you go to church?"

"Always."

"Do you wear your garments?"

"Sometimes."

"Do you break the Law of Chastity?"

"Always . . ."

I was used to men asking me questions about my food intake and sexual activities, but with Joey, it was different. I was not used to revealing my secrets and my sins to an *outsider*. Living out loud was uncharted waters.

I stepped into my new role like Frederick the mouse in the dead of winter. These were the sunshine days, my new identity burning bright, and I needed to soak up the sights, sounds, and sun in my new skin before I had to go back into hiding, back to the sad performative reality of a life with my feet planted in two opposing worlds. A 7–10 split.

By this point, I had learned to live with snake eyes and had forever given up hope of a spare.

However, in a matter of months, the lone and dreary world was suddenly blossoming with opportunity. And this casting process was my dress rehearsal. I was auditioning for the role of a lifetime: myself, no longer hiding behind the curtain of Mormonism.

I shared with Joey tales of my weekend escapades and the monikered men who filled them: Blondie and Man-Bun, the Felon and the Ghoster. I was a vibrant, single woman enjoying her glory days. *Friendly men in this town!*

I talked about Beauty Lab and our disruptive, irreverent marketing policies and unsurpassed customer service. I didn't hold back. I didn't play small. I didn't act like it was all an accident. I was a boss babe, kicking ass and taking names. *She works five to nine, makes six figures a year, and they call her the Tiger Lady.*

After our conversation, Joey told me to go through my friends lists on Facebook and Instagram in order to make a list of people I would want to watch on TV. That seemed easy enough. I had been analyzing people in terms of TV-network potential my entire life.

"She's dramatic, very Lifetime Movie of the Month."

"Likes to party, has more of a VH1 vibe."

"I'm not going to call her a *cow*, but I will say Animal Planet."

Joey would go through my lists of potential interviewees and ask me for their stats, unique identifiers, and the nature of our relationship.

They were interested in genuine connections, long-term friendships, diversity, representation, and an authentic sampling of "business-women in Utah."

I had never considered myself a businesswoman. I had still never taken a paycheck from Beauty Lab. I was a *whispers* divorced house-wife succeeding in an industry that I had no business even being in. I would have loved being celebrated for my marketing savvy, but resilience and entrepreneurship weren't on the list of Young Women Values. I didn't want to lead with qualities that men found unattractive.

The more Joey discovered about my life, the harder the questions became.

"Do your children know you drink?"

"Does your family know you date?"

"What will happen if they find out?"

At the time, the thought took my breath away like a dive into ice-cold water. *Impossible. It is considered sacred and never to be revealed.*

"They would freak out." *But they will never know.*

"What do you mean, freak out?"

"Everything would change. I'd risk so much: my family, my church, my friends, maybe even my customers."

I should have stopped the act right then and said directly to Joey, "I know I talk a good game, but this is just a dress rehearsal for me. I'm never going to be able to live openly as the person I'm introducing to you. She can only live in the shadows, not out, not loud, and certainly not proud."

This vibrant, empowered businesswoman had no place to lay her head in the real world. If I were to show up as myself, I would be cast out, shamed, struck dumb like Korihor, and eventually trampled under the feet of my people.

Every few weeks, Joey would interview me again, and it was an awakening. I fell in love with myself as the girl I was introducing him to. I had been absent in my life for so long. I could hear my voice describing myself, and I was reminded of Frederick warming the cave walls with just his words.

I felt warmer when I was living authentically, even if it was just during my conversations with Joey. I felt the ember flicker to life somewhere deep in my chest. *And if it is right I will cause that your bosom shall burn within you; therefore you shall feel that it is right* (Doctrine and Covenants 9:8).

The Glinda bubble of the gospel had transformed into the golden glow from the warmth of my words. I felt the ice around my heart beginning to melt away, but I knew it couldn't be. I couldn't lean in, it couldn't last. This girl was not meant to live free. *Nothing gold can stay.*

And so I made up my mind that I was going to play this thing out, and if they offered me the actual job, I would bail at the last second. I was going to revel in the casting process and pass the opportunity on to as many of my friends as I could think of. I knew a lot of women. I had lived in Holladay, Utah, in the same house for the last sixteen years. And that house was only a few blocks west of the house I had lived in while I went to high school. The families in these neighborhoods went generations deep, and I loved making friends. If you were to play six degrees of separation, you'd want me as your Kevin Bacon.

And Beauty Lab + Laser only increased my circle of influence. It was a magnet for the reality-TV-worthy. We specialized in lip injections and had a giant oil painting of Kylie Jenner hanging on our wall. She had changed her life when she changed her lips, and we celebrated her for it. Every hot wife, model, NBA WAG, and Jazz dancer graced the gates of our business and were considered cherished friends and fellow BeautyLabbers. I knew everybody. *She's connected, honey. Connected.*

Joey wanted a list of my top ten stars on the rise? No problem. I started making calls and naming names.

"Whitney Rose."

"How do you know Whitney?"

"I met Whitney a few years ago when she came to Beauty Lab looking for help with a chemical burn on her face. We fixed it, and then she hired me to do a boudoir photo shoot for her husband, Justin. We also think we might be related because we both are from the Robinson line in American Fork, Utah."

"Is Whitney Rose someone you would want to watch on TV?"

"Yes. Whitney Rose is 'Murica. She's true red, white, and blue, Brooks and Dunn fun. She is a contradiction from every country song lyric ever written. Whiskey in a teacup. Business sense and big boobs. Denim and diamonds, leather and lace. She is beautiful, but her looks aren't what she leads with. She's a tomboy in a tutu."

Justin and Whitney had both gone through the temple endowment and sealing like I had, but they had walked away from the church in order to be with each other. To many it seemed like they had traded their sacred eternal marriages for flimsy 'til death do us part. *Hasta la muerte!* Joey loved my dramatic description of the Roses and set up interviews right away.

Lisa was going to be thrilled! I couldn't wait to return and report and have her thank me for all my networking. First me, now Whitney. We were filling up the roster.

Lisa was not thrilled. She called to let me know. We discussed how Whitney might not be a good fit for the type of show she was curating. *Trashy? Very TLC.* She was looking for Sotheby's and I had given her Sturgis. Whitney was a little too young and a little too all over the place. A little bit country and a little bit rock and roll. Lisa was going for a classic "effortless cool" vibe. More John Legend than John Cena. But now that the wheels were in motion, there was nothing she could do to stop the work from progressing.

The casting process is like peeling off layers of an onion. Every detail of your life is examined and assessed, and as soon as you peel a layer, another one pops up.

"Can you send us photos of your house?"

"Can you send us photos of every room in your house?"

"Can you send us photos of your cars, your toys, your assets?"

"Can you send me the names and phone numbers of all the people in your life: nannies, stalkers, neighbors, lovers, teachers, customers, trainers, doctors?"

"Tell us how you spend your days."

"Tell us your goals."

"Tell us your goal weight."

"Tell us your gross income."

"Tell us your gross habits."

If you were born with any sense of competitiveness or ambition, it's hard not to play up your answers to the endless questions. It all felt innocuous and inventive. *We are trying to create a reality show here, not a docuseries.* We needed to be rich, crazy, fabulous, and messy. We knew what they wanted. We'd been raised on reality TV. And because there were no cameras around, because it was still just an *idea* of a show, we all worked overtime to give them enough that they might turn it *into* a show. It was a job interview for a new life, and I never dreamed I'd be one of the ones they hired.

The more questions we asked about the concept of the show, the fewer answers we got.

"It's a show about women in business in Utah."

"It's a show about Mormons in the modern-day world."

"It's a coed concept show similar to *Summer House*, only filmed in Utah and not in the summer."

"Think *Southern Charm*, only Salt Lake City."

They were cobbling together a cast, and once they found the people, they would figure out the format. It was about finding interesting, inspiring personalities who reflected both culture and conflict in the Beehive State.

Enter Mary M. Cosby. *Praise Jesus.*

Joey started asking me about Mary within a week of our first phone call. Casually at first and then more pressing.

"Do you know a woman named Mary Cosby?"

"Have you heard of the Faith Pentecostal Church?"

"Do you know anyone who is a member?"

"Is Mary the type of person who would come to Beauty Lab?"

When Joey had exhausted all possible connections, he settled on an old, run-of-the-mill dinner introduction and hoped we'd become fast friends. It was just to meet each other and break the ice. The fact that we were trying to form a friendship in order to make a TV show was just a wonderful surprise.

Michaline, our executive producer and the CEO behind the media company that first started ferreting around in Salt Lake City, flew to Utah about a month into the casting process and came straight to Beauty Lab to meet me and Dre. We laughed and talked about all the crazy things that make Utah and women in Utah unique. We loved her energy and trusted her. She seemed like a true girl's girl and someone who would put together a fantastic TV show about women supporting women.

I met with Michaline and Mary Cosby for dinner at the always-famous Valter's. Valter was there that night and in rare form. I arrived before Mary, which turned out to be a good thing, because when she walked through the doors, every spare hand in the restaurant was surrounding her.

"Hello Ms. Mary, let me take your coat."

"Hello Ms. Mary, here is a special chair for your purse."

"Hello Ms. Mary, we have some special items prepared by the chef for you tonight."

I had been eating at Valter's for years, and no one had ever offered me a chair for *my* purse. How had I never met or heard of Mary M. Cosby before?

It was time to order, and I realized I was nervous. Mary and I had exchanged brief greetings while she and her coat and her purse were being settled and seated separately. Arturo brought an amuse-bouche to the table and placed the plate in front of Mary. She didn't even look at the plate for more than a second, she just immediately recoiled and said quietly, "No." The plate was whisked away as quickly as it had appeared. I noticed that the surrounding waiters had similar plates prepared for me and Michaline, but now everyone stood frozen, scrambling to figure out their next move. Was Mary saying no, none of us could have the offensive dish, or was she just refusing it on her own behalf? Was the dish rejected because of her personal taste? A deadly allergy? A political boycott? We didn't know, and she wasn't talking. I tried to use my eyes to plead with the waiters to just accidentally set my plate down in front of me. I was curious, and I wanted to see it for myself and *then* reject it if necessary.

It didn't work. The waiters denied all of us the amuse-bouche. If Mary ain't happy, ain't nobody happy. A recurring theme whenever Mary was feeling quite contrary.

The rest of the dinner passed as can be expected when you're on a first date with the first lady of Faith Pentecostal. She was equal parts elusive and forthcoming, engaging and disinterested. I agreed with anything and everything she said, and when she corrected my grammar, my pronunciation, my diet, and my physical appearance, I hung my head in shame and thanked her sincerely.

Mary always smelled fabulous and always the same. She said it was a world-class perfume painstakingly developed by hand and by nose in the tiny parfumerie village of Grasse in the South of France. To me it smelled a lot like Dolce & Gabbana.

It might not have been a love match right out of the gate, but I was confident that with time and effort, I could sing her awake with a hymn or two. I wanted to get to know what her story was, how she became the person she is today, and when and where she learned that purses are entitled to their own chairs at restaurants.

The private purse chair was just one of Mary M. Cosby's many bits of wisdom:

1. Don't drink sparkling water. It hardens your ovaries.
2. You don't even know you look inbred.
3. Heat-wave death wine tastes the best.
4. You are the least attractive one. You need to be *humble*.
5. Take a seat and regroup. Your attitude *stinks*.
6. Don't get comfortable with me. You just stay in your small house with your snobby self.

Mary was an uninhibited force to be reckoned with, a truly original person with an original perspective on life and with an uncanny ability to read all of us like scripture.

CHAPTER 28

A DIVA IS A FEMALE
VERSION OF A HUSTLA

If we were going to film a sizzle reel, we needed a complete cast. There could be no empty chairs around our reality table. All of us had gone through several rounds with the casting director and his assistants. My friends lists had been plundered, my contacts far and wide fleeced in hopes of finding that final friend to complete our family.

Lisa Barlow and Meredith Marks sat at the head of the table, Mom and Dad, respectively.

I was next, the dutiful eldest daughter, grateful to be included but still unsure of what it would take in order to stay.

Mary M. Cosby had her spot, and she didn't care who was seated at the table as long as there was a chair for her purse.

Whitney Rose was on the short list, securing her seat in a role declared by Mary Cosby: little girl.

Our family was incomplete, insufficient, it was clear. We weren't sure what kind of show they were making, but we were sure it needed more players. Five is good for a basketball team, but it is not good for a sizzle reel.

All of us were dynamic women, but we were missing our spark, our ignition. Enter from trapdoor downstage center, bedazzled microphone in one hand and "WERK" fan open in the other: Jen Shah.

Jen was a BeautyLabber, and she was fabulous. Full stop. Every time she came by, she would be dressed head to toe in Gucci silks and four-inch heels. When she walked into a room, she led with her charisma. She had street smarts and survival instincts. But the magical part about Jen Shah was also the part that made her fallible and human. She was messy, and she owned it. Queen Bee may be debatable, but there was no doubt that in this group, Jen Shah was MVP.

Joey had been in my phone asking for more diversity. "We need representation. It's really important."

What I'd wanted to say was that perhaps Salt Lake City wasn't the most target-rich environment for such casting choices; it is, after all, the whitest corner of the whitest part of the Book of Mormon Belt. Net 60 percent of the state is Mormon, 90 percent of the state is Mormon-adjacent, and they've only let Black folks have full privileges in the church since 1978. However, I remembered Jen Shah. She tends to leave a pretty indelible mark on all she meets. I asked the employees if they thought Jen would be interested in a show about businesswomen supporting other businesswomen in the Mountain West. They texted her, and almost immediately, she responded, "Yes, have them call me."

Six weeks later, we had a call sheet, a production crew, and a sound team to film what would forever be known as *Utah: Untitled*.

✳ ✳ ✳

Filming the sizzle reel was like filming a tiny, mini-episode of reality TV. It required a full production crew, craft services, and mandatory union breaks. I was thrilled to receive an actual call sheet with my name and scheduled scene locations. *I think I'm gonna like it here.*

On some days I filmed at home, on others I filmed at Beauty Lab + Laser. The ladies came into the lab and we filmed them interacting with our staff and some of them getting our signature procedures (O-shot anyone?).

However, the sizzle's penultimate scene was a huge, fancy dinner that Jen hosted at a mansion in Little Cottonwood Canyon. We sat in chairs adorned with faux sheepskin furs from IKEA in front of a raging fireplace in the middle of June. Lisa offered Whitney unsolicited advice about her fashion choices: "It's a little too Utah." Later that night around the dinner table, Whitney tried to mitigate an argument between the ladies and Jen told her to be quiet but couldn't quite remember her name.

Imbued with the energy of table flips and dinner-party interrupters from years past, Whitney loudly responded to Jen's slight, "It's Whitney FUCKING Rose." It was a moment of Housewives soap-opera flair, and I was sure she had secured her spot on the cast with her dramatics. I was wrong.

In the following days, we wrapped up our interviews and confessionals. I wanted to look professional, so I leaned on the only working girl script I knew.

Well, we're businesswomen. Do you have some sort of business woman special? I'm due in Tucson later—some business thing, you know. I'm just a woman in business.

I mean, it wasn't like I claimed I had invented Post-it Notes, but

I channeled the best Romy and Michele I could imagine. It was completely wrong, but somehow completely right.

About a week after wrapping the sizzle reel, I flew out to Burbank to complete the wrap interviews. They told me I was the only woman of the six that they were flying in, and although I wasn't sure I believed them, it still felt special. Like I wasn't just a puppy in the pile. *You like me! You really like me!*

Being called to Burbank confirmed that the show was happening. For the entirety of the sizzle, I was wrestling with reality. I was still thinking the best-case scenario would be one hopeful season of a TLC docuseries sandwiched between *My 600-Lb. Life* and *Hoarding: Buried Alive*. But for me, just sitting in that production office, answering questions candidly and authentically, it felt like I was turning a corner. I was being cast in a role I'd been waiting for permission to fulfill my entire life. I could be myself, unequivocally, without obligation to represent the church, my family, or my dwindling faith.

Just a few years before, I was in the darkest part of my life, upside down in the depths of my own grief and shame. No hope of a future that I could cobble together without feeling overwhelming despair. I still choked on the word divorce. Despite the success of my children, my business, and even my church callings, "broken home" still loomed over my head like a black rain cloud. And I couldn't shake the hopelessness that surrounded me. I was successful, but I was still sad and defeated.

When producers asked me my level of happiness on a scale from one to ten, I answered "zero" without hesitation. I no longer felt obligated to be apart of the church or its trademark cult of happiness. I wasn't plastering a smile on my face and calling it fortitude. I was broken, and I was embracing it. And yet somehow these producers had seen potential light beyond my darkness. They saw a woman in business blazers and garment-appropriate cap sleeves and said, "I want her. I want the bad Mormon."

For the first time in my life, I felt wanted for my flaws, not just my facade. They wanted me because I had been divorced, because Billy had left, because I raised my daughters alone. They wanted me not because I hit the brass rings but because I failed trying. There I sat, not being asked to move to New York or pack my bags for Hollywood. I didn't have to trade everything for a bus ticket and a handful of dreams. No, I could stay at home, film in my backyard, highlight my business. They were asking me to just wake up and be who I was, and that was both more and less than anyone in my life had ever asked of me.

I wanted to believe I was still Eve, Mother of All Living. That I had a kingdom, a throne. A place in heaven with God and my family eternally. But over the course of my life, I had sacrificed so much for these things of great worth that I failed to see the worth within myself. And in the end, even Eve partakes of the forbidden fruit. Why was I fighting the inevitable? It was like holding my hand up to prevent a wave from crashing on the sand.

During my mission and in my marriage, I had been drowning, clinging to the church as a sort of life preserver. I was just a drop in the ocean, failing to see my value and my worth outside of the picture-perfect image. But as I slowly began to swim ashore, flanked by the support of my daughters, of my friends, and of my business, I realized that my potential had been capped, suffocated, snuffed out by the very bumpers I thought were helping me to bowl. When you dream of something for so long, it can at times imprison you. It becomes your kryptonite.

It was time to let go. It had *been* time to let go. And this sizzle reel and these producers who saw through the scar tissue to the heart of who I truly was were confirmation enough that the church's love was not as unconditional as I had once believed. *You are not a drop in the ocean; you are the entire ocean in a drop.*

After filming the sizzle reel and interviewing in Los Angeles, I came home and went to the bishop. I told him of my plans to be on TV and the effect it would have on my future in the church.

"Don't do it," he urged. "It's not worth it. But if you do, I'd encourage you to consider carrying around a glass of milk if you're at parties with alcohol."

For a month, I thought about what the bishop had told me. And one day, in an instant, I realized that I didn't have to do what the bishop said. I could do whatever I wanted. I wasn't beholden to him or to any other man. And maybe he was wrong. Maybe God wanted me to walk around parties with a martini instead of milk. Maybe instead of going to the temple to redeem other lost souls, I could focus on redeeming my own. On that plane over Death Valley, I had decided. I had made the choice to live my life as an out-of-the-closet, nonpracticing Mormon. In fact, it wasn't really a choice at all. It was an inevitability.

I wasn't coming out like every other person who left the faith. No, I was coming out on television. Two weeks had passed since I'd left California, and the only thing we had been told was that the sizzle was shown to a room full of executives. Every network exec in the room wanted the show, but ultimately, Bravo won out.

They were still telling us that they weren't quite sure what the show would be. They tossed around ideas similar to a *Mexican Dynasty*, a *Texicanas*, or a *Ladies of London*. All we knew was that it was going to be a show that centered on our lives as women living in Utah.

I was riding high.

I was going to be on television, my seat at the table seemed secure, and the possibilities were endless. Business at Beauty Lab was booming, and despite being convinced that I had been abandoned at sea, it appeared the tide was turning.

It was time for Hot Girl Summer.

Jen Shah was in New York City for work and told me to get on a plane. It didn't take much convincing.

Jen Shah never disappoints.

I arrived at her Midtown apartment early in the morning after taking the red-eye from SLC. The city felt different this time: more vibrant, more impressive. I couldn't be sure if it was New York that had changed or just my ability to see it clearly, but it didn't matter. I was there, and I felt electric, alive, but also tired. As soon as I got to Jen's apartment, I decided to first experience the city that never sleeps by sleeping in the city. I climbed into bed with Jen and immediately passed out.

When Jen finally woke me up a few hours later, she was determined to make up for lost time. Our first stop was the Gucci store on Fifth Avenue. We were ushered back to a private suite lined with clothes and refreshments. We ate macaroons and sipped champagne while we tried on racks of Gucci ready-to-wear. It was early August, and the dressing room was not only sweltering but full of clothing for the fall and winter seasons. Signature logo wool dresses, angora blanket shawls with interlocking G's, fuzzy mohair sweaters for cuddling up around the fire. Neck-prickling fabrics. We were there to shop for the cold season in Utah, so we had to imagine ourselves in a mood to bundle up.

It was ninety-eight degrees with 90 percent humidity in Manhattan, but I purchased a leather bomber jacket, full-length harem pants, and an oversize sweater anyway. I was feeling myself. Feeling alive. Feeling sweaty. Hot Girl Summer, indeed.

Jen was in the city to host her company's dinner party at Tao Downtown followed by clubbing at 1 OAK. I planned on turning up and getting down. Jen was the ultimate wingman, and tonight was *Top Gun*. Dinner was supposed to start around nine, but Jen's makeup artist didn't get to the apartment until nine. Stuart, Jen's former first assistant, finally left us to go meet up with all the employees who were waiting patiently at the restaurant.

By the time we left her apartment, we had invited the entire glam squad and I think one of Jen's neighbors to join us. We piled everyone into her Escalade, and Al, our driver, drove us to Tao like an inflated clown car. Grown-ass adults sitting on each other's laps with their butts balanced on arm rests. It was a chaotic *Eight Is Enough* without Dick Van Patten—sure, Mormons believe in no empty chairs, but we also believe in *enough* chairs.

By the time we arrived, the party of eight had been seated and served and were passing the dishes around the table for the final time. *We were late, honey. Late.*

But we were also with Jen Shah.

Jen cleared some stragglers from the table adjacent to her employees and made sure everyone had a place to sit. She flagged down a

waiter and ordered a second round of all of our favorites: shishito pep-
pers, chicken wing lollipops, and the wagyu teppanyaki. Then she sent
the waiter over to the "kids' table" where her glam squad sat and where
chairs kept getting added. Our group was snowballing. Every few steps,
we'd add another friend to our entourage and another name to Jen's
VIP guest list. By the time we got to 1 OAK, Jen had become the Pied
Piper of the Meatpacking District.

The owners' table at 1 OAK is the only way to play. We had bottle
service with sparklers and Veuve Clicquot. The table is right in the
center of the club, roped off with security. It was Shahmazing. Jen's
employees were funny and dynamic and deeply appreciative of her
generosity. She worked her way around the table, making sure everyone
was included and happy with drinks in hand.

When she landed on me, she asked, "Is there any guy here you like?
If you point him out, I'll make it happen." *Talk to me, Goose.*

I think she half expected me to say no, but I actually had someone
in mind.

He was six-foot-six, with long black dreadlocks, a T-shirt, and
designer moto jeans. I had noticed him the second I walked into the
club and briefly made eye contact.

He was easy to point out to Jen because he stood a few inches taller
than everyone else in the crowd.

"Him. He's the one."

She didn't hesitate, and I watched in awe and horror as she started
gliding through the pulsating throng of people directly to him. I was
trying to casually stand on the bench at our table so that I could have
a little perspective on the situation. I also felt responsible for Jen, all
five-foot-two of her, and I didn't want her getting trampled. She was so
small compared to the other patrons that I couldn't even see her in the

crowd. I could only tell where she was by the path she carved, parting the Red Sea like the prophetic figure that she is.

He was surrounded by a bevy of women, but she cut through them like a salmon swimming upstream. They started talking, and I saw his head begin to turn toward our table.

My prayer came out instinctively, fervently, and surprisingly with a Jersey accent.

Oh my God! Noooo! Please do not let him see me watching him, God, dear Lord Jesus and Baby Jesus. Help me, Lord!

Some of God's greatest gifts are unanswered prayers.

Despite my attempts to seek refuge in the bush like Tamra Judge, I was busted. We locked eyes; he excused himself from his friends and started walking to our table with Jen. The two of them together looked like Sylvester the Cat and Tweety Bird. *Sorry, Goose, but it's time to buzz the tower.*

She presented her conquest with a sense of duty: "Heather, this is Six-Six."

Hot Girl Summer is *happening.*

The night advanced from there until it was inarguably time to go. Outside the club, Jen and I stood on the curb. I didn't want to leave, but where to go and what to do? Over Jen's shoulder, I saw my part-time lover walk out of the club and saunter over to us. He invited us to an after-after-party in East Harlem. It was four a.m. But a woman on a mission is bound not by time. I begged Jen to let me go, like a teenage daughter begs her parents.

"Absolutely not," Jen said. "Heather, that was cute in the club, but you're gonna die. We're gonna go to Cafeteria, and then we're gonna go home. No one is going to Harlem."

I was so determined to twist Jen's arm that I tried to convince her of Six-Six's trustworthiness.

For a moment, I saw her wheels turning. She had the weight of the world on her shoulders, but Jen Shah doesn't crack under pressure. She's no shrinking violet. On the curb outside 1 OAK, I sat back and watched her do her thing.

She called over Six-Six's brother in order to have a recommendation of character. She asked for their driver's licenses and took pictures, front and back, of each. She asked for a background check, which, as a felon on parole, Six-Six fortuitously had saved as a PDF on his phone.

She asked the brother to drive his car around. She and Stu took a picture of the license plate. They got both of their numbers. They shared locations.

"OK, Heather. You can go. But call me on your phone and leave me on speaker for the entire night. I'll mind my business, I'll turn a deaf ear. But if I hear even one muffled scream or if you dare end the call, I will have all of NYPD up their fucking ass in 3.5."

Mama signed the permission slip. *You never leave your wingman.*

We fooled around in the backseat of his brother's car like two teenagers. It was dark and sexy and illicit, and I reveled in it. But as the morning approached and the sun started to rise, I began to feel very different about attending an after-after party in Harlem.

There's a reason last call occurs when it is still dark outside. I didn't have a mirror on me in the back of the car, in the light of day, I had enough street smarts to accurately imagine what I looked like. *Different is nice, but it sure isn't pretty. Pretty is what it's about. I never met anyone who was different who couldn't figure that out.*

It turns out that it's not at the stroke of midnight but actually it's at six a.m. that the spell is broken. With an understanding kiss goodbye, Six-Six called me a car to take me back home to Jen's apartment. No shame, no regret, no cover story. When you can't be Eve, it feels good to be the snake every once in a while.

CHAPTER 29

STARTED FROM THE BOTTOM, NOW WE'RE HERE

About a month after our adventures in New York City, I got a call from our producer. It was early October 2019, two or three months after Bravo had picked up the still unnamed, unannounced show.

"Hey, Heather. We have some exciting news to share with you. We have a title for the show: *The Real Housewives of Salt Lake City*. The cast is officially Lisa Barlow, Mary M. Cosby, Heather Gay, Meredith Marks, and Jen Shah."

Full-body chills.

My stomach was in my toes. My head was in the clouds. Never had I dared to dream a dream as big as this. A dream as big as *Housewives*. I was the girl who posted Andy Cohen's picture on my Instagram. I cherished every line from *The Real Housewives of New York City*, ate at Javier's whenever I was in Orange County, laughed in shock and awe at the peaches in Atlanta, and cheered for *Potomac* when they burst onto the scene. I was a fan. A family van, "go to sleep," rich bitch, table flip, "let's talk about the husband" type of fan. And here I was, being called up to the big leagues. I was blazing a new trail, trading in covered wagons for Sprinter vans. *Throw me in. I'll swim.*

Instinctively, I knew that I'd never be the housewife I had always wanted to be by the church's standards. But now, I had the opportunity to reclaim the title on my own terms. The only qualification was a simple, four-letter word: *real*.

Bravo executives required the same qualification. One month before filming, they came to Salt Lake City to meet us personally and vet us for the show. They told us they'd be looking at every aspect of our lives.

For some reason, I didn't think they'd actually come to my house, and so I had done zero prep and was, as Lisa would say, "in media res." Bravo executives sat in my living room on my cat-torn sofa with bright blue painter's tape to cover up the chipped wood trim. "We are remodeling," I offered casually.

They came to my business, interviewed my employees, and observed how our business was run. They did an extensive background check, giving me insight into Six-Six's ready-to-share PDF—a matching lovebird necklace of sorts, one might say. They did a credit check and went through all of our social media. And as someone who had learned to hide different parts of myself from the different people in my life, I found the thought of being known so intimately by many both thrilling and terrifying.

When they called us initially, Whitney was not a cast member. However, when the execs came to Salt Lake, they invited the original five of us to dinner and included a few hopefuls, Whitney Rose and Angie Harrington. During the dinner, they told Whitney that they were intrigued by her but that she had been edited out entirely from the sizzle reel. No moment of "Whitney FUCKING Rose," no moment of *Housewives* drama. It was a wake-up call to the fickle world we were joining. If Whitney could be edited out like the woman in the Van Halen pic, how disposable were the rest of us?

With filming set to begin for Season 1 in a matter of days, Beauty Lab was bumping. Dre and I were starting to see the fruits of our labors. We had taken the industry by storm, and everyone in Zion knew that Heather Gay and Dre Robinson were soon to be med-spa moguls.

We were invited to participate on a panel of business experts and act as judges for the Silicon Slopes Shark Tank. The event took place almost three years to the day after we launched the Mini Lip Plump. It was an honor to participate in such an esteemed event, and we loved meeting the entrepreneurs and hearing their pitches. We also discovered our latest software developer while we were there. It was a payoff moment for us as both business partners and friends. The last three years had been lean in every way, but now Beauty Lab was making more money than ever, we were about to be a part of *The Real Housewives of Salt Lake City*, and now the business community was recognizing us as colleagues and contenders.

Driving home from Silicon Slopes, we talked about what a full-circle moment it was.

"We did it, Dre. We got through the cold, hard winter days and survived. Now is our chance to soak up the sun and enjoy life a little more."

We were content and hopeful as we drove home to Holladay.

About twenty minutes later, I dropped Dre off in the Beauty Lab parking lot. She had left her car there and needed to finish some last-minute things at the office. I waved goodbye and headed home. I caught a glimpse of my face smiling in the mirror and laughed. It felt good to be successful. It felt good to be recognized. It felt good to feel good.

I was almost halfway home when I saw the text from Dre. I assumed she had left something in the car and needed me to drive back, so I opened it. The message appeared on my screen like a mirage.

"My brother is dead."

Dead? Like in trouble for doing something dumb? Or dead like . . . I dreaded what it might mean.

I didn't understand, it didn't make sense, so I called her. She was still at Beauty Lab.

"Dre, what's going on? Are you OK?"

One of our employees picked up the phone and filled me in as much as possible.

Dre's brother, Tim, was dead.

Even now, the words sting when I see them on the page. Tim was gone. Dead by suicide at the age of thirty-seven, leaving a huge void in the lives of everyone he loved, especially Dre.

Tim was Dre's younger brother by just ten days short of two years. He was her person. Our first fan and greatest cheerleader at Beauty Lab, he never missed a Saturday. He played the guitar and piano beautifully. He loved sports, skateboarding, the outdoors, and anything that could be done on a board, water or snow. He loved to thrill his family and friends with his stunts.

Tim touched the hearts of all who knew him. He found great joy in helping people. Behind the scenes, he served his family and friends often, helping with comfort, counsel, encouragement, and love, with no expectation or recognition.

Because of Tim, *we all have been changed for good.*

Reeling with grief and clinging to a connection with Tim, Dre and I started the Don't Leave Foundation as a way to honor him. The Don't Leave Foundation provides free laser treatment to individuals with self-harm or addiction scars. It is dedicated to treating each individual free of charge until the scars that trigger them are faded or gone all together.

In our community, self harm is rampant. We could book our entire schedule at Beauty Lab + Laser with Don't Leave patients.

In a culture that believes perfection is attainable, we often internalize the pain of falling short.

When you're instilled with the idea that your worth is directly related to your obedience, it's easy to feel small. After all, fetters and shackles aren't that different.

Losing Tim was devastating for all of us. We were riding the wave at its crest, and it quickly and unexpectedly, came crashing down.

The day after Tim died, I sat in Whitney's backyard and filmed my very first scene as a Real Housewife. I put my feet on the cold tile floor, but before I stood up, I thought of Tim.

I was done shutting down, done turning it off, done performing my reality. If I was going to do this, I was going to do it right. Not just for me but for Tim. For Dre. For my blue-eyed banditti: Ashley, Georgia, and Annabelle. For every person who ever felt like they weren't enough, like they didn't belong, like they couldn't be their whole self and still be loved.

I had a platform. I had the benefit of my whiteness, cisness, straightness. I had the benefit of financial stability. I had the benefit of a new chapter, a reprieve, a second lease on life, and I didn't want to squander it. If I was going to speak out, I was going to roar. I was going to commit.

Therefore, if ye have desires to serve God ye are called to the work.

CHAPTER 30

I THINK LIFE CHOSE
ME AFTER ALL

Filming *The Real Housewives of Salt Lake City* has changed my life. It is an absolute fever dream, an opportunity I never could have prepared for nor dreamt of. It's like being on an episode of *Survivor* and *Project Runway*. Fighting in full glam to not be voted off by your fellow Housewives or America.

I had been raised to be a lowercase-*h* housewife my entire life. But none of my mom's three-by-five note cards could have prepared me for a SWAT team dropping down on our party bus in the Beauty Lab parking lot, or Lisa dropping hot-mic moments about her friend of ten years, or Whitney spinning on a pole while she stirs the pot, or Mary spinning an entire season around smelling like hospital. And amidst all of this chaos, all you really want is a second to catch your breath in order to talk about the serious things, the colossal things, like Meredith and her dumb family that poses.

The second I agreed to be a Real Housewife, I became a Bad Mormon. I had never meant to cut the holes in the curtain. But now that they were there, the holes made it easier for the cameras to see the sacred secrets hidden behind the veil.

Recently, as I was dropping my daughter Annabelle off at her new job, I asked her casually if her boss was Mormon. "He *seems* like he might be," she replied.

As we pulled up to the restaurant, I noticed that she quickly and quietly removed the tiny cross earrings she was wearing. We made eye contact, and she explained, "Just in case he is . . ."

I gave her an understanding nod, but I still felt compelled to say something. "It's just a cultural thing. They see the cross, and they know that you aren't their type of Christian. *Welp, she's not a Mormon. I don't know who she is or what she's capable of.*"

It's not their fault. They are just drawn that way.

Mormons don't wear crosses. We don't have crucifixes in our homes, we don't have crosses on our Bibles or the Book of Mormon. There are no crosses anywhere in our churches or temples. Our meetinghouses are marked with long spires and white steeples, but Mormons don't believe in the cross, and if you want to let us know you aren't part of the group, wearing a cross is a surefire confirmation.

Otherness can be a heavy cross to bear in a very insular community.

When we first started filming, there was a tiny part of my pioneer girl's heart that still believed I could perhaps be both a housewife and a Housewife. A part of me believed that I, too, could take off my silver cross earrings before anyone noticed. I tried to wrestle with ways I could be on the show while not doing anything to openly offend my friends or family.

Ninety-nine percent of the time, I can wear modest clothing and carry around milk in a glass.

The first few months of being a Housewife was glorious. It was a rebirth. *I can breathe for the first time.* I wanted to celebrate with the people I loved most in my life, and the majority of them were still active members of the church.

Because my fame seemed to come at the sake of my salvation, it held no value for my friends or family. Instead of being my trumpet of success, it became the elephant in the room. There was no way I could be myself in a way that would not disappoint them.

The first time I ordered a drink on camera, I was at the bowling alley with Whitney, no gutter bumpers in sight. I asked for a Tito's with water and lime.

I didn't know what to order. I didn't know the lingo, I didn't know what would sound cool. Ordering drinks never rolled off my tongue, it always felt secretive and shameful. I didn't know about terroir or reposado, neat or dressed. All these words were completely foreign, but I was bowling with the big girls now, and I wanted to learn fast.

When we filmed the Beauty Lab baby shower, I wore a one-shoulder, one-piece white Halston jumpsuit. I hadn't been wearing my garments for years, but I still felt exposed. I had been watching Lisa like a hawk, curious to see how she was going to navigate wearing her garments on camera. What was the right thing to do? My entire left shoulder was bare, and it was clear I was not wearing what many called my magic underwear at a time when I needed the most protection. I felt guilty being brazen about it, defying the rules publicly. It had nothing to do with betraying my sacred covenants with God. It had everything to do with betraying my family and friends. But it fit, it zipped, and it was white.

My prayer came out short and sweet and in my pioneer-girl voice.

I'm sorry, but if you are truly my friends, if you truly care, please give me a pass on the dress code this one time, and let me bare my shoulder and still retain the love of my friends and family.

At Mary's *Women Helping Women in Business Philanthropic Glam Met Gala* luncheon, I drank wine. And I figured that everyone would excuse me because I was, after all, at Valter's, where it would be far more sacrilegious to abstain than to indulge.

So much of my life had already been wasted on useless endeavors. Hours spent in robes and veils watching elderly people reenact the creation story inside the temple. Hours spent pondering why the Lord wanted my hand held in a cupping shape. Hours spent studying and teaching scripture that was written by the hand of man, not the hand of God. An emperor prancing around in his new clothes while everyone fawned over his artistry.

When I learned some of the truths about Joseph Smith, I wanted to shout, "But he hasn't got anything on! He's just taken bits and pieces from his favorite scriptures and jumbled them on the page."

Even if I didn't call myself a Mormon and even if I wanted to be free from it, I still didn't want to hurt anyone—not my friends, not my family, and especially not God. I'm a people pleaser. I'm a middle child. I'm a Cancer. I'm a white on the color chart. I just wanted peace. But there was no way for me to be who I was and not inadvertently break the hearts of my family.

After the first season, there were throngs of people in my DMs who gave me the freedom to fly; their words and affirmations became the wind beneath my wings. When you're taught at the age of eight to "choose the right," you believe that every decision, good or bad, is followed by its immediate consequence. And yet here I was being disobedient and being blessed. There was no way I couldn't second guess my every step.

It was the external validation from the fans that let me know that what I was doing had meaning. More than that, it was actually helping and healing people who related to me and my story.

The love from the audience gave me the strength to face the most important conversation I needed to have: telling my daughters that I wanted to leave the church.

If they stayed Mormon, as I had raised them, I would be cut out of the major milestones of their life. I would never see them get married. I wouldn't be a part of their eternal family. If I left the church to give my daughters autonomy and choice, that choice could be one that ultimately excluded me from their lives.

I sat them all down on camera and told them that I wanted to leave. Not only was I coming out to my daughters, but I was also coming out to myself. I had never said the words out loud before. Instead, they hung over my head, clouding every interaction. It was time.

Even though I believed that my kids loved me, I didn't want to burden them with something they didn't ask for, especially when they'd already had their little, gentle, unbreakable hearts burdened with so many of my mistakes—my separation, my divorce, my business, my guilt.

"So, I've been wanting to talk to you guys about something. For me as your mom, I can tell you that in the last few years, I've had a lot of realizations that I probably haven't articulated. I probably haven't said it out loud, but you've felt it. As a mom, for so long, especially when your dad and I divorced, I felt like in order to be a good mom, I had to just toe the line, show no deviation, put my head down, be the best single Mormon mom I could be, which really didn't work. I think for anyone who gets divorced, it's like you are labeled as failing at something. Of course, I didn't just feel like I failed in society. I felt like I failed you guys. I didn't get married and have children to get divorced. I don't want a broken family. It's come to where I owe it to you to be honest about where I'm at. And honestly, I don't know where I'm at. I don't ever want to take away from your faith or your Mormonism. I want to date, I want to go out, I want to drink, and I want to do all these things. And there's so much shame, and there's so much fear. I don't want to be associated with a church that has a racist past or homophobic doctrine or doesn't believe women are equal to men. I don't want it for myself, and I definitely don't want it for you, either."

When they responded the way they did, when they supported me, hugged me, and loved me, I felt held in a way that no man and no institution could ever imitate. Our embrace as our own little family was stronger and more permanent than any Patriarchal Grip. My honesty was a relief to them just as much as it was for me. *Why did I wait so long?*

The Real Housewives of Salt Lake City changed everything.

The cameras were a mirror to the world I had built without Billy. They saw my daughters living and loving as their most authentic selves. They saw my business, Beauty Lab + Laser, run hand in hand with my very best friend. They saw my life in a time of transition—messy and confusing but all the while beautiful.

Watching the show, I was able to take a step back and see my life through a wider lens. Things that were unclear to me—things lost in the rote of the everyday, lost in the routine of dead-inside duty—were made visible, the veil removed and the death stare broken.

I didn't need a figurehead to lead me. I didn't need a figurehead to raise a family, to be a mom, to be an example for my daughters. For so long, I had been committed to becoming a housewife, to hiding the most important parts of myself in order to be as appealing as possible. In pursuit of that title, I had lost myself, resigned to the fact that it would never be.

So much had been lost, but so much had been gained. Persecutions may rage, mobs may combine, armies may assemble, calumny may defame, but I'm exactly where I need to be with the people who matter most. My church may be absent, my marriage may be null, my faith may be questioned, but I'm a mom, a sister, a daughter, a friend, a businesswoman, and a Housewife.

Does that not matter?

And the truth is that as long as it matters, it's the only thing that does.

After the first season aired, the warmth I received from my daughters, from my friends, and from the fans melted the frozen berg that I had for so long attributed to my demise.

Housewives are survivors. Sure, we are a little flawed—a little damaged, dented, and burnt—but we are still our own champions. We get out there every day and are unapologetically ourselves. This community of strong and resilient women fortified me, buoyed me, and allowed me to see myself objectively.

Would I risk my eternity, my church, my community, my family, for a *sizzle reel*?

Yes. A thousand times, yes.

I clapped my hands for joy and exclaimed: This is the desire of my heart.

EPILOGUE

During the reunion episode immediately after Season 1 aired, Andy Cohen asked me if I was surprised at being declared the "fan favorite." Surprised didn't begin to cover it. I replied, "I just didn't think there was an audience for the mess that I am."

Being cast on *The Real Housewives of Salt Lake City* introduced me to a worldwide audience far beyond anything a church-bred, sensible Utah girl like me could have imagined. I had long considered the things I would lose when people "found out" about my church exodus. But I never considered the things I would gain.

As soon as the show began airing, I suddenly had new friends, a new family: Housewives from every franchise, Bravolebrities, reality-TV fans, devout and former adherents from all the major and minor religions. Families in every form, folks from every faith, background, and culture. All of them seeking *me* out, celebrating *my* story, replacing *my* exile with their empathy.

People understood the struggle of being true to yourself even when it causes pain to the ones you love most. Accepting who you are when it contradicts your faith and your family feels, in a sense, like coming out. And I'm grateful I didn't have to go through it alone. Instead, I was lifted up by the thousands of people saying they liked me, they accepted me, they related to me.

The *Real Housewives* franchise is both powerful and far-reaching. Each new episode is like an ocean wave crashing on the shore, leaving new treasures and connections in my in-box. I'm flooded with messages of encouragement from all over the world. In an instant, my life went from fearing I was losing everything to thousands of people telling me I *was* everything.

The warmth of the new friends I was making took away the chill that rippled through my closest devout circles, an army of angry Mormons expressing disappointment, letting me know that I was wrong. I never knew so many were so concerned about my salvation. Websites were dedicated to fact checking my statements and campaigning to discredit me and my experiences. I responded by embracing my newfound fame in a different way. I was baptized into a new faith. *Now, as ye are desirous to come into the fold of God, and to be called his people.*

Fans began to collaborate and brainstorm endless memes, polls, and awards celebrating my shortcomings and successes. *Willing to bear one another's burdens, that they may be light.*

They championed my fears and failings through all the ups and downs. *Comfort those that stand in need of comfort.*

They grieved with me when my father passed away. *Mourn with those who mourn.*

They stood as examples of hope, a future, and loving acceptance. *Stand as witnesses of God at all times and in all things, and in all places.*

The community of kindred spirits that surrounds me now is

truly a covenant people committed to sacred, not secret, principles of unconditional love, acceptance, and grace. *They clapped their hands for joy, and exclaimed: This is the desire of our hearts.*

After so many years frozen in regret and despair, I know now that I am not alone. Throw me into the icy Arctic, I'll emerge holding a snowflake. I belong to a greater community. One that reaches far beyond the television screen. A community of beautiful outsiders like me who are imperfect in every single way. I know this is where I belong, and if it weren't for *The Real Housewives of Salt Lake City,* I would never have known just how many of us were out there.

When each passing season ends and a new season approaches, the question always remains: *Will I be invited back to the fold?*

This is the only excommunication I fear now.

I know I need to stay serious and acknowledge the gravity of the situation, but I can't help but press down hard on my lower lip to keep from smiling. *Is this really happening? Does reality television seriously want* me?

And the feeling is both terrifying . . . *and thrilling.*

In the name of the Father, the Son, and Andy Cohen. Amen.

ACKNOWLEDGMENTS

1. If I Didn't Have You to Wake Up To

Ashley, Georgia, and Annabelle. You are my world. I'll never let go, girls.
I'll never let go.

2. Families Can Be Together Forever

Mom and Dad. I shaped my view of all that I am and all that I ever
hope to be based on your examples. Despite the ways I've disappointed
you, I hope you know that I still try to honor you every single day.

Jenny, Tyler, Nancy, Logan, and Casey. The smartest, funniest people
in any room. You've honed my skills, pushed me to be stronger, and
laughed with me through it all.

3. Closer to Fine

Dre Robinson. My right-hand man and Daddy Dre to my daughters.
For showing me what true loyalty looks like. For teaching me that
the less I seek my source for some definitive, the closer I am to fine.
Dreather Forever!

4. The Book of Love

Natasha Simons. For endless patience, thoughtful guidance, unending compassion, and scores of support.

The entire team at Gallery and Simon & Schuster. The editors, designers, publicists, marketers, and more that have made this book the success that it is.

My agent and friend, Steve Troha. I'll always like you the most.

John Jardin. Anonymous Wombat and the frog in my pocket. This book exists today because of you.

5. Take A Bow

Team BLL and all the BeautyLabbers. Your loyalty and continued patronage is the life force behind our business, our future, and our purpose here on earth.

Every follower, every fan, every friend. All the teachers both past and present. For showing me the way and opening my eyes to a reality outside the marshmallow world.

6. It's In Every One Of Us

Michaline and Joey. For choosing the bad Mormon.

Andy, Noah, Jenna, Sheonna, Kemar, Lori, Lisa, and the entire team at Shed Media, Bravo, and beyond.

7. Dancing On My Own

To the community of outsiders, of others. To the survivors. To the folks who find out who they are then do it on purpose. We may never truly find where we belong, but at least we're all looking together.

ACKNOWLEDGMENTS

I am deeply grateful to everyone who has crossed my path whether it be in person, in the pages of a book, in the scenes on my screen, or in the posts on my phone. Your words are a part of my inner dialogue and the context within which I view my life. *Beloved, Baby Island, Family, Dear Mr. Henshaw, Mandarin Orange Sunday, Prince of Tides, The Rime of the Ancient Mariner.* Shane and Ben, Scheana Shay, Hannah Gadsby, Gordon Korman, Walt Whitman, Peter Spier, Kristin Cavallari, Dave Quinn, SYCMU, Betches, Fat Carrie Bradshaw, Sarah Jessica Parker, Felicity, *My So Called Life, Degrassi Junior High, Kids Incorporated,* Stephen Kellogg. Roald Dahl, Robert Frost, Rumi, Leo Lionni, Toni Morrison, Advntrmates, Samuel Taylor Coleridge, Laura Ingalls Wilder, E.B. White, Allan W. Eckert, Glennon Doyle, Joseph Smith. Lauren Conrad, Lisa Rinna, Kim Zolciak-Biermann, Kelly Bensimon, Phaedra Parks, Kyle Richards, Paige Davis, the kids from *The Real World: New York*, Tom Cruise, Diane Keaton, Trixie Mattel, Gene Wilder, Bill Paxton, Harry Dean Stanton, Leonard Nimoy, Macaulay Culkin, Angela Lansbury, Tom Hanks, Peter Scolari, Chris Hansen, Julia Louis-Dreyfus, Lisa Kudrow, Mira Sorvino, Darth Vader, The Indigo Girls, Brandi Carlisle, Kristin Chenoweth, Madonna, Yaz, Dolly Parton, Samia, Janis Joplin, Kelly Clarkson, Fleetwood Mac, Eurythmics, Cutting Crew, Dar Williams, Styx, R.E.M., Christine and the Queens, Noah Cyrus, Rihanna, Carole King, Kanye West, Blake Shelton, Michael McLean, Kodaline, Paul Simon, Florence and the Machine, The Beatles, Beyoncé, Drake, Leonardo DiCaprio, Kate Winslet, Celine Dion, *For the Love of Willadeen, Savannah Smiles, Gilligan's Island, Scary Movie, Annie, Defending Your Life, The Wizard of Oz, Grease 2, Cannonball Run, Big Bad Mama, Fraggle Rock, Hillstreet Blues, Anchorman, The Jetsons, Mean Girls, Rushmore, Apocalypse Now, The Partridge Family, Sleeping Beauty, The Sound of Music,*

ACKNOWLEDGMENTS

Little Shop of Horrors, Evita, Survivor, Project Runway, Sex and the City, Top Gun, Romy and Michele's High School Reunion, Clueless, Veep, Mad Men, Breaking Bad, Seinfeld, RHOA, RHOBH, RHONJ, RHONY, RHOP, RHOD, RHOC, RHOM, Don't Leave, Live Love Lab. Life is Short. Buy the Lips.

Don't miss the next book from Heather Gay.

Keep reading for a sneak peek . . .

ONE

GOOD-TIME GIRL

I would've loved to have been a Good-Time Girl in college!" Really, I would've loved to have been *anything* in college. I would've loved to have experienced day drinking, to have experienced a hangover, to have woken up in a stranger's bed after a tawdry one-night stand. The truth is, I was not a Good-Time Girl. And worse, I wasn't even *adjacent* to any Good-Time Girls. In fact, no one I knew in college was having a good time at all by any standard college definition. We were at a no sex, no drinking, no fraternizing, church-owned university, where good times were relegated to Harry Potter theme parties and Family Home Evening groups.

I knew what college was supposed to be like; I had seen the movies and had visited Greek Row at the University of Utah. But Brigham Young University (BYU) was not like any college ever represented on-screen or off. Everything was loaded, fraught with potential judgement: who you dated, what you studied, how you worked, how you relaxed. We were observing each other, noting everyone's level of righteousness, devotion to the faith, and their ability to be a good husband or wife in the future. I can't remember going to one single college party in the traditional sense. No red Solo cups, no socks on the doorhandles, no keg stands. I can't remember even hearing about a house party and, if there was one, it was no wilder than a game of Twister, fully clothed, with a couple of empty two-liter bottles of Sprite. Twister and Sprite is not necessarily a *Bad*-Time, but it's definitely not the image that popped to mind the first time I heard the phrase "Good-Time Girl." That image was one of a college girl on Spring Break in micro-shorts with a tank-top yanked up to her chin. A Mardi Gras girl flashing all her fellow students. But there were no beads nor Bourbon Street at BYU. If I flashed anyone, it could have only been on accident. An inadvertent act done during a heated game of Twister while trying to place my right hand onto someone else's blue circle.

There were no sororities, no fraternities, no wet T-shirt contests. No actual twisting of body parts off the Hasbro mat. Like the aliens sang in the movie *Waiting for Guffman* about life on Mars, "BORING! BORING! BORING!" These were quintessential college experiences I wanted to have, but I didn't know where to find them, or where to find even the BYU version of them. If you don't drink in college, what do you even really do? If a Good-Time Girl flashes her tits in the forest, does it even make a sound if she's completely sober? Imagine how brazen you'd have to be to live a Mardi Gras life on a tap water cocktail.

Yet, somehow, despite all of these factors, the nickname was bestowed upon me years after it was impossible to prove otherwise.

This moniker originated through a story that is, quite frankly, absurd and embarrassing. It's so embarrassing, in fact, that I almost don't even want to speak it into existence. I'd rather die in a blaze of glory as someone known for flashing her boobs rather than the pathetic version of how the name actually came to be.

It all began when I was twelve years old, sowing my wild oats at a Brigham Young University summer retreat called Academy for Girls. It was the closest thing to a military academy that my parents could find that didn't involve shaving my head or wearing a uniform.

Academy for Girls was a camp for Mormon girls between the ages of twelve and eighteen from all over the world. We came to Provo, Utah, to experience the BYU campus for six spiritually uplifting, platitude-packed days and five fun-filled nights. We stayed in the freshman dorms and attended classes on etiquette, poise, handicraft, religion, and homemaking. There were no boys and no Mardi Gras beads, but there were definitely boobs—two on every attendee, in fact. We heard mention of one coed activity, a dance held with the neighboring Academy for Boys, but that was only for the girls who were fourteen and up. I, at a pudgy, prepubescent twelve wasn't eligible for *that* type of fun, so I had to create my own.

Our counselor stayed on the same floor as us in a locked room at the end of the hallway. Once she went to bed, there was no rousing her, and it was after lights-out that we had our best adventures. Each counselor went by a made-up name they chose for themselves in order to give an air of anonimity and an extra element of fun. My counselor chose the nickname Kare spelled K-A-R-E, as in Care Bear with a funky K—which I thought was a fail, and a less than valiant effort. When I learned later that Kare was just short for her real name, Karen, I knew my instincts had been right. She was phoning it in! It felt like a rip-off, especially when I met the other camp counselors who had names like Lickety Splits and Rainbow Sunshine. Meanwhile, I got stuck with

Kare . . . spelled wrong. Like many things in any twelve-year-old girl's life, it was a letdown.

Our days were spent dressed in modest attire, attending seminars in giant auditoriums on campus. We ate in the cafeteria, and, every other day, we had supervised outings. Our excursions were held on campus and limited to root beer floats in the Cougareat and visits to the BYU Dairy for a single scoop of ice cream—vanilla, mostly.

Part of our requirement at Academy for Girls was memorizing the standards that were listed explicitly in the official church pamphlet, *For the Strength of Youth*. It was a two-by-three paper notebook outlining a clear set of criteria that all devout Mormon kids should aspire to. It dictated appropriate hairstyles, appropriate clothing choices, and appropriate physical adornments. In the fine print, it made crystal clear that there should be no more than one piercing per earlobe.

Naively, I thought the only place you could get a piercing was at the Claire's boutique in the mall. That procedure involved a highly untrained, definitely not OSHA-certified, sixteen-year-old store clerk and definitely not a medical device piercing gun. But, as it turns out, if you have a needle, an ice cube, and a willing accomplice, you can pierce just about anything just about anywhere . . . and at Academy for Girls, we aimed to do just that.

I didn't know I wanted a second piercing until they told me I couldn't have one. This was my only chance. I had barely gotten my parents to take me to Claire's for my initial piercing, and there was no way I would convince them to take me for a second round.

I bravely volunteered to go first. We set up our make-shift clinic in the room farthest from our counselors with added pillows squeezed into the space between the carpet and the doorframe to muffle the sound of my screams. Four girls held me down while my friend Aimee numbed my earlobe with a melting ice cube—I can still feel the trickle of water that trailed down my neck and into the collar of my shirt. She took a needle and sprayed it with hairspray because "the alcohol would kill the germs" and proceeded to slowly, with zero finesse, push the needle through my ear. I felt every single layer of flesh give way with an audible pop. I barely survived the first earlobe without passing out before I managed to tell the group through sweaty tears that I needed a break. I took a few melty ice cubes and my bruised ego back to my room. As I left, I promised we could pierce the other earlobe the following night, but we all knew it was a lie. Regret had set in like a thick blanket over the thrill of rebellion, and I took the rogue earring out the next morning hoping that the hole would seal before my parents arrived for the final banquet.

Disappointed in my own cowardice, I now had something to prove.

The next day, we discovered an old wheelchair in a utility closet on our dorm room floor. One of the more brazen girls in our group got in the chair and pulled a twin-sized blanket over her head as if she were some sort of crazed patient from a mental facility. Taking my cue, I joined in, playing the role of Maniacal Hospital Attendant. I embraced my reign of terror with extra fervor. Once the lights were out, we began barging into girls' rooms unannounced. She would fling open the door to their room, and I would push the wheelchair as fast as I could straight up to their bedside and scream, "BOOBIES!" Then, from under the blanket, my crazed patient would reach out and attempt to give them a titty twister. It was pretty hard for her to find the titties given the blanket, the darkness of the room, and their terrified screams. I did my best to guide and direct her outstretched hands with slight adjustments to the wheelchair. From behind, I pushed and pivoted and encouraged her to "Grab higher!" and "To the right! To the right! You're skimming her elbow!" We only retreated when contact was actually made or when the screams became too intense. The wheelchair moved sluggishly across the Berber carpeted floors, but I was amped up on adrenaline and my new persona and found the strength to invade as many rooms as possible before our counselor, Kare, woke up and our cover was blown.

As I had hoped and prayed, this little prank gave me quite the reputation among the Academy for Girls attendants. The Terrorizing Titty-Twister Twins were talked about far and wide. As notorious as I felt then, I was equally as confident that once I walked off campus, that reputation and its sins would be far behind me. But I should have known that God never forgets. I never repented appropriately and because I hadn't taken it to Him in prayer, He in turn sent it right back down into the hands of Lisa Barlow. Which, even next to the legendary wrath of God, was much more damning.

Flash forward three decades to 2019 and the reveal of the cast of *The Real Housewives of Salt Lake City*. After hearing our names announced together for the first season, Lisa Barlow discovered that her neighbor also knew me. We hadn't seen each other since we were twelve at the Academy for Girls, but, apparently, I had left an impression. Unbeknownst to me, my reputation as the nefarious Titty Twister had stuck with her. It was the one anecdote she remembered, and she readily shared it with Lisa, who proceeded to conflate a lot of the details. And sure, Lisa might not be the greatest listener, but considering the facts, even I would have been confused: "I knew Heather . . . BYU . . . a lot of fun . . . boobies! . . . Got in trouble . . . pretty wild." Based on those CliffsNotes, Lisa assumed that this was a tale about college coeds in their early twenties.

This was a side to me that Lisa had never imagined. And yet . . . it tracked. Suddenly, I was a Good-Time Girl: "Heather Gay thinks every day is Mardi Gras at BYU"; "Honor code, what?!" Boobs and blankets at twelve somehow turned into flashing and flirting at twenty.

Perhaps that's why, when I first heard about the accusation in Season One of *Salt Lake City*, I found it so offensive. I had never even been to Mardi Gras, let alone earned a string of beads. As a student, I worked forty hours a week at two jobs, took a full class load, started a small business, and did everything I could to scrape by. I was focused on succeeding and surviving at work and school, and even that came secondary to finding a boyfriend. Yet here I was wearing the scarlet letter without having had any of the scarlet fun. *"I would've loved to have been a Good-Time Girl in college!"*

Once I didn't have to hide, I realized that Lisa Barlow had it right all along. I was born a Good-Time Girl, and now I'm less afraid to say it out loud. It's easily the truest, wildest, most authentic part of myself. But for most of my life, it was also the part of myself that I thought was weak, rebellious, and wrong. The life that had been ascribed to me did not make room for Good-Time Girls, only Good Little Girls, and that ideology was reinforced in every interaction I had with my parents, my siblings, my teachers, my friends, and my church. I tried to hide who I was like the world's worst-kept secret all my life, and it's taken me years to realize this.

Following Season One, when I started to work on the first draft of my memoir, *Bad Mormon*, I began going through all my old scrapbooks and journals and stumbled upon letters, photos, and notes reminding me that this had never really been a secret. One letter in particular was written to my best friend when I was twenty-three, just a few weeks before I finished my missionary service in the South of

France. During this eighteen-month-long mission, my life had been dedicated to daily prayer, scripture study, and full-time service. My every waking moment was entrenched in serving the Lord and proclaiming the Gospel. Every thought, every conversation, every agenda was about God, getting closer to God, bringing people to God, and becoming more like God. I talked to thousands of people, in French and in English, about His eternal Plan of Happiness and my hopeful eternal glory.

And even after ALL of that, I still couldn't purge myself of the desire to want more. In that letter, I confided my fears and my dreams—the tangible longing for a bigger life, the acknowledgment of the real me screaming to get out. It's who I always was, and I knew it even back then. I tried to fill my bucket with enough illicit reserves to get me through the life that was planned for me, but it wasn't enough. It was never enough. It was never enough because I always wanted more. To get more, I'd have to give up the safety and control that I'd been taught to aspire to. And now I'm trying really hard to believe that my ambition isn't something to be ashamed of, and that it might actually even be an attribute.

When I revisited this specific letter, I had the perspective of someone who had made bad choices and still been blessed. I had everything *I* ever truly wanted. I suddenly saw everything with the lens flipped for the very first time. I no longer needed to hide the things that made me the most myself.

The Mormon part of me still clings to the belief that my current success and happiness are not real. That any temporary blessings are fruit from the Poison Tree and can never last. But I'm trying to remember that this is a lie. In fact, it's the exact opposite. I've just found a way to acknowledge and honor my authentic self for perhaps the first time ever. I didn't get here because I betrayed my church or my family; I got here because I *stopped* betraying myself.

Now, with perspective, the nickname of Good-Time Girl is something I'm proud to claim. After all, it's much cooler than Kare with a funky K. I'll wear my scarlet "GTG" proudly emblazoned across my chest, and I'll be delighted that she finally feels welcome.

ABOUT THE AUTHOR

Heather Gay is a star of Bravo's *The Real Housewives of Salt Lake City* and the cofounder of Beauty Lab + Laser, an innovative cosmetic medical practice based in Salt Lake City, with its own behind-the-scenes podcast, *Live Love Lab*. A graduate of Brigham Young University, Heather lives in Salt Lake City with her three daughters. *Bad Mormon* is her first book.